Racine

Plays and Playwrights Series

EDITORS
Kenneth Richards & Peter Thomson

CONGREVE
Harold Love

SHERIDAN AND THE DRAMA OF GEORGIAN
ENGLAND
John Loftis

Forthcoming

BRECHT
Jan Needle and Peter Thomson

GOLDONI
Kenneth Richards and Laura Richards

P. J. Yarrow

Racine

BASIL BLACKWELL
Oxford

British Library Cataloguing in Publication Data

Yarrow, Philip John
    Racine. – (Plays and playwrights series).
    Bibl. – Index.
    ISBN 0 631 17950 X
    1. Title 2. Series
    842′.4 PQ1905
    Racine, Jean – Criticism and interpretation

Set in VIP Bembo by
Western Printing Services Ltd, Bristol
Printed in Great Britain by
J. W. Arrowsmith Ltd,
Bristol

Contents

9

Acknowledgements

Many years ago, a reviewer referred to the feeling of nausea that overcame him whenever a new book on Racine was published. As the flood has certainly not abated since, can yet another be justified?

Of the many studies of Racine, some—particularly, perhaps, those devoted to special aspects of his work—are excellent. Nevertheless, there is still room for a modest little book that would treat Racine as a man who lived at a particular time in a particular country, who wrote for a particular kind of stage and a particular public, who did not ignore his predecessors and rivals, and who wrote plays that both pleased his own contemporaries and are still acted and read three centuries later;—that, without striving after novelty or saying anything not fully justified by the text, would provide the reader, clearly and in small compass (after all the volume of Racine's plays is not great), with the information needed to understand and appreciate his plays. It was with this aim in mind that the present book was written.

In the last resort, however, it was, it must be confessed, written because the invitation to write it was irresistible. I am deeply grateful to the General Editors of the series and to Blackwell's for giving me the opportunity. I am grateful, too, to the University of Newcastle upon Tyne for a term's leave of absence; and to Dr Enid L. Duthie and Professor J. Lough for reading part of this volume in typescript—they are, of course, in no way to blame for its shortcomings.

I

The Seventeenth-Century
French Theatre

When Racine began writing, there were three theatres in Paris: the
Hôtel de Bourgogne; the Marais theatre; and the theatre of the
Palais-Royal. Racine's first two plays were performed in this last by
Molière's company, which shared it with a company of Italian
actors. The theatre of the Palais-Royal had one unusual feature:
instead of being flat, the floor rose in tiers towards the back of the
hall. Built by Richelieu, it had fallen into disrepair during the score of
years that separated his death from the installation of Molière's
company (1661); and the spectators at *La Thébaïde* and *Alexandre*
had, over their heads, no ceiling, but merely a sheet of blue canvas
hanging from ropes. Molière's company, which performed on the
best days (Tuesdays, Fridays, and Sundays) was considered inferior
in tragedy, but excelled in comedy, his own plays constituting
the best part of its repertory. The Italians, who had the other four
days, also performed comedies—improvised comedies in their own
language—, delighting their foreign audience by their vivacity and
their consummate comic technique, their miming and their acrobatic
skill.

Apart from the first two tragedies, and *Esther* and *Athalie*, acted at
Saint-Cyr and Versailles by schoolgirls, Racine's plays were all
staged at the Hôtel de Bourgogne, where the actors had a higher
reputation for tragedy than Molière's company. Molière gives an
impression of the declamatory style of the Hôtel de Bourgogne in

the first scene of his *Impromptu de Versailles*; and Gabriel Guéret, in a satirical review of the state of literature in 1668, puts these words into the mouth of Montfleury, the great tragic actor of the Hôtel de Bourgogne, who had recently died of apoplexy after playing the part of Oreste in Racine's *Andromaque*:

> I wore out all my lungs in these violent spasms of jealousy, love and ambition. I had to compel my temperament a thousand times to exhibit on my face more passions than there were in La Chambre's characters. I was often obliged to cast terrible glances, to roll my eyes furiously in my head like a madman, to inspire dread by my grimaces, to imprint on my forehead the glow of indignation and of frustration, to follow it simultaneously by the pallor of fear and surprise, to express the transports of rage and despair, to shout like one possessed, and in consequence to dislocate all the joints (*démonter tous les ressorts*) of my body to make it supple for these different impressions. If anyone, therefore, should wish to know what I died of, let him not ask whether it was of fever, of dropsy, or of gout, but let him know that it was of *Andromaque*. (*Le Parnasse réformé*)

Comically exaggerated as this passage may be, it helps us to imagine what a seventeenth-century performance of *Andromaque* was like. Racine preferred the style of acting of the Hôtel de Bourgogne[1] to that of Molière and his company, who, in contrast, says Molière ironically, were 'ignorant people who recite as one speaks; they do not know how to rant the lines, and to pause at the finest places'.[2]

The Hôtel de Bourgogne, built in the sixteenth century, had been modernized in 1647, to compete with the Marais theatre, rebuilt after a fire three years earlier. It was long and narrow—109 feet by 44. The stage, raised 6'4" above the floor at the front and sloping backwards, occupied the whole width of the floor and was 45' deep, providing an acting area of some 32' in width and perhaps a little less in depth. The side and the rear walls of the hall were lined with a double row of boxes, with a gallery over the boxes at the sides. The cheapest part of the house was the *parterre* or pit, where the spectators mostly stood —though there were benches beneath the boxes along the side walls, one of which was said to be used by playwrights. At the back of the

---

[1] See below, p. 31.   [2] *Les Précieuses ridicules*, scene 9.

pit, level with the stage and sloping very gently backwards towards the rear boxes, was the *amphithéâtre*. Apart from the spectators in the pit, the boxes, the amphitheatre, and the gallery, there were also spectators seated on the stage itself, one of the most expensive parts of the house. According to a record kept in 1672 and 1673 by one of Molière's actors, Hubert, the number of spectators on the stage varied during that period from none at all to thirty-six; they must have considerably reduced the space available to the actors.

The curtain was raised before the performance began, and not lowered until after it was over. When the spectator went in, he was confronted by the stage set for the performance, with chairs on it in readiness for the wealthy young noblemen who wished to see the play from that vantage point and to display themselves. The play began with the actors of the first scene coming forward on to the stage. A notebook kept by the stage-designers of the Hôtel de Bourgogne records the settings and properties used for Racine's plays. The action of *La Thébaïde* and *Mithridate* took place in the conventional palace of seventeenth-century French tragedy (*palais à volonté*), furnished in the second play with an armchair and two stools for the council scene. *Britannicus* is in another palace, this time with two doors and curtains, and two armchairs for the fourth act. *Bérénice* takes place in a closet adorned with monograms and furnished with an armchair, *Bajazet* in a 'salon turc', and *Phèdre* in a vaulted palace. *Andromaque* is set out of doors: it requires a palace with pillars, and the sea and ships in the distance. The only plays in which we leave palaces are *Alexandre* (war tents and pavilions), *Iphigénie* (tents, with the sea and ships in the background), and Racine's only comedy, *Les Plaideurs*, which takes place in a street and requires two houses at the back of the stage and two at the sides.

The actors were sumptuously attired. According to Chappuzeau, who published a valuable little book, *Le Théâtre françois*, on the theatre of his day in 1674, they scorned sham gold and silver, which tarnished quickly, with the result that a single Roman costume might cost 500 écus or 1500 livres. It is not certain how literally Chappuzeau's phrase, 'costume à la romaine', is to be taken. The actors and actresses seem to have worn contemporary dress, with some concessions to historical accuracy—corslets and plumed helmets or hats for classical tragedies, and turbans for an Oriental play such as *Bajazet*.

During the intervals, a small string orchestra played, and two men went round snuffing the candles. A tempting variety of drinks could be bought at the bar. When the play was over, the orator of the company—one of the actors—came forward, thanked the audience, announced the next production, and encouraged the audience to come to it.

Chappuzeau's little book provides the reader of Racine with some interesting pieces of information. When one company announced a play, the other—by 1674, the amalgamation of the Marais company with Molière's had reduced the number of French companies to two—tried to put on a similar play in competition. This is probably how at least one of Racine's plays came to be written.[3] To avoid disputes between actors, the author was usually entrusted with the casting of the play, possibly seeking the advice of a member of the company. He would also attend rehearsals to advise and criticize the actors.

Except during the fortnight before Easter, there were normally three performances a week—on Fridays, Sundays, and Tuesdays. The other four days of the week, says Chappuzeau, were less suitable, since three of them—post days or market days—were busy days for the bourgeois, and Thursdays were given up to outings. The first performance was usually given on a Friday, in the hope of attracting a large audience on the following Sunday. New plays were ordinarily put on between October and Easter, when the court was in or near Paris.

The theatre-going public seems to have been comparatively small, and to have consisted of the elements mentioned by Chappuzeau—the bourgeois, including the well-to-do merchants of the fashionable rue Saint-Denis, and the gentlemen and ladies of the court and the salons. The bourgeois themselves occupied the pit; their wives, and the gentlemen and ladies of fashion the rest of the house. The audience, however, was far from decorous, since soldiers, pages, and lackeys often forced their way in without paying, injuring or killing the porters if they attempted to hinder them, and continuing their unruly conduct inside the theatre. In 1673, the invasion of the Hôtel de Bourgogne by a group of armed men was the occasion of an edict for the purpose of preventing disorder in the theatre (Jan. 9). Before this, says Chappuzeau, 'half the pit was often

[3] See below, pp. 25 and 51.

full of disorderly people; some went into the boxes; the audience was large and the takings small'. But as Molière's theatre was the scene of a riot on Jan. 13, 1673, and as further edicts were needed, it would be naïve to regard the edict of that year as the dawn of a bright new day.

The prices were high, ranging from 15 sous for a place in the pit to 5 livres 10 sous[4] for a seat in one of the best boxes or on the stage. For the first performances of new plays, these prices were raised.[5] As such increases must have discouraged the plebeian members of the audience from attending the crucial first performance of a new play; as the proportion of the takings contributed by the pit was, in any case, smaller than that contributed by the occupants of the more expensive parts of the house; and as the actors were reluctant to put on new plays in summer when the court was away: it seems probable that they paid more heed to the taste of the aristocratic part of the audience—in so far, that is to say, as there was a difference. Moreover, it seems that the success or failure of a play was to some extent decided by the readings of it given by the playwright in salons before the first performance. The seventeenth-century French theatre—unlike Elizabethan drama—does not appear to have reflected popular taste.

Seventeenth-century tragedy, though influenced by Aristotle, Horace, and their commentators, bore very little resemblance to the tragedy of Greece and Rome. It was divided into five acts, and written in verse. It was supposed to have a moral purpose, to inculcate virtue and to serve as a warning against vice; though, in the last resort, both writers and spectators cared more about entertainment than about moral aims. It observed the principles of propriety (*bienséance*) and verisimilitude. Propriety entailed, amongst other things, the avoidance of whatever might shock the audience, not only because of its violence and indecency, but also because of its unfamiliarity, its unlikeness to seventeenth-century French manners. Verisimilitude meant the avoidance of what was improbable, but hampered the playwright less than one might imagine, since Thomas Corneille says that 'anything that can happen without doing

[4] A sou was the twentieth part of a franc or livre. The livre was worth at least as much as the English pound of today.

[5] The price of the cheaper tickets was doubled; that of the other seats was not increased proportionately.

much violence to the common order of nature must be considered probable' (preface to *Timocrate*), and Rapin in his *Réflexions sur la Poétique* (1674) allows the transformation of Niobe into a stone, providing it is effected by a god.

A consequence of the principle of verisimilitude—and of the unchanging stage set—was the unity of place, of time, and of action. The time allowed was a day, though this was variously interpreted. D'Aubignac, in his *Pratique du Théâtre* (1657), recommended that the action should last from sunrise to sunset, or vice versa; Corneille, in his *Discours*, was prepared to allow up to thirty hours. In any case, a logical consequence of the unity of time, drawn by D'Aubignac, was that the dramatist must begin his play as near to the crisis as possible and avoid a multiplicity of incidents. A consequence of the unity of place was the linking of scenes, the stage never being left empty from the beginning of an act to the end, and the arrival or departure of one or more characters marking the beginning or end of a scene. It followed from the principle of verisimilitude that the entrance or the exit of a character should be justified, not arbitrary; and from the principles of propriety and verisimilitude that each main character should normally be accompanied by a confidant or confidante.

Suspense, created by *péripéties*—reversals of the situation producing the characteristic alternation of hope and fear—was essential. Although a tragedy was predominantly serious in tone, it did not necessarily end unhappily; D'Aubignac, indeed, deprecates the use of the term tragi-comedy to describe a play with a happy ending, precisely because it told the audience what the ending would be, and reduced the suspense, and by Racine's time the distinction between tragedy and tragi-comedy had virtually ceased to exist. For D'Aubignac, a tragedy is 'something magnificent, serious, grave, and suited to the agitations and great reverses of the fortune of princes', and may end 'either by the misfortune of the main characters or by such prosperity as they might have wished for'.

A tragedy showed a conflict between characters or within a character (between love and duty, for instance), and a love interest was essential. The characters were of royal rank, and the subject taken from history or legend. Historical truth might seem to be required; but as history might be changed in the interests of verisimilitude or propriety—in other words, anything improbable or alien to seventeenth-century manners might be eliminated—, and as

D'Aubignac authorized the alteration not only of details, but of the main historical action, the historical residue was sometimes very slight indeed. Nor should it be assumed that the historical or legendary subject was always the starting point. Often, no doubt, a dramatist wrote a play about some historical event that caught his imagination or suited his purpose: Corneille's *Cid* was an adaptation of a Spanish play that had appealed to him, and the story of the Horatii and the Curatii enabled him to depict different attitudes to war and patriotism in *Horace*. Sometimes, clearly, the dramatist started with a situation, and then looked round for historical characters to place in it. When, two years after *Andromaque*, Quinault wrote a tragedy, *Pausanias*, which is remarkably like *Andromaque*, it seems likely that he began with the situation of *Andromaque* in mind, and looked for a different set of names. Campistron, in the preface to his *Andronic* (1685), says that, wishing to dramatize Saint-Réal's *Don Carlos*, but feeling unable to give the characters their real names, he cast around until he found a similar episode in the history of Constantinople. Probably Racine chose his subjects by both methods. When he wrote *Esther* and *Athalie*, he treated subjects that had struck him as suitable for his purpose; but was the starting point of *Andromaque* the Greek story of Andromache or Corneille's *Pertharite*? of *Mithridate*, the history of Mithridates or Corneille's *Nicomède*?

Stage directions are rare in seventeenth-century tragedy. D'Aubignac, indeed, held that all the poet's ideas about the stage set and the costumes, movements, and gestures of his characters should be expressed in his verse. This should be borne in mind when reading Racine. Lines such as

Vous vous troublez, Madame, et changez de visage,
(*Britannicus*, II, 3, 1. 527)
Approchez-vous, Néron, et prenez votre place,
(*Britannicus*, IV, 2, 1. 1115)
J'entends gronder la foudre, et sens trembler la terre,
(*Iphigénie*, V, 4, 1. 1698)

and passages such as those in which Junie, Phèdre, and Thésée give their impressions of previous interviews with Britannicus (11.1001–9), Hippolyte, and Aricie (11.743–52, 1451–2) are in effect stage directions worked into the text.

Tragedies were written in verse, in twelve-syllable lines (or alexandrines), arranged in rhyming couplets, with masculine and feminine rhymes alternating. A number of stylistic features recur constantly, and, since Racine perfected, but used, the style of his contemporaries, deserve a brief mention; the examples quoted are taken from plays performed in the ten years immediately preceding Racine's first tragedy.

Longer speeches often consist of quatrains or groups of four lines. Stichomythia—alternate lines spoken by characters in a verbal duel—, though less common and less prolonged than earlier in the century, still occurs. So do *stances*, the lyrical expression of an emotion or a dilemma in stanzas consisting of lines of varied length—in Montfleury's *Trasibule* and in Thomas Corneille's *Antiochus*, for instance.

The alexandrine, with its caesura after the sixth syllable, falls naturally into two halves, the second of which, with lyrical or dramatic effect, may repeat, or contrast with, the first, or may resemble it in form while contrasting with it in meaning. Such symmetrical lines may show the strength of an emotion, emphasize a dilemma, or give point to an argument or idea.

> On me vole son cœur, on me vole sa foi. . .
> > (Thomas Corneille, *Persée et Demétrius*, IV, 5)
> Ou la main de la sœur, ou la tête du frère. . .
> > (Thomas Corneille, *Pyrrhus*, III, 2)
> Et vous trahir ici, c'est vous être fidèle.
> > (Quinault, *La Mort de Cyrus*, III, 3)

Paradoxical lines like this last are common:

> C'est être criminel qu'avoir trop de vertu.
> > (Montfleury, *Trasibule*, I, 1)
> Rome n'est plus dans Rome, elle est toute où je suis.
> > (Corneille, *Sertorius*, III, 1, l. 936)

Sometimes, two symmetrical lines may be juxtaposed:

> Il sert dans son parti, vous commandez au vôtre;
> Vous êtes chef de l'un, et lui sujet dans l'autre. . .
> > (Corneille, *Sertorius*, I, 3, ll. 301–2)

Here, not only do the two hemistiches in each of the two lines contrast with each other, but the two lines are formed on the same pattern, and express the same antithesis (reversing the order). Sometimes, two lines are formed on the same pattern without internal symmetry:

> Sophonisbe, en un mot, et captive et pleurante,
> L'emporte sur Eryxe et reine et triomphante . . .
>
> (Corneille, Sophonisbe, II, 1, ll. 427–8)

And, of course, more complex formal patterns are found. In the following quatrain, for instance, the antithesis is expressed first in whole lines, then in hemistiches, and finally in whole lines again:

> Je vous l'*ai pris* vaillant, généreux, plein d'honneur,
> Et je vous le *rends* lâche, ingrat, empoisonneur;
> Je l'*ai pris* magnanime, et vous le *rends* perfide,
> Je vous le *rends* sans cœur, et l'*ai pris* intrépide,
> Je l'*ai pris* le plus grand des princes africains,
> Et le *rends*, pour tout dire, esclave des Romains.
>
> (Corneille, Sophonisbe, V, 4, ll. 1661–6)

Another common feature is a series of lines or couplets beginning in the same way, with the same word or phrase.

> *Stratonice.*
> Ah, je n'en doute point, et mon cœur interdit,
> En *croit* bien plus encor que vous n'en avez dit;
> *Je crois qu'*auprès de vous le Prince a l'injustice
> De me rendre toujours quelque mauvais office;
> *Je crois qu'*il ne peut voir mon hymen qu'à regret,
> *Je crois que* mon bonheur fait son tourment secret,
> *Je crois qu'*il veut m'ôter ce que j'obtiens de gloire,
> *Je crois qu'*il vous y porte.
> *Séleucus.*
> Ah, c'est un peu trop croire.
>
> (Quinault, Stratonice, III, 1)

> *J'aime* en Sertorius ce grand art de la guerre
> Qui soutient un banni contre toute la terre,
> *J'aime* en lui *ces* cheveux tous couverts de lauriers,
> *Ce* front qui fait trembler les plus braves guerriers,
> *Ce* bras qui semble avoir la victoire en partage.
>
> (Corneille, Sertorius, II, 1)

In the second example, the repetition of the demonstrative pronoun takes over from the repetition of 'j'aime'.

Verbal repetition of one kind or another is very common, particularly the reduplication of a word in a hemistich (usually the first):

Ce cœur, ce lâche cœur osait trop accorder.[6]
(Thomas Corneille, Commode, IV, 2)
Jetez, jetez, mon fils, les yeux sur cet objet:
Cherchez, cherchez en lui le meurtrier d'un père . . .
(Montfleury, Trasibule, I, 5)

This is, clearly, a convenient way of filling a line with the requisite number of syllables; but it is often more than mere padding. There is no doubt of its effectiveness in the following example:

Vous direz à la Reine . . . —Hé bien! je lui dirai?—
Rien, Seigneur, rien encor; demain j'y penserai.
(Corneille, Sertorius, IV, 3, ll. 1519–20)

Less frequently, a word is repeated several times in a passage. The repetition of the word *croire* in the passage from *Stratonice* above is a good example. In the following passage, also from Quinault, the repetition of the words *haïr* and *aimer* emphasizes the persistence of the heroine's hopeless affection:

Mon père à le *haïr* tâche de m'animer;
Mais lui-même autrefois m'ordonna de l'*aimer*.
Si j'*aime* injustement, j'*aimai* d'abord sans crime,
J'en reçus de sa bouche un ordre légitime,
Et d'ordinaire on sait beaucoup mieux obéir,
Lorsqu'il s'agit d'*aimer*, que lorsqu'il faut *haïr*.
Je l'*aimai* par devoir, je l'*aime* par coutume:
Et dès qu'on a souffert qu'un premier feu s'allume,
Julie, on s'aperçoit qu'il est si doux d'*aimer*,
Qu'on peut malaisément s'en désaccoutumer.
(Agrippa, II, 1)

Sometimes, too, a character repeats the words of another—ironically, triumphantly, broodingly, reproachfully, regretfully, to express surprise, as an effective retort, and so on.

[6] Cf. Mon cœur, mon lâche cœur s'intéresse pour lui?
(Andromaque, V, 1, l. 1404)

Elpidie.
Vous perdez un amant, et moi je perds un fils . . .
Aristide.
Quoi, vous perdez un fils, et je perds un amant?

(Montfleury, *Trasibule*, IV, 6)

Corneille is particularly fond of this device. Here are two examples of several in his *Sophonisbe*.

Il vous la doit, Madame.—Il me la doit, Barcée,
Mais que sert une main par le devoir forcée?[7]

(II, 1, ll. 479–80)

In Act I, scene 4, Sophonisbe encourages her husband to continue fighting:

En tout événement Cyrthe vous tend les bras,
Vous tiendrez, et longtemps, dedans cette retraite.
Mon père cependant répare sa défaite,
Hannon a de l'Espagne amené du secours,
Annibal vient lui-même ici dans peu de jours.

(ll. 358–62)

In Act III, scene 6, having been defeated and taken captive, he reminds her ruefully:

Me les promettiez-vous, alors qu'à ma défaite
Vous montriez dans Cyrthe une sûre retraite,
Et qu'outre le secours de votre général
Vous me vantiez celui d'Hannon et d'Annibal?

(ll. 1065–8)

Stylistic patterns such as these are of a piece with the declamatory delivery, the stylized stage sets, and the conventional costumes of the seventeenth-century French theatre.

The greatest dramatist of the seventeenth century before Racine was Corneille—both a predecessor and a contemporary of Racine's, since his first play was performed ten years before Racine's birth, and his last in 1674, just after *Iphigénie*. As we shall see, Racine owed a good deal to Corneille. He also owed something to another

[7] Cf. Il vous doit son amour.—Il me le doit, Albine . . .

(*Britannicus*, I, 1, l. 20)

dramatist of the first half of the century, Rotrou, whose *Hercule mourant* (1634?) may have influenced *Andromaque,* whose *Antigone* (1637) was certainly used by Racine in writing *La Thébaïde,* who wrote an *Iphigénie* before Racine (1640), and whose *Bélissaire* (1643) suggested a scene of *Britannicus.* In it, Théodore, jealous of Bélissaire's love for Antonie, tells Antonie that, if she lets Bélissaire know that she returns his love, she (Théodore) will put him to death; she then listens from a place of concealment to the interview between Bélissaire and Antonie.[8]

Though the second half of the century should not be contrasted too sharply with the first half, there are some differences between them. A more pessimistic conception of human nature came to prevail, partly, perhaps, as a result of the Fronde. Men were seen as motivated by self-interest, and unable to control their passions (in Pascal, La Rochefoucauld, and Mme de Lafayette, for instance); and stoicism, the prevailing moral philosophy of the first half of the century, gave way to epicureanism, and to the conviction that it was not only impossible, but wrong, to curb the passions (Saint-Evremond, La Fontaine). Love played an even more important part than previously in the tragedy of the age—perhaps because, after the failure of the Fronde, the central government enjoyed absolute power, and noblemen and parlements were deprived of political influence. 'The public wants love, lots of it and of all kinds; it must be treated thoroughly,' wrote Chappuzeau. Whereas Corneille, whose career had begun in the age of Richelieu, maintained that tragedy should deal with characters in danger of losing their lives or their states, or of banishment, and invented the term 'comédie héroïque' for a play—such as *Tite et Bérénice*—in which the only danger is that of losing a lover or a mistress, Racine, in the preface to his *Bérénice,* insists that a play about love can be a tragedy: 'It is not necessary that there should be bloodshed and corpses in a tragedy'. In the decade before Racine's first play, the demand for love had been exploited by a number of dramatists, particularly Quinault and Corneille's brother, Thomas.

'All for love' might serve as a title to many of their plays. In Thomas Corneille's *Timocrate,* the seventeenth-century play that ran

---

[8] Cf. *Britannicus,* Act II, scenes 4–6. There is a similar episode in Quinault's *Mariage de Cambyse.*

longest, the hero, Timocrate, has no sense of responsibility to his subjects. His only motive in waging war is to win Eriphile, the daughter of the queen of the country he is fighting, and his troops have orders to shed no blood. Darius, in his tragedy of the same name, is interested, not in recovering his kingdom, but in marrying Statira; and he does not reveal his identity until he is sure that he is loved for himself alone, and not for his rank. In Quinault's *Astrate,* Astrate, the sole survivor of the dispossessed royal house, loves the queen, the daughter and successor of the usurper, and fights for her against his own side:

J'écoute mon amour, et n'entends rien de plus.

(IV, 4)

Lovers are remarkably devoted, disinterested, and submissive. In Thomas Corneille's *Bérénice,* Philoxène, who, as a prince, loved Bérénice, a commoner, remonstrates with her for continuing to love him when the situations are reversed, and he turns out to be a commoner whilst she is a princess. In his *Commode,* Electus loves Marcia, but, though she returns his love, she wants to marry the emperor; so Electus sinks all personal feelings, and does all he can to bring about her marriage with Commode.[9]

Sans cesse tout pour vous, et jamais rien pour moi.

(II, 2)

In Quinault's *Mort de Cyrus,* the first sight of Thomiris on the battlefield so unnerves Cyrus that he falls in love with her on the spot, loses the battle, and is captured by her. Thomiris loves Cyrus, but marries Odatirse, who threatens to kill Cyrus if she does not. Cyrus kills Odatirse, but Thomiris feels that it is now her duty to avenge her husband, and Cyrus gives himself up:

Vous avez résolu que l'assassin périsse,
Et puisque je le suis, il faut que j'obéisse;
Vos désirs sont mes lois, et voulant mon trépas,
C'eût été vous trahir que ne me livrer pas.

(V, 4)

He is duly executed. Antiochus in Quinault's *Stratonice* does, it is true, venture to criticize Stratonice; but he immediately afterwards dismisses the unfortunate Zabas who dares to agree with him.

---

[9] Cf. Euchérius in Thomas Corneille's *Stilicon.*

Théodat in Quinault's *Amalasonte* is disobedient in one respect: he refuses to obey the queen's command to keep away from her. However unjustly she treats him, he will love no one else:

Près d'elle un mal pour moi vaut mieux qu'un bien ailleurs.

(IV, 1)

Similarly Démétrius in Thomas Corneille's *Persée et Démétrius* refuses to leave Erixène, though his life is in danger if he stays. Finally he kills himself because he thinks she does not love him.

Some of Racine's lovers are reminiscent of these devoted heroes of Thomas Corneille and Quinault. But these writers also have lovers of another kind, selfish and unscrupulous, who threaten to kill their mistress's father (*Commode*), brother (Thomas Corneille, *Pyrrhus*), lover (Thomas Corneille, *Camma*; *La Mort de Cyrus*) or child (Corneille, *Pertharite*; Montfleury, *Trasibule*), unless she marries them, and anticipate Pyrrhus and Néron. Corneille's *Toison d'Or* also contains two lovers who are far from disinterested. Jason, who is glib and fickle, has deserted Hypsipyle, and is paying his addresses to Médée with the object of winning the golden fleece; but when Hypsipyle follows him to Colchos, Médée finds him making love to her. Absyrte, Médée's brother, is prepared to take advantage of his sister's magic arts to win Hypsipyle's love, and declares: 'je ne suis pas homme à servir mon rival' (V, 1, l. 1848).

Love, in the heroines, too, is an irresistible force, winning easy victories over dignity, duty, or responsibility. Eriphile in *Timocrate* loves and encourages the adventurer, Cléomène. Statira in *Darius* loves the adventurer, Codoman, without thought of the future.[10] Some—Constance in Thomas Corneille's *Maximian,* Thomiris in *La Mort de Cyrus*—refuse to marry men to whom they are promised, because they love others. Antigone, in *Pyrrhus*, is engaged to Pyrrhus, but she cannot help loving Hippias:

Aimer quand on le veut passe notre puissance . . .[11]

On aime bien souvent quand on le veut le moins.

(I, 1)

---

[10] Cf. Titus in *Bérénice* (ll. 1089–95).
[11] Antiochus in Quinault's *Stratonice* also says:

. . . on n'aime pas toujours ce qu'on voudrait aimer.

(I, 6)

Médée in *La Toison d'Or* similarly says:

Je veux ne t'aimer plus, et n'en ai pas la force.

(II, 2, l. 765)

She tells Jason that he should have sacrificed his companions to his love of her, and she herself betrays her father and her country for love of him. Hypsipyle, in the same play, abandoned by Jason pursues him to Colchos and abases herself to plead with him:

Il n'est pas glorieux pour une grande Reine
De montrer de l'amour, et de voir de la haine,

(III, 3, ll. 1168–9)

he comments.

Jealousy makes women cruel to their rivals, like Fatime in Quinault's *Généreuse Ingratitude*, who falsely tells Zaïde, in order to make her suffer, that she, Fatime, is to marry Zaïde's lover, or Corneille's Médée, who says:

Je ne croirai jamais qu'il soit douceur égale
A celle de se voir immoler sa rivale . . .[12]

(IV, 3, ll. 1576–7)

Corneille's Sophonisbe marries Massinisse—and brings about her own downfall—in order to stop him marrying her rival. Not infrequently, jealous women want to kill their false lovers. Marcia, in *Commode*, asks her lover, Electus, to kill Commode, whom she does not love but wants to marry, because he has decided to marry her sister. Zaïde, in *La Généreuse Ingratitude*, urges her brother to kill her lover whom she believes faithless; but she tells her confidante:

Si cet ingrat périt, il faudra que je meure,
Je sens dans mon esprit triompher tour à tour,
La rage et la tendresse, et la haine et l'amour;
Je suis son ennemie, et je suis son amante,
Quand mon dépit s'accroît, ma passion augmente;

Cf. Vous que j'ai plaint, enfin que je voudrais aimer.—
Je vous entends. Tel est mon partage funeste:
Le cœur est pour Pyrrhus, et les vœux pour Oreste.

(*Andromaque*, II, 2, ll. 536–8)

[12] Cf. Erixène in Thomas Corneille's *Persée et Démétrius*.

> Et quoiqu'il soit aimable, et qu'il m'ait pu trahir,
> Je ne le puis aimer, et ne le puis haïr.
>
> (IV, 4)

Médée says that her love

> va jusqu'a à la haine, et toutefois, hélas!
> Je te haïrais peu, si je ne t'aimais pas.
>
> (II, 2, ll. 770–1)

Oscillation between hatred and love is the main theme of Quinault's *Amalasonte*. Queen Amalasonte is in love with Théodat, and he loves her; Amalfrède, too, loves him, but her love is not requited—a typical Racinian situation. In the course of the play, Amalasonte is repeatedly led to believe Théodat unfaithful. Whenever this happens, she wants to put him to death, though not without hesitation:

> Que voulez-vous, Madame?
> Je ne le puis savoir.—Ce que je veux, hélas!
> Comment le saurais-tu, si je ne le sais pas?[13]
>
> (II, 2)

When, however, she believes that he has been murdered, she wants to avenge his death:

> Hélas! je me flattais quand j'ai cru le haïr . . .[14]
>
> (III, 5)

Finally, persuaded that Théodat has tried to kill her, Amalasonte sends him a poisoned letter; but the moment it has gone, she repents. Although she thinks that he has died faithless, she laments his death. Amalasonte, a queen with the power to put her lover to death, is a foretaste of Racine's Roxane, as well as of Hermione; and, like Roxane, she is credulous, easily persuaded of her lover's innocence:

> Un criminel qui plaît est toujours innocent.
>
> (II, 4)

Amalfrède swings from love to hatred and back again like Amalasonte. Just after she has declared,

---

[13] Cf. Je crains de me connaître en l'état où je suis.
(*Andromaque*, II, 1, l. 428)
[14] Cf. 'Qui te l'a dit?' (*Andromaque*, V, 3, l. 1543). See below, p. 35.

Sa perte est maintenant mon unique désir,
Je sens que je verrais sa mort avec plaisir,

(III, 3)

her brother tells her that he has killed Théodat, and she bursts out:

Quoi, tu m'as pu ravir un objet si charmant,
Et tu crois échapper à mon ressentiment?

(III, 4)

The chief difference between Amalfrède and Amalasonte is that the former has no moral scruples, and misleads the queen into believing, not only that Théodat is unfaithful to her, but that he has even attempted to kill her.

There are other things in the plays of the period that anticipate Racine. It has been observed that the intensity of the emotions of Racine's characters increases when they are in one another's presence, and diminishes when they are apart. Lisandre, in *Le Feint Alcibiade*, has the same experience:

L'absence a fait en moi son effet ordinaire,
Cléone que j'aimais cesse enfin de me plaire . . .

J'ai revu Léonide, et sa vue en mon âme
A fait renaître un feu des cendres de ma flamme . . .[15]

(III, 1)

So has Cyrus, who says:

Plus un objet est proche, et plus il est puissant . . .

(*La Mort de Cyrus*, II, 1)

Racine's characters scrutinize one another, and divine states of mind from facial expression and behaviour (or betray themselves involuntarily by the same means). There are plenty of examples in Corneille, Thomas Corneille, and Quinault; indeed, this is a

---

[15] A dead metaphor revivified by its context. Cf.

L'amour n'est pas un feu qu'on renferme en une âme:
Tout nous trahit, la voix, le silence, les yeux;
Et les feux mal couverts n'en éclatent que mieux.

(*Andromaque*, II, 2, ll. 574–6)

On craint que de la sœur les flammes téméraires
Ne raniment un jour la cendre de ses frères.

(*Phèdre*, II, 1. ll. 429–30).

recurring feature of French drama from Alexandre Hardy onwards, due perhaps to French court and salon life. One passage of Quinault is worth quoting because it is particularly reminiscent of Racine:

> Il m'aime; ce n'est pas qu'il me l'aie osé dire;
> Pour contraindre sa flamme, il n'a rien épargné;
> Le silence toujours sur sa bouche a régné;
> Mais un cœur pour parler, n'a-t-il qu'un interprète?
> Ne dit-on rien des yeux, quand la bouche est muette?
> L'amant qui craint le plus de rien faire éclater,
> N'en dit toujours que trop, à qui veut l'écouter;
> En vain pour se contraindre, on prend un soin extrême;
> Tout parle dans l'amour, jusqu'au silence même.[16]
>
> (*Astrate*, II, 3)

Heroes—like Oreste—sometimes delude themselves into thinking that they are no longer in love. Zégry, in *La Généreuse Ingratitude*, ill-treated by Fatime, persuades himself that he has ceased to love her; but when he hears Ormin dwelling on her faults, he is impatient with him, and acknowledges:

> Ma flamme est une erreur, mais cette erreur m'est chère,
> Tes fidèles conseils ne sont pas de saison,
> L'amour n'a pas fait place encore à ma raison . . .
>
> (I, 5)

In *Stratonice*, whenever Zénone attempts to talk of the king, Stratonice turns the conversation to the prince, whom she is supposed to dislike—one thinks of Pyrrhus in Act II, scene 5 of *Andromaque*:

> *Z.* Mais contre Séleucus quel sujet vous anime?
> Madame, il n'a pour vous fait voir que de l'estime.

---

[16] Cf.   Tout nous trahit, la voix, le silence, les yeux . . .

> (*Andromaque*, II, 2, l. 575)

J'entendrai des regards que vous croirez muets . . .

> (*Britannicus*, II, 3, l. 682)

There are early examples of such scrutiny in Hardy, *Félismène,* Act III; Corneille, *Mélite*, II, 6, *La Suivante*, I, 8; and Du Ryer, *Les Vendanges de Suresnes*, IV, 2.

S. Zénone, il est certain, mais le Prince son fils
    N'a pour moi jusqu'ici fait voir que du mépris.
Z. Le Roi cherche à vous plaire avec un soin extrême.
S. Le Prince Antiochus n'en use pas de même.
Z. Le Roi vous aimera, bornez-y vos souhaits.
S. Mais le Prince son fils ne m'aimera jamais.
Z. Vous nommez tant ce fils, à vos désirs contraire,
    Qu'on dirait qu'il vous touche un peu plus que son père.

(II, 2)

In *La Mort de Cyrus*, hatred is the origin of love. When Thomiris
defeats and captures her enemy Cyrus, she begins by hating him, or
thinking that she hates him; but hatred gives way to love:

Sitôt qu'avec ses yeux les miens se rencontrèrent,
De nouvelles ardeurs en mon cœur s'allumèrent.
Je pris pour haine alors ce qui vint m'enflammer;
Et croyant mieux haïr, je commençai d'aimer.
J'attribuai d'abord tout mon trouble à ma haine,
Je n'y resistai point, je le souffris sans peine;
Et quand je m'aperçus de l'erreur de mes sens,
J'y voulais résister, mais il n'etait plus temps.

(I, 5)

One is reminded of Eriphile in Racine's *Iphigénie*.
    Both in *Stratonice* and in Thomas Corneille's *Antiochus*, as in
Mithridate, a son is in love with his father's bride to be. Antiochus,
like Phèdre, conceals his love, but falls sick, the victim of a myster-
ious languor. Like Phèdre, too, he says:

De quel front accepter les droits au diadème,
Si je n'ai pas appris à régner sur moi-même?
Et par quel âpre soif du vain titre de roi,
Prendre un empire ailleurs que je n'ai pas sur moi?[17]

(I, 1)

Incest is the subject of two plays, Quinault's *Mariage de Cambyse* and

[17] Cf.   Moi régner! Moi, ranger un État sous ma loi,
        Quand ma faible raison ne règne plus sur moi!
        Lorsque j'ai de mes sens abandonné l'empire!
                                    (*Phèdre*, III, 1, ll. 759–61)

Thomas Corneille's *Pyrrhus*, in both of which a brother and a sister are in love. But although love between brothers and sisters is far worse than Phèdre's love for a mere stepson, these two pairs of brothers and sisters have little sense of guilt, oppose little resistance to their passion, and confess their mutual love in charming love scenes. A sense of guilt indeed would be out of place, since it turns out in both plays that one of the pair was changed in infancy, so that they are not related.

Quinault's plays have a good deal of charm, which lies partly in his style; and just occasionally one comes across lines that in their simplicity or their harmony are not unworthy of Racine. The dying queen, for instance, tells her lover, Astrate:

> J'aimais beaucoup le trône, et moins encor que vous.
> Le jour avec vous seul m'aurait pu faire envie;
> Mais sans trône, et sans vous, que faire de la vie?
>
> (*Astrate*, V, 5)

Lavinie in *Agrippa* believes her lover to be dead, yet hopes:

> Votre fils ne vit plus, je ne puis m'en flatter,
> La nature le dit, et je n'ose en douter:
> Mais ce doute est si doux, que l'Amour qui murmure
> Voudrait bien s'il osait, démentir la Nature.
>
> (IV, 3)

The alliteration and the assonance of the third line recall Racine. Another line with an almost Racinian ring is this:

> Tout me nuit, tout me perd, et tout me désespère.[18]
>
> (*La Généreuse Ingratitude*, IV, 9)

That Racine owed something to Thomas Corneille and Quinault is probable; but the distance between him and them is enormous. Some of their plays are simple and good—Thomas Corneille's *Ariane* and *Comte d'Essex*, Quinault's *Amalasonte* and *Stratonice* (a charming study of the dawn of love, not unworthy of Marivaux), for instance. But they pay no attention to realism of setting or historical truth, they are sometimes complicated, they use disguise and confusion of identity too freely, and they are often highly improbable. In *La*

[18] Cf.   Tout m'afflige et me nuit, et conspire à me nuire.

(*Phèdre*, I, 3, l. 161)

Généreuse Ingratitude, Zélinde, disguised as a man, runs away from home in pursuit of her faithless lover; she is captured by pirates, and sold to none other than her lover. In *Timocrate*, two countries are at war: Cléomène, the mainstay of one side, is the king of the other, in disguise. In *Bérénice*, *Darius*, and *Astrate*, a man of unknown parentage turns out to be the rightful ruler of the kingdom. In *Le Feint Alcibiade*, Alcibiade's twin sister passes herself off as her brother, and follows her faithless lover to Sparta. In *Le Mariage de Cambyse*, sisters, and in *Pyrrhus*, brothers, were exchanged in infancy. In *Agrippa ou le faux Tibérinus*, Tibérinus and Agrippa are doubles; Agrippa kills Tibérinus and passes himself off as him. Dramatists take full advantage of the opportunities for double-entendre afforded by such situations.

Misunderstandings and dilemmas are frequent. In Quinault's *Coups de l'Amour et de la Fortune*, Roger's successive acts of devotion to Aurore are attributed by her to his rival; exactly as Amalasonte is led, time and time again, to believe Théodat unfaithful. The queen in *Timocrate* vows to put Timocrate to death if he falls into her hands, and to reward the man who delivers him up to her with the hand of her daughter: what is she to do when he gives himself up? In *Le Feint Alcibiade*, the supposed Alcibiade, concealed in the queen's apartment, saves the king's life: is the king to punish him for being where no man should be, or to reward him? What is Thomiris to do, when, having vowed to punish the murderer of her husband, she finds it is her lover, Cyrus? And Astrate, who is in love with the queen, but who finds that he is the rightful heir to the throne of which she is the usurper, and son and brother of men for whose deaths she is responsible?

Playwrights are also fond of making their characters express unexpected and unlikely opinions, explicable only by motives of which the audience is ignorant. In *Timocrate*, the queen holds a council to discuss whether she should give her daughter to her enemy Timocrate or not. Cléomène, who loves her daughter, somewhat surprisingly recommends that she should be married to Timocrate. Although he explains this opinion in different ways to different people, the real explanation is that he himself is Timocrate. In *Le Feint Alcibiade*, the king asks his wife and his favourite whether he should send Alcibiade away or not. As we believe the queen to be in love with Alcibiade, and the minister to be jealous of him, we are somewhat taken aback when she urges the king to send him away, and he recommends that he be allowed to stay. In *Stratonice,* Séleucus tells Stratonice that he would like her to marry his son (with whom she is secretly in love) instead of himself; she refuses. Agrippa, in the play of that name, tells Lavinie that he really is Agrippa, not Tibérinus; to prove it, he sends for his father—who denies it.

Finally, there is a good chance that anyone reported dead in a play by Quinault will still be alive. Fabrice, in *Le Fantôme amoureux,* is chased by the duke's guards and killed; in fact, they have killed the wrong man, with the result that throughout the play Fabrice is taken for a ghost. Théodat in *Amalasonte* is twice believed to have been killed; and Lisandre and Agis, in *Le Feint Alcibiade,* both believed to be dead, have in fact been saved by Alcibiade.

Racine avoids all such improbabilities. He makes no use of disguise (except in his one comedy), and little of concealed identity; and he makes his characters speak and behave naturally. Nevertheless, when Eriphile in *Iphigénie* turns out to be the daughter of Helen, and Joas in *Athalie* to be the rightful heir to the throne, and when, after being reported dead, Porus, Mithridate, and Thésée walk on to the stage, the seasoned theatre-goer must have felt himself to be on familiar ground.

2

From *La Thebaïde* to *Andromaque*

From letters and other documents, a good deal is known about the life of Racine, but very little about the vital years in which he wrote the first ten of his twelve plays. Between January 1664 and the beginning of 1685, there is a gap in his correspondence, with only one or two insignificant notes surviving from the intervening years. Even about the events before and after this period, there is a good deal of uncertainty: on almost every point of interest in the life of Racine, the evidence is confused or conflicting.

Jean Racine, the first child of Jean Racine and Jeanne Sconin, was born in La Ferté- Milon, some forty-five miles north-east of Paris, in December 1639. His father was a minor legal official; his paternal grandfather, another Jean Racine, was a comptroller in the salt warehouse of La Ferté-Milon;[1] and his maternal grandfather, Pierre Sconin, was both an official in the office responsible for waterways and forests and president of the salt warehouse. In short, on both sides of his family, he belonged to middle-class officialdom.

In January 1641, Racine's mother died after giving birth to a daughter, Marie; and when, in February 1643, his father died too, the paternal grandparents took charge of Jean Racine, and the maternal grandparents of his sister. After the death of Racine's paternal grandfather in September 1649, his widow, Marie des Moulins,

---

[1] This was the office that administered the gabelle or salt tax, responsible for seeing that every household purchased its due amount of salt, and for preventing the smuggling of salt from areas where it was cheap or untaxed to areas where it was dear.

decided to retire to the famous convent, Port-Royal, where she had a number of relatives, including a daughter, Racine's aunt, Agnès de Sainte-Thècle; and Jean Racine went with her.

Port-Royal at that time had two branches, governed by a single abbess—one in Paris (Port-Royal de Paris) and one outside, between Sceaux and Versailles (Port-Royal des Champs). A peculiar feature of Port-Royal is that it had attracted to its neighbourhood a number of men, the *solitaires*, who lived in pious seclusion at Les Granges outside Port-Royal des Champs. In addition, a number of sympathizers had built houses nearby, such as the duc de Luynes at Vaumurier, M. du Gué de Bagnols at the château de Saint-Jean des Trous, and M. Maignart de Bernière at the château du Chesnay. Under the influence of the nuns' director, Saint-Cyran, Port-Royal—particularly its men—had become the centre of the movement known as Jansenism, which upheld the doctrine of predestination, stressed the omnipotence of God and the helplessness of man without Grace, and practised an austere religion in opposition to the relative laxity of the Jesuits. Under Saint-Cyran's influence, too, the *solitaires* had begun to educate boys, and established a school in Paris in 1646, where a small number of boys were taught in classes of five or six. Through the hostility of the Jesuits, the school was dispersed in the summer of 1653—different groups going to the château du Chesnay, to Les Granges (with Nicole), to the château de Saint-Jean des Trous, and to Sevrans near Livry. The school at Les Granges was closed in 1656; the others in 1660.

As Racine was certainly educated at Port-Royal—some have even detected the influence of Jansenism in his tragedies—, it is disappointing that we do not know exactly how long he lived there, nor how his time was spent. The facts are that he was educated at Port-Royal from an uncertain date (possibly 1649)[2] until 1653; that

---

[2] It is generally assumed that Racine accompanied his grandmother to Port-Royal in 1649, shortly after her husband's death. But the evidence is conflicting, and both an earlier and a later date for his first arrival at Port-Royal are possible.

On the one hand, Racine stood godfather at christenings in La Ferté-Milon on November 17, 1649 and on March 6, 1650; and Marie des Moulins's presence at Port-Royal is not attested before May, 1652. On the other, Racine says in a letter to Mme de Maintenon (March 4, 1698) that his aunt, Agnès de Sainte-Thècle, taught him the knowledge of God in his

he then spent two years at school in Beauvais, returning to Port-Royal for three further years; that at some time he was at the château de Saint-Jean des Trous and at Le Chesnay, as well as at Les Granges; that he was taught by Nicole, Antoine Le Maître, and Hamon, at whose feet he asked to be buried; and that he acquired a sound knowledge of Greek from Lancelot.

On leaving Port-Royal, Racine spent a year reading philosophy at the collège d'Harcourt, one of the constituent colleges of the University of Paris. He then lived with his cousin, Nicolas Vitart, the duc de Luynes's steward, frequenting taverns, writing verse, and incurring the wrath of Port-Royal. In November 1661, at the invitation of his uncle Sconin, vicar-general of the cathedral of Uzès, he went thither to read theology with a view to entering the Church and obtaining a benefice. He remained there at least until the following July, possibly longer, before returning to Paris empty-handed.

The career of few dramatists can have begun less auspiciously. In 1660, a play of his, *Amasie*, was turned down by the Marais theatre; in 1661, a tragedy about Ovid was rejected by the Hôtel de Bourgogne; and Molière's biographer, Grimarest, says that a play on the subject of *Théagène et Chariclée* was refused by Molière's company in 1662. The following year, according to Grimarest and Boileau's friend, Brossette, Molière, looking for someone to write a play to compete with Boyer's *Thébaïde* at the Hôtel de Bourgogne, remembered the young man who had brought him *Théagène et Chariclée*, and advised him to adapt Rotrou's *Antigone*.[3] Racine set to work; by November 1663 he was engaged on the fourth act; and his first extant play, *La Thébaïde*, was performed by Molière's company on June 20, 1664.

childhood. Now, if we accept her own statement that she entered Port-Royal at the age of fifteen (i.e. in 1641 or 1642), this seems to imply that they were together at Port-Royal well before 1649. But the *Nécrologe de Port-Royal* says that she was a novice in 1647, and Racine's friend, Vuillard, says that she looked after her nephew before entering Port-Royal, where she took her vows in 1648 (letters of April 30, 1699 and June 3, 1700).

[3] See Grimarest, *La Vie de M. de Molière*, ed. G. Mongrédien, 1955, pp. 55–6, and the *Correspondance de Boileau-Despréaux et de Brossette*, ed. A. Laverdet, 1857, p. 519. Boyer's play was a failure, and never published.

Since plays by Gilbert entitled *Théagène et Chariclée* and *Les Amours d'Ovide* were performed in 1662 and 1663 respectively, Racine may have been engaged in similar competitions before.

Rotrou, like the sixteenth-century dramatist, Garnier, who had also written an *Antigone,* had made a single play of the story of the sons of Œdipus and of that of their sister, Antigone. This duplicity of action was no more possible in 1664 than the changes of scene of Rotrou's tragedy; so that Racine had to make a five-act play out of the first two acts and a half of Rotrou's. This he did by turning the skirmish with which Rotrou's play opens into two, by increasing the love interest, and by developing the rôle of the brother's uncle, Créon, who now becomes the villain of the piece and his son's rival as well.[4] His debt to Rotrou, however, is considerable. He owes his opening and his characters to him—Rotrou's Antigone, like Racine's, prefers Polynice to Etéocle; Rotrou's Polynice, like Racine's, proposes the single combat in order to put an end to the bloodshed; Rotrou's Etéocle, like Racine's, has the support of the people of Thebes; and Racine has developed the hints in Rotrou's play that Créon is a villain and a tyrant.

Racine owes a good deal to Corneille, too. *La Thébaïde* recalls *Horace*—one deals with war between brothers, the other with war between two states closely united by friendship and marriage ties. In both, vain attempts are made to prevent the war; in both, there is an ambiguous oracle; and in both, general bloodshed is averted by a combat between representatives of the two sides. Like Sabine in *Horace*, Jocaste more than once asks the combatants to take her life. In both plays the narrative of the fight is split into two parts, the first report giving a misleading impression of the outcome. Moreover, the *stances*—or lyrical monologue in stanza form—of Antigone in the fifth act recall the famous *stances* of Rodrigue in Corneille's *Cid*.

Racine's chief debt to Corneille, perhaps, is the dramatic technique of his play, the use of *péripéties* to maintain suspense until the end of the play. *La Thébaïde* opens (like Rotrou's *Antigone*) with a report that fighting has broken out. This turns out to be false. Then the oracle is consulted, and delivers an ambiguous prophecy. Jocaste and Antigone have an interview with Polynice, but he is deaf to their entreaties. Fighting again breaks out, but peace is restored by the suicide of Ménécée, which seems to fulfil the oracle. Jocaste, however, expresses pessimism in a speech (11.675–90) which neatly

---

[4] As he is in love with his niece, Antigone, his love is incestuous, a curious anticipation of *Phèdre;* but Racine makes nothing of this in the play.

summarizes the *péripéties* of the play so far and foreshadows what is to come. The meeting of the brothers, the climax of the play, is postponed until the fourth act, and is dramatically more effective than it is in Rotrou's play. In *Antigone*, the meeting is not pre-arranged: Polynice summons his brother to the walls of the city, and proposes the single combat to him. In Racine's play, the meeting is arranged beforehand, and differences of opinion about it arouse the interest of the audience: Antigone hopes that it will bring about a reconciliation, Créon expects that it will make matters worse, and Etéocle believes that it will achieve nothing. In fact, it leads to the single combat, the first report of which tells of Polynice's triumph, followed shortly afterwards by news of his death and of Hémon's. Créon is now confident that Antigone will marry him; but she commits suicide.

Not only is suspense maintained, but the characters are more sharply contrasted than in *Antigone*, or for that matter any other previous treatment of the subject. Polynice is the better of the two brothers—'plus doux et soumis', according to Jocaste (l. 1033), 'vertueux', according to Antigone (l. 1268). He is Antigone's favourite brother, and she has even sent her lover, Hémon, to serve him, a detail invented by Racine. Polynice, moreover, hates the war that has been forced upon him, and proposes the single combat to put an end to the bloodshed. He is also in the right. Œdipus having ordained that the brothers should reign alternately, Etéocle began and then refused to give the throne up, on the grounds that the people did not want him to. In claiming the throne, Polynice is not only claiming his due; he is obeying his father's commands, and upholding royal authority against the demagogy of his brother:[5]

[5] Quinault's play, *Les Coups de l'Amour et de la Fortune*, deals with two sisters, who are at war for the throne of Barcelona. Like Etéocle and Polynice, they have an abortive meeting. As in Racine's play, it is the sister who enjoys the sympathies of the audience (Aurore) who upholds the rights of the legitimate heir against the doctrine of popular sovereignty:

Stelle.   Le peuple à qui le Ciel a concédé les droits
            D'interpréter les Dieux et de créer les Rois,
            Par ses émotions a bien dû vous apprendre
            Qu'il révoque l'arrêt que vous avez fait rendre,
            Que votre soin ne sert qu'a vous faire haïr,
            Et que ce n'est qu'à moi que l'on doit obéir.

Jocaste.	Il a pour lui le peuple.

Polynice.   Et j'ai pour moi les Dieux.

(IV, 3, l. 1166)

Antigone and Hémon are on his side; so is Jocaste:

L'un a pour lui le peuple, et l'autre la justice.

(III, 3, text of 1664)

Etéocle is the more violent of the two brothers, hates his brother more than his brother hates him, expresses his hatred at far greater length, is quite in the wrong, and is a demagogue into the bargain (ll.488–96).

Just as the brothers are less sharply contrasted in previous treatments of the subject, so Créon is less villainous. In *La Thébaïde*, he is the wicked uncle of legend. Ambitious, crafty, and double-faced, he has inflamed the mutual hatred of the brothers, and induced Etéocle to turn Polynice out of Thebes. He is almost devoid of paternal affection.

Despite all this, however, *La Thébaïde* is quite unlike a play by Corneille, and is curiously anticipatory of Racine's later work. The subject is taken from Greek mythology like those of some of Racine's finest and most characteristic tragedies, and the play depicts a family rent by strife and hatred, the victim of fatality and heredity. Rivalry, mistrust, and hatred between brothers or half-brothers recur in *Britannicus*, *Bajazet*, and *Mithridate*.[6] Moreover,

---

Aurore.   Sachez que si le peuple à mon règne s'oppose,
               Ses mouvements font voir l'équité de ma cause;
               C'est un monstre privé de tout discernement,
               Qui cherche le désordre avec aveuglement,
               Et qui s'émeut toujours, tant son audace est grande,
               Contre les souverains dont il faut qu'il dépende:
               Mais enfin son courroux ne doit pas m'alarmer,
               Avec un seul regard je puis le désarmer.

(I, 3)

Compare, too, Racine's *Alexandre*:

Taxile	Le peuple aime les rois qui savent l'épargner.
Porus.	Il estime encor plus ceux qui savent régner.

(I, 2, ll. 223–4)

It is with Porus that the audience's sympathies lie.

[6] Hatred and rivalry between sisters is the subject of Quinault's *Coups de*

the hatred of the two brothers is exacerbated by physical proximity, like the emotions of several of Racine's later characters. The characters of *La Thébaïde* are unheroic, not lacking in courage, but controlled by their passions, rather than in control of them. Jocaste, in need of physical support, faintly foreshadows Phèdre:

> Olympe, soutiens-moi; ma douleur est extrême.
>
> (I, 3, l. 44)

Like Phèdre, too, she blames the gods for their injustice and cruelty. Although the love interest is secondary, the situation is one that recurs continually in the later plays: A and B love one another, and one of them is loved by the jealous and unhappy C. In *La Thébaïde*, as in *Mithridate* and *Phèdre*, the jealous and unhappy lover is the father of the successful one. The play is comparatively simple, and it ends unhappily. As in *Britannicus*, the climax is a crucial interview, postponed until the fourth act, which, in fact, fails to bring about the reconciliation hoped for. Moreover, this outcome is carefully prepared, since Créon forecasts what will happen (11.875–90). The theme of the play is reinforced by the recurrence of the word *sang,* used in its literal sense of 'blood' and in its metaphorical sense of 'family', sometimes used with effective irony in both senses at once, as in Creón's line:

> Et le sang reprendra son empire ordinaire.
>
> (III, 5, l. 808)

Finally, Créon's madness or near madness at the end anticipates the states of mind of Oreste and Néron at the end of *Andromaque* and *Britannicus*.

Racine's play with its mixture of derivative features and of features characteristic of his future work, is extremely interesting, but not a great play. The subject is lacking in universal appeal, there is little attempt to evoke the background, and there are none of those passages of magnificent poetry that abound from *Andromaque* onwards. Moreover, some of the characters are either inconsistent or imperfectly adapted to the situations in which they find themselves. Polynice, for instance is depicted as deeply affected by the war that he has started, which is hard to reconcile with his expressions of *l'Amour et de la Fortune*; between brothers, of Thomas Corneille's *Persée et Démétrius*.

ruthless ambition in Act IV, scene 3 (ll. 1127–30, 1159–60).[7] Créon, the character whom Racine has most transformed, is the most incoherent. Although we are told that everything that has happened is his work, that it was he who induced Etéocle to refuse to give up the throne to Polynice, and who brought about the meeting in order to inflame their hatred (11.851–2, 875–90), we see little of this in the play. His affection for his sons seems to fluctuate strangely. At one moment, he says:

> Mais il me reste un fils; et je sens que je l'aime,
> Tout rebelle qu'il est, et tout mon rival même.
>
> (III, 6, ll. 871–2)

At another, after the death of both his sons as well as both his nephews, he remarks:

> Il n'est point de fortune à mon bonheur égale,
> Et tu vas voir en moi, dans ce jour fortuné,
> L'ambitieux au trône, et l'amant couronné.
>
> (V, 4, ll. 1422–4)

His love for Antigone is quite out of character. It is inconceivable that an ambitious, unscrupulous man like Créon, who says

> Le trône fit toujours mes ardeurs les plus chères . . .
> Je ne fais point de pas qui ne tende à l'empire,
>
> (III, 6, ll. 843 and 848)

should become demented from thwarted love and remorse.

Racine learned from his mistakes. He is careful to let us know that Acomat's desire to marry Atalide is purely political:

> Quoi? vous l'aimez, Seigneur?—Voudrais-tu qu'à mon âge
> Je fisse de l'amour le vil apprentissage?
>
> (*Bajazet*, I, 1, ll. 177–8)

Mithridate, torn between his love for Monime and his ardent desire to prosecute the war against the Romans, is a much more convincing and moving character than Créon.

---

[7]Some of the incoherence is due to the fact that sixteenth- and seventeenth-century editions of Seneca gave Polynices some of the speeches of Eteocles in the corresponding scene in his *Phoenissae*.

Alexandre was first performed by Molière's company on December
4, 1665. On the 18th, the actors were surprised to learn that the play
was also being performed by their rivals at the Hôtel de Bourgogne
with the connivance of Racine—it appears, indeed, from Robinet's
rhymed news sheet of December 20, that they had already performed it privately at the comtesse d'Armagnac's the previous
Tuesday (December 14). According to Racine's eldest son, the
reason for this shabby action was that Racine

> did not approve of the over-uniform delivery customary in
> Molière's company. He wanted the verse to be given a certain
> sound which, together with the rhythm and the rhymes, can be
> distinguished from prose . . .[8]

The play was successful. While it was performed at the Palais-
Royal, the takings were high, and it remained in the repertory of the
Hôtel de Bourgogne, and afterwards of the Comédie-Française, for
at least twenty years. Intended as a compliment to Louis XIV, to
whom it was dedicated when it was published,[9] *Alexandre* established Racine's reputation as a dramatist. Saint-Evremond in exile in
England wrote an essay on it. Nevertheless, the modern reader, for
whom this is Racine's least interesting play, may feel some sympathy
with Corneille, who is said, after hearing Racine read it to him, to
have told him that he was unfitted for drama.

Alexandre is unlike *La Thébaïde* in many respects (including the

[8] Jean-Baptiste Racine also says that his father preferred what he calls the
'recitative' of the Hôtel de Bourgogne, because it was 'more majestic and
displayed the tragic verse to better advantage than the actors of Molière's
company'. But Racine did not like delivery to be too unnatural either.
Jean-Baptiste adds that he could not bear 'those exaggerated and yelping
tones that actors like to substitute for natural beauty, and that might, so to
speak, be noted down like music'. (L. Vaunois, *L'Enfance et la Jeunesse de
Racine,* 1964, pp. 201, 207)

[9] A comparison between Louis XIV and Alexander the Great in 1664 may
seem unlikely; but as early as 1657 the *Gazette de France* had written: 'For,
although our great Monarch, having been born in the midst of triumphs
and victories, is altogether warlike, as he has shown in several campaigns, marching at the head of his armies, and taking part more gaily in
the labours of his soldiers than in the delights of this flourishing court:
nevertheless as he is of a disposition no less gentle than courageous, he
has no less inclination for peace than for war . . .'

happy ending), but it has two things in common with it: it owes a
great deal to Corneille, and it is quite unlike Corneille in its general
character. Porus, the implacable enemy of Alexandre, and the pro-
Greek Taxile are rivals for the hand of Axiane, who favours Porus
and shares his hatred for Alexandre; exactly as, in Corneille's
Nicomède, Nicomède, the implacable enemy of Rome, and his
brother, Attale, who has been brought up in Rome, are both aspir-
ants to the hand of Laodice, the queen of a neighbouring country,
who prefers Nicomède and shares his hatred for Rome. The line,

> Comment prétendez-vous que je vous traite?—En roi.
> (V, 3, l. 1500)

is clearly an echo of the line,

> Ne soyez l'un ni l'autre.—Et que dois-je être?—Roi.
> (*Nicomède*, IV, 3, l. 1318)

The character of Alexandre owes something to that of César in
Corneille's *Mort de Pompée*. Alexandre is in love with Cléofile, as
César is in love with Cléopâtre; he profits from the treachery of
Taxile, as César does from that of Ptolomée, without having to
reward it; and, in the last resort, like César, he is not prepared to
subordinate military achievement to love. Racine, in fact, points out
the resemblance between Caesar and Alexander in this respect in his
second preface; love, he says, never disturbed either of them exces-
sively. The magnanimity of Alexandre at the end recalls that of
Auguste in Corneille's *Cinna;* and it wins over Porus and Axiane, as
that of Auguste wins over Cinna and Emilie. Indeed, if the relationship between Taxile, Axiane, and Porus is reminiscent of *Nicomède*, it
is no less reminiscent of *Cinna*; and, like Maxime in that tragedy,
Taxile is driven to treachery by love. The speech in which Porus
describes the ardour of his men (11.123 ff.) reminds one of Cinna's
description of his fellow-conspirators; and there is something of
Emilie, as well as something of Cléopâtre and of Laodice, in Axiane.
Finally, the political scenes are written in imitation of Corneille;
though Racine's are decidely inferior, because the content is
slight.

Although *Alexandre* anticipates *Mithridate*, it is not particularly
characteristic of Racine. There is too much love, or rather too much
gallantry, in it: Alexandre, in the middle of his campaigns, sighs for

Cléofile, corresponds with her, and wages war only to come to her—which is not easy to reconcile with his determination to leave her for further conquests. Taxile changes sides because Axiane prefers his rival, Porus. Porus cares more about winning military glory and Axiane's hand, than maintaining the independence of his country. Saint-Evremond was not altogether wrong when he said that he could recognize nothing of Alexander but his name in Racine's play, and that Porus was purely French.

But if all this makes us think of Thomas Corneille or Quinault at their most dated, there are at least no disguises or false identities, and the plot is not absurd. Moreover, there are features that are more characteristic of Racine. The situation is the typical one: Porus and Axiane (a character invented by Racine) are mutually in love, with Taxile as the unsuccessful rival. The play is simple, containing, as Racine stresses in his preface, 'few incidents and little matter'. The style marks an advance on that of *La Thébaïde*, and contains some excellent passages; for example

> Tant d'États, tant de mers qui vont nous désunir
> M'effaceront bientôt de votre souvenir.
> Quand l'Océan troublé vous verra sur son onde
> Achever quelque jour la conquête du monde;
> Quand vous verrez les rois tomber à vos genoux,
> Et la terre en tremblant se taire devant vous,
> Songerez-vous, Seigneur, qu'une jeune princesse,
> Au fond de ses États vous regrette sans cesse,
> Et rappelle en son cœur les moments bienheureux
> Où ce grand conquérant l'assurait de ses feux?
>
> (III, 6, ll. 915–24)

But whereas *La Thébaïde,* with obvious weaknesses of construction and characterization, provides an interesting foretaste of what is to come, *Alexandre* gives us Racine's form with an unoriginal and uninteresting content.

Between *Alexandre* and *Andromaque*, two important events occurred in Racine's life. Nicole remarked in a pamphlet that a dramatic poet was no better than 'a public poisoner, not of the bodies, but of the souls of the faithful'. Racine took this as a personal insult, and attacked Port-Royal in two entertaining, but mordant, letters

(1666),[10] which in later life he bitterly regretted: the breach with Port-Royal was complete. More important, Racine fell in love with the widowed actress, Mlle Duparc, who became his mistress (or possibly wife),[11] and who, under his influence, left Molière's company at the end of March 1667 and joined the Hôtel de Bourgogne. She bore Racine a daughter, who died at the age of eight or thereabouts. It was she who appeared in the title role of *Andromaque*, first performed by the Hôtel de Bourgogne at court on November 17, 1667, and publicly in Paris the following day.

Andromaque, Racine's first great success and his first great play, is a love tragedy, one in which the catastrophe is brought about by the passion of love—an overwhelming, destructive passion (in the three Greeks, at least). This conception of love is not completely new in French tragedy; something like it can be seen in Thomas Corneille and Quinault, particularly in *Amalasonte*; but Racine expresses it infinitely more powerfully, and shows the same passions at work in his men as in his women. Whereas Amalasonte and Amalfrède to some extent anticipate Hermione, Théodat is a docile and submissive lover, and Odatirse who, in *La Mort de Cyrus*, uses a similar kind of blackmail to Pyrrhus, is the villain of the play.[12] Pyrrhus and Oreste in *Andromaque* are neither submissive lovers nor, for all their violence, villains; they arouse our sympathies, and make us feel, 'There, but for the grace of God . . .'

Love in *Andromaque* robs its victims of pride, honour, self-control, resolution, and self-knowledge. In the first scene, we learn that Oreste had thought his love for Hermione to be extinct, but 'je me trompais moi-même' (l. 37); that Pyrrhus has wavered 'plus de cent fois' between Andromaque and Hermione (l. 115), and that he may

> dans ce désordre extrême,
> Épouser ce qu'il hait, et punir ce qu'il aime;
>
> (ll. 121–2)

and that Hermione is

> Toujours prête à partir, et demeurant toujours . . .
>
> (l. 131)

[10] Only the first of these was published.
[11] See below, p. 41.
[12] See above, p. 13.

In Act II, scene 1, Hermione says

Je crains de me connaître en l'état où je suis,

(l. 428)

and the rest of the scene brilliantly illustrates her lack of self-knowledge, her continual self-deception. She indulges herself in day-dreams of Pyrrhus's returning to her (ll. 436–40). If realism asserts itself for a brief moment ('Mais l'ingrat ne veut que m'outrager', l. 440), she immediately finds pretexts for remaining at Pyrrhus's court (ll. 441–4). At the end of the scene, she deludes herself into thinking that she might transfer her affections to Oreste, but his approach pricks the bubble:

Ah! je ne croyais pas qu'il fût si près d'ici.

(l. 476)

Hermione never quite abandons hope. When Pyrrhus, from pique, decides to marry her, she convinces herself that he must love her (l. 846). Even after she has ordered Oreste to kill him, she does not know whether she loves him or not; until the news of his death clarifies her feelings, and she upbraids Oreste with the famous question, 'Qui te l'a dit?' (l. 1543). Similarly, Pyrrhus in Act II, scene 5, has made up his mind to abandon Andromaque; but he betrays his real feelings by speaking of her continually, and wondering what effect his decision will have upon her.

Pyrrhus, Oreste, and Hermione are tossed backwards and forwards between love and hatred.

Il faut désormais que mon cœur,
S'il n'aime avec transport, haïsse avec fureur,

(I, 4, ll. 367–8)

says Pyrrhus, and his words are constantly echoed by Hermione. In their despair, the three Greeks lose their self-control, and become cruel and violent. Oreste insults Pyrrhus when he accedes to his demands, plans to abduct Hermione so that she may share his torments, and murders Pyrrhus. Pyrrhus threatens to hand Astyanax over to the Greeks, in order to compel Andromaque to marry him. Hermione wants to make Andromaque suffer (l. 447), rebuffs her when she appeals to her—thereby compelling Andromaque to consent to marry Pyrrhus, and bringing about the final catastrophe—, tells Oreste,

tout ingrat qu'il est, il me sera plus doux
De mourir avec lui que de vivre avec vous,

(IV, 3, ll. 1247–8)

orders him to kill Pyrrhus (he had already thought of doing so on his
own account, l. 733), and even contemplates killing Pyrrhus herself:

Quel plaisir de venger moi-même mon injure,
De retirer mon bras teint du sang du parjure,
Et pour rendre sa peine et mes plaisirs plus grands,
De cacher ma rivale à ses regards mourants![13]

(IV, 4, ll. 1261–4)

Occasionally, they strike heroic attitudes; but they are attitudes.
Pyrrhus tells Andromaque that he will protect Astyanax with his
own life (l. 288); he then promises to hand Astyanax over to the
Greeks, giving Oreste false reasons for his action (II, 4), and finally
agrees to save him only if Andromaque will marry him. Hermione
observes that

L'amour ne règle pas le sort d'une princesse:
La gloire d'obéir est tout ce qu'on nous laisse.

(III, 2, ll. 821–2)

But in fact her father has ordered her to leave Epirus unless Pyrrhus
agrees to Astyanax's death (ll. 406–8), and this is a mere pretext for
obeying the promptings of her love. Except, of course, in the noble,
steadfast, devoted wife and mother, the Trojan Andromaque herself,
love in *Andromaque* is madness, 'fureur'; and the tragedy ends
appropriately with the lines:

Sauvons-le. Nos efforts deviendraient impuissants
S'il reprenait ici sa rage avec ses sens.

(V, 5, ll. 1647–8)

The influence of the seventeenth-century salon is strong. The

---

[13] Cruelty may also be unconscious, as when in answer to Pyrrhus's
question, 'Me cherchiez-vous, Madame?', Andromaque replies:

Je passais jusqu'aux lieux où l'on garde mon fils,

(I, 4, l. 260)

or Hermione tells Oreste that she would like to love him (II, 2, l. 536), or he
tells her that Pyrrhus does not love her (II, 2, l. 549).

politeness of the characters can be a source of dramatic effect, when it fails to conceal the underlying animosity or brutality, or when the mask of politeness and decorum falls and the real feelings break through. A good example of this is Hermione's outburst,

Je ne t'ai point aimé, cruel? Qu'ai-je donc fait?

(IV, 5, l. 1356)

provoked by Pyrrhus's suggestion that she had never loved him, but was to marry him only for political reasons (a taunt, self-deception, or an attempt to preserve her dignity?[14]) Moreover, the characters scrutinize one another, spy on one another, observe words, gestures, and facial expressions (ll. 574–5, ll. 1442–8); and the consciousness of being observed increases their sufferings:

Vous veniez de mon front observer la pâleur,
Pour aller dans ses bras rire de ma douleur.

(IV, 5, ll. 1327–8)

They are also quick to seize the implications of remarks, and well versed in the lore of the human heart.

Vous que j'ai plaint, enfin que je voudrais aimer,

(II, 2, l. 536)

says Hermione. Oreste immediately understands:

Tel est mon partage funeste:
Le cœur est pour Pyrrhus, et les vœux pour Oreste.

(ll. 537–8)

Her pretexts for remaining in Epirus do not conceal her real reason from Oreste (ll. 570–3). When Oreste thinks that Hermione's wrath against Pyrrhus gives him grounds for hope, Pylade immediately dashes his hopes to the ground: 'Jamais il ne fut plus aimé' (1.748)—a remark that echoes Oreste's own words in an earlier scene,

Hermione.
Ah! ne souhaitez pas le destin de Pyrrhus:
Je vous haïrais trop.
Oreste.   Vous m'en aimeriez plus.

(II, 2, ll. 539–40)

[14] See R. C. Knight, '*Andromaque* et l'ironie de Corneille' in *Actes du premier congrès international racinien*, 1962, p. 25.

pointing the contrast between his clear-sightedness then and his self-deception now. The confidants are as penetrating as their masters: Phoenix accurately interprets Pyrrhus's continual references to Andromaque (II, 5), and Cléone realizes that Hermione still loves Pyrrhus—

> Il vous aurait déplu, s'il pouvait vous déplaire,
>
> (II, 1, l. 426)

—and knows that apparent calm after a severe blow, whether in Oreste or in Hermione, is a bad sign (ll. 834, 1141).

In his prefaces, Racine gives as the source of this tragedy a passage of Virgil, relating how Pyrrhus, married to Andromache, discarded her, seized Orestes's wife, Hermione, and was killed by Orestes in revenge. There is not much of *Andromaque* here; but Racine is certainly right in saying that his play owes little to the *Andromache* of Euripides. In the Greek play, Andromache is the concubine of Neoptolemus (another name for Pyrrhus); her child, Molossus, is her child by him, not the son of Hector; Hermione, Neoptolemus's wife, is jealous of Andromache, because Andromache has borne him a son, whereas she is barren; Hermione runs away with Orestes; and Neoptolemus does not appear. If one were to speculate on the origin of *Andromaque*, one might suppose that Racine began with the intention of writing a love tragedy like *Amalasonte*, in which love should be a destructive force; that the idea of a chain of lovers, like that in Corneille's *Pertharite*—in which Garibalde loves Eduige, who loves the usurper, Grimoald, who loves the widow of the former king, Rodelinde, whose task is to save the life of her young son[15]—came next; and that it was only then that Greek names were fitted to the characters. But if that were so, the association with the Trojan War, brought by the Greek names, is an integral part of the play.

The Trojan War gives the characters heroic stature. Hermione is

---

[15] Cf. Oreste, in love with Hermione, who loves Pyrrhus, who loves his captive, Andromaque, who is faithful to her dead husband, Hector, and anxious to save the life of her son, Astyanax. Like Hermione, Eduige promises to marry Garibalde if he kills Grimoald; but Garibalde, unlike Oreste, knows exactly how she would feel and behave if he did, and refuses (II, 1). Grimoald, like Pyrrhus, tries to make Rodelinde marry him by threatening to kill her son if she does not. The resemblance between *Pertharite* and *Andromaque* was first pointed out by Voltaire.

the daughter of Menelaus and Helen; Oreste, an important legendary figure in his own right, is the son of Agamemnon and Clytemnestra; Pyrrhus is the son of Achilles; and Andromaque is the widow of the great Trojan hero, Hector, slain by Achilles, and the pathos of her situation is enhanced by the haunting memory of the manner of her husband's death:

> Dois-je oublier Hector privé de funérailles,
> Et traîné sans honneur autour de nos murailles?
>
> (III, 8, ll. 993–4)

Moreover, the wretched, pitiful state of the characters of the play is in sharp contrast with the greatness of their parents. When Oreste hesitates to kill Pyrrhus at Hermione's behest, she reflects on her own ineffectiveness compared with the power of her celebrated mother (ll. 1477–84). Oreste, the ambassador of the Greeks, cares nothing for the Greeks, and does his best to fail in his mission in the hope of winning the hand of Hermione. Both are helplessly tossed about by their passions. So is Pyrrhus, the unworthy son of his father, who himself fought at Troy. Not only, as both Oreste and Céphise point out, is he undoing his father's work, but his exploits at Troy were those of a butcher (ll. 999–1008). The meaning of the line,

> Hector tomba sous lui, Troie expira sous vous,
>
> (II, 2, l. 148)

and of Hermione's statement that his deeds obliterated those of his father (l. 467) is made clear by Hermione's taunt:

> Du vieux père d'Hector la valeur abattue
> Aux pieds de sa famille expirante à sa vue,
> Tandis que dans son sein votre bras enfoncé
> Cherche un reste de sang que l'âge avait glacé;
> Dans des ruisseaux de sang Troie ardente plongée;
> De votre propre main Polyxène égorgée
> Aux yeux de tous les Grecs indignés contre vous:
> Que peut-on refuser à ces généreux coups?
>
> (IV, 5, ll. 1333–40)

The other Greeks, who—without Achilles—fled before Hector (ll. 185–6, 209–12), and who displayed greed and brutality at the sack of Troy were no better. Racine does not glorify war in *Andromaque*.[16]

---

[16] Nor had he in *Alexandre*, e.g. ll. 697–704, 1337–41.

The Trojan War influences the events of the play, the action of which takes place only a year after the fall of Troy. Without the Trojan War, there could scarcely be a play: Astyanax would not be in danger, were he not the son of Hector, growing up with a sense of grievance, of wrongs to be avenged. Without the Trojan War, a solution might be found; but Andromaque, even if she could bring herself to marry again, cannot marry Pyrrhus, whose father killed her husband, and who himself killed her father. The characters of *Andromaque* are the prisoners of their past.

Finally, the Trojan War inspired Racine with some of the finest passages in his tragedy—this moving evocation of the desolation caused by war, for instance:

Je songe quelle était autrefois cette ville,
Si superbe en remparts, en héros si fertile,
Maîtresse de l'Asie; et je regarde enfin
Quel fut le sort de Troie et quel est son destin.
Je ne vois que des tours que la cendre a couvertes,
Un fleuve teint de sang, des campagnes désertes,
Un enfant dans les fers . . .

(I, 2, ll. 197–203)

Andromaque is a stark tragedy. The characters are in a situation from which there is no escape, and the play moves inexorably to the final catastrophe. Pyrrhus is murdered, Hermione kills herself, Oreste goes mad, and Andromaque is left to restore order. In it, Racine revealed himself for the first time as a great poet, equally capable of vivid narrative, of evocative description, of moving expressions of emotion. *Andromaque* is a memorable expression of suffering humanity.

3

From *Les Plaideurs* to *Bajazet*

Mlle Duparc died on December 11, 1668—in childbirth, according to Boileau, as reported by Brossette. Robinet, listing those present at the funeral in his news sheet of December 15, describes one of the playwrights, the one most concerned,—usually taken as an allusion to Racine—as 'half dead'. Eleven years later, Mme Voisin, the notorious fortune-teller and purveyor of magic spells, abortions, and poisons, in the course of the interrogations that followed her arrest, claimed to have been intimate with Mlle Duparc, as well as with her daughters and her stepmother, and stated that Racine had married Mlle Duparc secretly, that he was madly jealous, that he had refused to let her see Mme Voisin and Mme Voisin's maid (who was also a midwife) during her last illness, and that rumours of his having poisoned her had gone round. On January 11, 1680, Louvois wrote to an official of the *chambre ardente*, the tribunal examining Mme Voisin, telling him that he could have a warrant for Racine's arrest whenever he wanted. Racine was not arrested.

It is not impossible that Racine and Mlle Duparc were secretly married, and it is perhaps more likely that she died in childbirth than that she was poisoned.[1] What seems certain, however, is that Racine was passionately in love with her, and that she and her stepmother had some questionable acquaintances of whom he disapproved. These are the circumstances in which Racine wrote *Andromaque*, *Les Plaideurs*, and *Britannicus*.

[1] See A. Chagny, *Marquise du Parc*, 1961, pp. 154–79.

Les Plaideurs, Racine's only comedy, was first performed at the Hôtel de Bourgogne in the winter of 1668. It was apparently not successful until it won the approbation of Louis XIV at Versailles. From Racine's preface, we learn that he originally thought of adapting the *Wasps* of Aristophanes for the Italian actors, but abandoned the idea when Scaramouche—the actor Tiberio Fiorilli —went back to Italy (April 1668); that several friends encouraged him to write the play, and even contributed to it (at dinners in a tavern, according to Louis Racine); and that such knowledge of legal terms as he had was due to a law suit of his own (possibly about a priory[2]).

Racine's remark in the preface, that he was merely translating Aristophanes, is quite untrue; in fact, he adapts only part of the Greek play, and his debt to Aristophanes is slight. What he owes to him is the idea of a judge attempting to break out of his house in order to go to the law-courts, and eventually prevailed upon to stay at home and try a lawsuit between two dogs, one of whom had stolen a cheese—in Racine, this becomes a lawsuit between a dog and the capon he has killed. Aristophanes's attack on a democratic institution becomes in Racine's play a scathing satire on the French legal system of his period. The Philocleon (or Pro-Cleon) of Aristophanes is a juryman, one of some 6,000 such; and he is kept at home by his son, Bdely-cleon (or Anti-Cleon), who considers that a juryman's life is futile drudgery—the remuneration is derisory, the work is hard, and the power he exercises is negligible. Racine's judge is kept at home, not because his labours are ill rewarded, but because he has gone mad; his profession is, indeed, extremely lucrative. Racine's play is an attack on the corruption and venality of the law, its interminable delays, and the rapacity of all those connected with it, from magistrates down to their domestic servants. Racine has added a love interest, two crackbrained inveterate litigants, Chicanneau and the comtesse de Pimbesche,[3] and makes two servants act as counsels for the

[2] According to Louis Racine and to D'Olivet (see Pellisson and D'Olivet, *Histoire de L'Académie française*, ed C.–L. Livet, 1858, vol. II, p. 341).

[3] According to the Dictionary of the French Academy (1694), the word *pimbêche* then meant a meddlesome busybody. Cotgrave gives: 'a wilie queane, subtile wench, cunning drab; one that can finely execute her Mistresses knavish devises' (*Dictionarie of the French and English Tongues*, 1632 edition).

prosecution and the defence, and in so doing parody the forensic eloquence of the time.

Even at its most fantastic, Racine's play is a surprisingly faithful reflection of the reality of the age—in which lawsuits, it should be remembered, were a common enough misfortune: 'everyone', says Mme de Nemours in her memoirs, 'has lawsuits or is afraid of having them'. Perrin Dandin receiving his clients from his attic window may seem incredible; but Tallemant des Réaux tells of a M. de Portail, a counsellor in the parlement of Paris, honest but crazy, who had turned his attic into an office, and never spoke to people except through the window. The scene in which Chicanneau and the countess quarrel was based on a similar scene between the président de Lionne and the comtesse de Crissé in the office of Boileau's brother; it was Boileau who mentioned it to Racine, and, according to the *Ménagiana*, the comtesse de Pimbesche wore a dress of the same shade of pink as the comtesse de Crissé, and, like her, a mask over her ear. In the last act, the styles of various barristers of the time (including Racine's old master, M. Le Maître) are parodied; in particular, the exordium of L'Intimé's speech, taken from Cicero, had been used by one, Gautier, in the case of a pastry cook against a baker.

Racine parodies not only barristers, but also Corneille—particularly, and particularly wittily, a line from *Le Cid*,

Ses rides sur son front ont gravé ses exploits,

(I, 1. l. 35)

quoted almost exactly, but in a context that changes the meaning of *exploits* from military to legal deeds (l. 154). Corneille, we are told, was deeply offended. Another literary debt—a more surprising one, perhaps—is to Rabelais. The name of the judge, Perrin Dandin, comes from Rabelais's Third Book; and Racine's Intimé, who, like his father, regards being beaten as a source of income, reminds one of the *chiquanous* in Book IV, who may also have suggested the name Chicanneau.

Racine's comic technique owes a good deal to Molière. The scenes in which the attitudes of characters undergo sudden reversals half-way through (I, 6, 7; II, 2) and the one in which Chicanneau cannot speak for the countess's interruptions (I, 7) recall Molière. The scene of double-entendre in which Léandre visits Isabelle in disguise, and they speak of their love in front of Chicanneau, who thinks they are talking of a lawsuit (II, 6), reminds one of similar scenes in *L'Amour Médecin*, *Le Médecin malgré lui*, and *Le Sicilien*. Chicanneau and the comtesse de Pimbesche are monomaniacs, like so many of Molière's characters; and the distorted professional outlook of Perrin Dandin recalls Molière's doctors. Perhaps Racine repaid some of his debt: Perrin Dandin's invitation to Isabelle to watch torture being administered is rather like Thomas Diafoirus's invitation to Angélique in *La Malade imaginaire*, three years later, to attend a dissection.

The great comic writer, however—Aristophanes, Rabelais, Molière—is indulgent. Aristophanes's Philocleon is mistaken, and his son may get the better of him in argument; but he is well-meaning, and worth twice his son in endurance and vitality. Rabelais and Molière show us human folly and selfishness, but virtue and good sense as well. In *Les Plaideurs*, apart from the colourless lovers, Léandre and Isabelle, all the characters are selfish or mad or both. Perhaps that is why it is easier to admire than to like this brilliant comedy.

Britannicus (December 13, 1669) is a tragedy on a subject from Roman history, chosen perhaps with Corneille in mind. Some of Corneille's best plays had treated Roman subjects; *Othon* (1664) had dealt with an intimate of Nero who eventually succeeded him (he is mentioned in *Britannicus*); like *Attila* (1667), *Britannicus* has a cruel and crafty ruler as one of its main characters; and Agrippine, loath to relinquish power to her son, is reminiscent of Cléopâtre in *Rodogune*. The play was not immediately successful: the audience at the first performance was diminished by a rival attraction, the execution of a nobleman, the marquis de Courboyer; and there was some adverse criticism. However, it established itself, and, declares Racine in the second preface, 'If I have done anything solid and deserving of praise, most connoisseurs agree that it is this same *Britannicus*'.

It is one of his finest works and, except for *Esther* and *Athalie*, the one in which he is most faithful to history. His main source is Tacitus, on whom, as he tells us in the second preface, his characters are based, and who suggested some of the most striking passages in the tragedy. In Tacitus, we read how Agrippina married her uncle, Claudius, and got him to adopt Nero (her son by a previous husband, Ahenobarbus) in place of Britannicus (his son by a previous wife, Messalina); how she married Nero to Britannicus's sister, Octavia; how she poisoned Claudius and made Nero emperor in his stead, with the help of Burrus; how Burrus and Seneca, Nero's tutors, united against Agrippina; how Agrippina was excluded from power, and her ally, Pallas, deposed; how she threatened to put Britannicus in Nero's place: how, mistrustful of Britannicus's ambition, Nero poisoned him (with a rapid poison prepared by Locusta) at a banquet; and how, later, Nero had his mother assassinated, and divorced Octavia in order to marry Poppæa.

In Tacitus, as he says, Racine found his characters—Agrippina, greedy for power, arrogant, employing 'severity and menaces—she could give her son the empire, but not endure him as emperor';[4] Nero, at first a good ruler, though with latent vices, honouring his mother, then escaping from her control, and displaying unconcern when Britannicus died of poison in his presence; Burrus, with his 'soldierly efficiency and seriousness of character'[5]—though Racine modifies his character, and turns him into a well-meaning, slightly obtuse soldier, with little insight into the real character of his pupil; and Britannicus, young, but not devoid of ambition.

Many passages of Racine's play recall Tacitus, though often the context or the content is changed. Tacitus's description of Agrippina as 'the daughter of a great commander and the sister, wife, and mother of emperors'[6] becomes dramatic when it is used by Agrippine herself to cow Burrhus:

> Moi, fille, femme, sœur, et mère de vos maîtres!
>
> (I, 2, l. 156)

The real Britannicus annoyed Nero by addressing him as

[4] The quotations are taken from Tacitus, *The Annals of Imperial Rome*, translated by Michael Grant, Penguin Classics, 1959 reprint. This one comes from p. 271.

[5] Op. cit., p. 274. Louis Racine says that criticisms of Pyrrhus's violence made Racine resolve to portray a 'parfaitement honnête homme' in his next play, and he quotes Boileau:

> peut-être ta plume aux censeurs de Pyrrhus
> Doit les plus nobles traits dont tu peignis Burrhus.
>
> (Epître VII)

[6] Op. cit., p. 261.

'Domitius', but this was before the death of Claudius. How much more dramatic the insult becomes when it is put into the mouth of Britannicus in the course of a quarrel with Néron in the middle of the play (l. 1040)! Agrippine's great speech in Act IV, scene 2, is in germ in Tacitus:

> Agrippina was alarmed; her talk became angry and menacing. She let the emperor hear her say that Britannicus was grown up and was the true and worthy heir of his father's supreme position—now held, she added, by an adopted intruder, who used it to maltreat his mother. Unshrinkingly she disclosed every blot on that ill-fated family, without sparing her own marriage and her poisoning of her husband.[7]

Racine has turned Agrippina's threat into an appeal to Néron for gratitude, and developed it into one of his most memorable scenes. The speech in which Agrippine relates how the days have gone when

> mon ordre au palais assemblait le sénat,
> Et que derrière un voile, invisible et présente,
> J'étais de ce grand corps l'âme toute puissante,
>
> (I, 1, ll. 94–6)

and recalls the day on which, as she was about to take her seat beside Néron, he

> Se leva par avance, et courant m'embrasser,
> Il m'écarta du trône où je m'allais placer.
>
> (ll. 109–10)

is another reminiscence of Tacitus.[8] But both these episodes have been changed. Agrippina listened to the discussion of the senate on one occasion only, and on that occasion the senate did the opposite of what she wanted; and the text of Tacitus does not suggest that Nero prevented her from sitting beside him, but that he went towards her to save appearances, to make it look as if she were sitting beside him at his invitation:

[7] Op cit., pp. 279–80.

[8] Op. cit., p. 276. Another minor change is that Racine's Burrhus secretly got the army to swear fidelity to Néron (ll. 857–8, 1185–6), whereas in Tacitus, 'the palace gates were suddenly thrown open. Attended by Sextus Afranius Burrus, commander of the Guard, out came Nero to the battalion which, in accordance with regulations, was on duty' (p. 273).

Again, when an Armenian delegation was pleading before
Nero, she was just going to mount the emperor's dais and sit
beside him. Everyone was stupefied. But Seneca instructed
Nero to advance and meet his mother. This show of filial
dutifulness averted the scandal.

In the first passage, Racine has exaggerated the influence of Agrippina; in the second, he has altered an attempt to cover up Agrippina's
effrontery into a brutal affront. *Britannicus* is more than Tacitus
versified.

The reader of Tacitus, of course, has no more read *Britannicus* than
the reader of Holinshed has read *Macbeth*. Not only has Racine
adapted what he borrowed for his own dramatic purposes, but he
condenses his original, selecting, bringing together, and linking
events that are scattered over a hundred pages of Tacitus. Moreover,
the rule of the unity of time compelled him to choose a precise
moment, a critical moment as the time of his play. He chose the
moment when Néron, in open revolt at last against Agrippine,
murders Britannicus, and appears in his true colours. Now this
moment is an invention of Racine's. The action of the tragedy begins
when Néron, encouraged by Narcisse, carries off Junie, to spite
Agrippine, who is clinging to power, supporting Britannicus, and
favouring his marriage with Junie. This action alarms Agrippine,
alienates Britannicus, and arouses the suspicions of Burrhus.
Moreover, Néron, at the sight of Junie, tearful and in her night attire,
falls in love with her; rivalry in love thus reinforces the political
struggle between Britannicus and Néron. But Junie, despite what
Racine says in his preface, owes nothing but her name and her
brother, Silanus, to the Junia Calvina of history. She is a creation of
Racine's; so is the mutual love between her and Britannicus, and the
rivalry in love between Britannicus and Néron. The rivalry, indeed,
is historically impossible, since the real Britannicus died at the age of
fourteen; Racine has prolonged his life and added three years to his
age. Narcisse, the confidant both of Britannicus and of Néron,
betraying the former to the latter, the evil genius of Néron,
encouraging his vices and his desire for independence, urging
him to reject Agrippine's demands and murder Britannicus, is
another creation of Racine's. There was a real Narcissus; but as a sup-
porter of Britannicus and an opponent of Agrippina, he was impri-

soned at the outset of Nero's reign, and committed suicide in prison.

These changes, additions, and inventions give this chapter of history a centre that is lacking in Tacitus—make it dramatic, in short. Moreover, they are completely credible and in keeping with the historical atmosphere.[9] It *was* love that led to the breach between Nero and Agrippina—but love for the freedwoman, Acte, not love for Junia Calvina or Junie. Sometimes, even, an invented detail enhances the historical atmosphere, and strikes one as being truer and more satisfying than historical fact—Locuste trying out her poison on a slave, for instance (ll. 1392–4); it is a pig and a goat in Suetonius.

Racine develops what is latent in Tacitus, imaginatively reconstructs what he does not say. The situation of Agrippine is one example:

Il faut qu'entre eux et lui je tienne la balance,
Afin que quelque jour, par une même loi,
Britannicus la tienne entre mon fils et moi.

(I, 1. ll. 68–70)

The climax of the play occurs in Act IV, scene 2. Agrippine, aware of her ability to overawe her son by her presence, has been trying to have an interview with him. At last she succeeds. Néron agrees, or appears to agree, to her demands; but when the interview is over, he goes his own way and has Britannicus poisoned. The interview is crucial, precisely because, by achieving nothing, it reveals Agrippine's impotence. The whole of this scene is based, as we have seen, on a brief, not particularly significant, passage of Tacitus.

Racine's greatest piece of imaginative insight in *Britannicus* is the evolving character of Néron, the 'monstre naissant', torn between on the one hand his early upbringing and his fear of Agrippine—

Tout: Octavie, Agrippine, Burrhus,
Sénèque, Rome entière, et trois ans de vertus

(II, 2, ll. 461–2)

—and, on the other, his passion for Junie, the example of immorality

[9] Except, perhaps, for the entry of Junie into the temple of the Vestal Virgins at the end. This was criticized by contemporaries, e.g. Boursault, who, in the account of the first performance of *Britannicus* in his *Artémise et Poliante*, wittily comments that she 'becomes a nun in the order of Vesta'.

set by previous emperors, the example of the ruthless ambition of his
own mother, and the latent vices he has himself inherited:

> je lis sur son visage
> Des fiers Domitius l'humeur triste et sauvage,
> Il mêle avec l'orgueil qu'il a pris dans leur sang
> La fierté des Nérons qu'il puisa dans mon flanc.
>
> (I, 1, ll. 35–8)

He begins by keeping out of Agrippine's way; then he has Junie
arrested and brought to the palace, and is smitten by her charms.
Love increases his restiveness, and brings out the worst in him. His
love is a cruel, sadistic love:

> J'aimais jusqu'à ses pleurs que je faisais couler
>
> (II, 2, l. 402)

(an ambiguous line: does 'which I caused to flow' imply 'because I
made them flow'?) and it makes him desire to inflict suffering on his
rival:

> Néron impunément ne sera pas jaloux.
>
> (II, 2, l. 445)

It also determines him—after a little hesitation—to repudiate
Octavie, the wife imposed on him by his mother. The cruel nature of
his jealousy is fully revealed when he compels Junie to make Britannicus believe she no longer cares for him by threatening to kill him if
she betrays her real feelings in the meeting which he will watch from
a place of concealment.[10]

> Elle aime mon rival, je ne puis l'ignorer;
> Mais je mettrai ma joie à le désespérer.
> Je me fais de sa peine une image charmante,
>
> (II, 8, ll. 749–51)

he says. By the end of the second act, he has come a long way from
the hesitant Néron of the second scene in it. By now it is fairly clear
what course he will eventually choose.

In Act III, surprising Junie with Britannicus, he begins to fulfil his
threat by having him arrested. This action is followed by the arrest of

---

[10] This episode is borrowed from Rotrou's *Bélissaire*. See above, p. 12.

Agrippine. The choice is finally made in Act IV, when, after being unmoved by Agrippine's alarming display of her lust for power and swayed by Burrhus's more disinterested and hence more effective entreaties, he yields to Narcisse's insidious arguments, and resolves, for political motives as well as from jealousy, to murder Britannicus. Burrhus and Narcisse, who represent the good and bad sides of Néron's nature,[11] are far removed from the usually colourless confidants of French classical tragedy. When, in the last act, Néron is able, impassive, to watch Britannicus die, it is clear to all that the monster has come to birth. Agrippina and Burrhus are doomed. Néron has asserted himself, but he is distracted by the loss of Junie, and ahead of him stretches a criminal future.

This magnificent tragedy is an admirable illustration of Aristotle's remark—annotated by Racine in his copy of the *Poetics*—that 'poetry is something more philosophical and more worthy of serious attention than history; for while poetry is concerned with universal truths, history treats of particular facts'.[12]

In 1670, Racine met and conquered another actress, Mlle Champmeslé, who joined the company of the Hôtel de Bourgogne with her husband in March. She remained his mistress for seven years; although, unlike Mlle Duparc, she seems to have led the kind of life commonly attributed to actresses, and not to have restricted her favours to him. Mme de Sévigné wrote to her daughter: 'There is a little actress, and Despréaux and Racine and their like with her: they have delicious suppers, that is to say wild revels (*diableries*)' (April 1, 1671). This is the Racine of *Bérénice* and *Bajazet*.

Bérénice was first performed at the Hôtel de Bourgogne on November 21, 1670, with Mlle Champmeslé as Bérénice and her

[11] Professor P. F. Butler, in his edition of the play (1967) and elsewhere, argues that it is a defence of Machiavellianism, that Narcisse is clear-sighted, and that Néron has to kill or be killed. This is hard to accept. Agrippine is powerless (ll. 837–856, 1258–68), and Britannicus—though momentarily deluded, presumably by Narcisse, into thinking that he has some backing—has no supporters (ll. 323–6, 905–913); moreover, through Narcisse, Néron is in his confidence. Narcisse is so far from clear–sighted in his estimate of the populace (ll. 1437–1452) that he is massacred by it.

[12] *Poetics*, translated by T. S. Dorsch in *Classical Literary Criticism*, Penguin Books, 1972 reprint, pp. 43–4.

husband as Antiochus. Exactly a week later, Corneille's *Tite et Bérénice* was put on at the Palais-Royal. The story that Henriette d'Angleterre simultaneously suggested the subject to both dramatists is now generally discredited, on the not altogether conclusive grounds that it first appeared half a century after the plays. If we reject it, the most likely explanation is that Racine, possibly at the instigation of the Hôtel de Bourgogne, wrote a play on a subject that he knew was being treated by Corneille. Not only had he been engaged in similar competitions before,[13] not only does he seem to have more or less consciously pitted himself against Corneille in some of his previous plays, but the subject of the play (the conflict between love and political expediency or responsibility) is more characteristic of the elder writer. Moreover, in one or two respects, Racine's play contradicts Corneille's, almost as if he were setting him right on points of historical fact or verisimilitude. Corneille's heroine is acclaimed by the people of Rome; Racine's imagines this happening, but events prove her wrong (ll. 298–300). Corneille's Tite is willing to abdicate for Bérénice's sake; Racine's Titus dismisses this course of action (ll. 1399–1402).[14] But this is mere conjecture: the question cannot be settled, and scarcely matters.

The subject of Racine's tragedy is a sentence from Suetonius quoted in his preface; but it is worth looking at it in its context (Racine's sentence, or rather the two quotations that he has made into a single sentence, is printed in italics):

> He was believed to be profligate as well as cruel, because of the riotous parties which he kept going with his more extravagant friends far into the night; and morally unprincipled, too, because he owned a troop of inverts and eunuchs, and nursed a guilty passion for *Queen Berenice, to whom he had allegedly promised marriage.* He also had a reputation for accepting bribes and

[13] See pp. 4, 25 above.

[14] Saint–Evremond condemned the readiness of Corneille's Tite to give up the throne and leave Rome as unhistorical and improbable (*Sur les caractères des tragédies,* in *Œuvres en prose,* ed. R. Ternois, vol. 3, 1966, pp. 332–3).

The fact that Racine's play was performed first is not necessarily proof that it was written first. Molière's company had spent nearly the whole of October at Chambord and a week of November at Saint-Germain, and it had begun to perform *Le Bourgeois Gentilhomme.*

not being averse from using influence to settle his father's cases in favour of the highest bidder. It was even prophesied quite openly that he would prove to be a second Nero. [. . .]

His dinner parties, far from being orgies, were very pleasant occasions, and the friends he chose were retained in office by his successors [. . .] *He sent Queen Berenice away from Rome, which was painful for both of them*; and broke off relations with some of his favourite boys [. . .][15]

Not quite the picture we get from Racine's play! So far from being a good influence, she appealed to the vicious side of Titus, and her dismissal was a necessary step in the rehabilitation of his good name.

Bérénice is clearly very different from *Britannicus*. However freely Racine may have treated history in his previous tragedy, he gives us the essential historical truth about Nero and Agrippina. In *Bérénice,* he is concerned with the poetic truth about two lovers, deeply in love, but constrained to separate by the duty or sense of responsibility of one of them—two lovers to whom he has given the names of Titus and Bérénice, but who have very little in common with the Titus and Berenice of history. He has added Antiochus, the usual Racinian third party, whose love for Bérénice is unrequited; but he has eliminated all the other characters who were present in the complex historical situation—the action takes place after (instead of before) the death of Vespasian, and there is no reference to Domitian and Domitia who figure both in Suetonius and in Corneille's play. Everything in the historical background that can illuminate the protagonists and their emotional predicament is vividly portrayed; everything else ruthlessly suppressed.

The main characters, Titus and Bérénice, are of the highest rank, elevated far above ordinary mortals, and surrounded by pomp and circumstance. Bérénice is beset by crowds of courtiers and cannot easily escape even for a moment from the oppressive court that surrounds her (ll. 53–4, 67–8). Titus is the son and heir of Vespasian, deified the previous night. We see him in the senate, redrawing the frontiers of Asia, so as to create a vast new kingdom for Bérénice, giving her sovereignty over a hundred new races (11.170–6, 523–7);

---

[15] Suetonius, *The Twelve Caesars*, translated by Robert Graves, Penguin Classics, 1972 reprint, p. 290.

above all, we see him enthroned in majesty, the cynosure of all eyes, in one of Racine's most magnificent, most evocative passages.[16]

The stage set is symbolic of the action; it consists of a closet, adorned with the entwined initials of Titus and Bérénice, and with two doors opening off, one into the apartments of Titus, the other into the apartments of Bérénice. Outside, invisible but ever-present in our minds, are Rome and—far away—the East. Although the Roman court may be sycophantic and contemptible, the Roman senate and people, represented on the stage by Titus's confidant, Paulin, are implacably opposed to the marriage of the emperor with a foreign queen. At the news of the separation of Titus and Bérénice, Rome is overjoyed and thus imprisons Titus in his decision. The word *Orient* occurs ten times in *Bérénice* and helps to create the atmosphere of the tragedy. The East, whence Bérénice and Antiochus come, and whither they return at the end, is the scene of the military exploits of Titus, aided by Antiochus, and the place where both Titus and Antiochus first saw and loved Bérénice. It is a scene of desolation and smoking ruins, a place of exile, associated with unbridled passion and unhappy love—the sufferings of Antiochus and of Cleopatra and her lovers (ll. 387–96), and the future sufferings of Bérénice herself. It is not without significance that the East is now nearly all subject to her:

> L'Orient presque entier va fléchir sous sa loi . . .
>
> (II, 1, l. 337)

Bérénice has often been described as an elegy. That there is something elegiac about it is implicit in Racine's remark in the preface about its 'majestic sadness'; but it is, as Théophile Gautier said, a 'dramatic elegy', not lacking in dramatic interest. Although we learn in Act II, scene 2, that Titus has made up his mind to send Bérénice away, we also learn that he has been unable to tell her of his decision. How will it be communicated? Will it be communicated, or will he change his mind? There are signs of vacillation (ll. 1135–6); Act IV ends, ambiguously, with Titus's words:

> J'espère, à mon retour,
> Qu'elle ne pourra plus douter de mon amour;
>
> (IV, 8, ll. 1253–4)

[16] See below, p. 148.

and, in the last act, he admits:

> Je suis venu vers vous sans savoir mon dessein:
> Mon amour m'entraînait; et je venais peut-être
> Pour me chercher moi-même, et pour me reconnaître.
>
>   (V, 6, ll. 1382–4).

One is reminded of Néron, determined to free himself from Agrippine's influence, but unable to face her. Bérénice, on her side, is convinced that Titus is about to marry her; and the audience wonders whether she is right or wrong, and, if she is wrong, how she will react to the news. Titus's decision and Bérénice's emotions, moreover, affect Antiochus, whose hopes are alternately raised when Titus resolves to separate from Bérénice, and dashed by Bérénice's indifference or hostility and by doubts about Titus's firmness of purpose, so that

> Tous mes moments ne sont qu'un éternel passage
> De la crainte à l'espoir, de l'espoir à la rage.
>
>   (V, 4, ll. 1299–1300)

It is only in the last moments of the tragedy that these three characters come to accept the situation.

What remains with one afterwards is the memory of the various aspects of love so poignantly described by Racine—the tender, undemanding affection of Bérénice, fondly repeating her lover's name (ll. 269–72), waiting patiently for the few moments that Titus can give to her (ll. 534–6); Titus, regarding those same moments as a necessary pleasure (ll. 423–4), and loving Bérénice without looking into the future, without thinking of the eventual outcome (ll. 1089–94); and the sufferings of love—those of Antiochus, solitary in the East ('Dans l'Orient désert quel devint mon ennui!', l. 234), leaving Rome because he cannot bear Bérénice's preoccupation with Titus:

>   Je fuis des yeux distraits,
>   Qui me voyant toujours, ne me voyaient jamais;
>
>   (I, 4, ll. 277–8)

those of Titus, resolving to send Bérénice away only after

> Des combats dont mon cœur saignera plus d'un jour,
>
>   (II, 2, l. 454)

but tongue-tied in her presence (ll. 473–6), listening to the senate, but unable in his misery to break his 'silence glacé' (l. 1378); and those of Bérénice, when the news has been broken to her, dishevelled, her dress disordered, asking for a sword or poison to kill herself, her eyes turned towards the emperor's apartments as if she were asking for him, distraught, but with none of the violence of Hermione (ll. 967–71, 1227–34). It is fitting that the play should end with the word 'Hélas!'

Saint-Evremond complained that Racine's Titus was in despair, whereas some grief at most would have been appropriate.[17] From a realistic point of view, he is right. In *Bérénice,* love and its torments are depicted as everlasting: after five years, Antiochus's love is as strong as ever it was (ll. 585–8), and Bérénice foresees an eternity of suffering:

> Pour jamais! Ah! Seigneur, songez-vous en vous-même
> Combien ce mot cruel est affreux quand on aime?
> Dans un mois, dans un an, comment souffrirons-nous,
> Seigneur, que tant de mers me séparent de vous?
> Que le jour recommence et que le jour finisse,
> Sans que jamais Titus puisse voir Bérénice,
> Sans que de tout le jour je puisse voir Titus!
>   (IV, 5, ll. 1111–17)

The real Bérénice, over forty years old, had been thrice married and had lived incestuously with her brother before she met Titus, who had been married twice; it is unlikely that either of them suffered quite so acutely as Racine's characters. Racine may possibly have had Louis XIV in mind in writing *Bérénice*—certainly the line,

> Vous êtes empereur, Seigneur, et vous pleurez!
>   (IV, 5, l. 1154)

or something very like it, was addressed to him by Cardinal Mazarin's niece, Marie Mancini, when they separated; but Louis XIV married and fell in love with Louise de la Vallière. Jean Racine, although half dead at Mlle Duparc's funeral, was not impervious to

---

[17] Op. cit., p. 332. Jane Austen would have agreed: 'I have no doubt of his suffering a good deal for a time, a great deal, when he feels that he must give you up;—but it is no creed of mine, as you must be well aware, that such sort of Disappointments kill anybody' (letter to Fanny Knight, Nov. 18, 1814).

the attractions of Mlle Champmeslé. After the death of Beatrice, Dante married Gemma Donati. But *Bérénice* is not concerned with everyday reality; it is an embodiment of the ideal love of Petrarch and *L'Astrée* and the *précieuses*, of the undying romantic ideal of the eternity of passion. Titus, Bérénice, and Antiochus are symbols:

> servons tous trois d'exemple à l'univers
> De l'amour la plus tendre et la plus malheureuse
> Dont il puisse garder l'histoire douloureuse.
>
> (V, 7, ll. 1502–4)

Bajazet, first performed at the Hôtel de Bourgogne on January 5, 1672, was the first of Racine's plays to be published without a dedication and with only a short preface, unlike the lengthy, virulent self-justifications that had accompanied its predecessors. Racine, it may be deduced, was growing in self-confidence.

Set in seventeenth-century Turkey, the tragedy tells a story related orally in France by a former French ambassador to the Sublime Porte, the comte de Cézy, and known to Racine at second hand, either from the chevalier de Nantouillet (as he says in the preface), or from the version given by Segrais in one of his *Nouvelles françoises* (1656–7). Less simple than *Bérénice, Bajazet* shows, it might be said, some of the characters of *Andromaque* in the situation and setting of *Britannicus*.

It is the two female characters, Roxane and Atalide, who remind one of *Andromaque*. Like Hermione, Roxane swings between love and hatred, according to whether she believes her love for Bajazet to be returned or not, finally having him put to death when she knows that he loves her rival. Like Hermione, too, she is credulous, easily persuaded that Bajazet loves her, however flimsy the evidence:

> Tu ne remportais pas une grande victoire,
> Perfide, en abusant ce cœur préoccupé,
> Qui lui-même craignait de se voir détrompé.
>
> (IV, 5, ll. 1298–1300)

This trait is, in fact, the mainspring of the action. In her cruelty and vindictiveness, Roxane is reminiscent, not only of Hermione, but of Néron. She longs to see her rival suffering before the body of her dead lover:

Toi, Zatime, retiens ma rivale en ces lieux.
Qu'il [Bajazet] n'ait en expirant que ses cris pour adieux.
Qu'elle soit cependant fidèlement servie.
Prends soin d'elle: ma haine a besoin de sa vie.
Ah! si pour mon amant facile à s'attendrir,
La peur de son trépas la fit presque mourir
Quel surcroît de vengeance et de douceur nouvelle
De le montrer bientôt pâle et mort devant elle,
De voir sur cet objet ses regards arrêtés
Me payer les plaisirs que je leur ai prêtés!
                                 (IV, 5, ll. 1319–28)

With all her violence, cruelty, and authority, however, Racine has managed to make Roxane a pathetic figure: all her power cannot compel Bajazet to love her, and, though she can put him to death, she is utterly dependent on him:

De toi dépend ma joie et ma félicité.
                                 (II, 1, l. 556)

Like Titus in *Bérénice*, Roxane's rival, Atalide, has loved without taking thought of the future (ll. 345–52), but her main dramatic function is to be jealous. Like Plautine in Corneille's *Othon*, she commands her lover to marry her rival in order to save his life, and she cannot help being jealous when he obeys; but Racine has enriched the borrowed episode.[18] Atalide's jealousy, due in part to the inaccurate account of the interview between Bajazet and Roxane given by the complacent or unobservant vizier, Acomat, leads Bajazet to speak constrainedly to Roxane, which arouses her suspicions; Atalide is thus directly responsible for the final catastrophe:

Enfin, c'en est donc fait; et par mes artifices,
Mes injustes soupçons, mes funestes caprices,
Je suis donc arrivée au douloureux moment
Où je vois par mon crime expirer mon amant.
                                 (V, 12, ll. 1721–4)

[18] There are one or two other reminiscences of Corneille in *Bajazet*. The scene (Act V, scene 4) in which Bajazet, accused by Roxane of having merely feigned love for her (l. 1480), at first tries to deny his guilt, but is silenced by being shown his letter to Atalide, is reminiscent of Act V, scene 1 of *Cinna*. The line, 'Mon unique espérance est dans mon désespoir' (l. 336) is an echo of a line in *Le Cid*, 'Ma plus douce espérance est de perdre l'espoir' (1.135).

The situation of *Bajazet* is not unlike that of *Britannicus*, with Bajezet's position in the struggle for power between Amurat and his sultana, Roxane, similar to that of Britannicus in the contest between Néron and his mother. More important, the background is similar to that of *Britannicus*. Racine says in his preface that his main aim was 'to alter nothing in the manners and customs of the nation'. This seems to be true, though the monogamy of the protagonists, particularly perhaps of Bajazet himself, is a little strange in the context of the seraglio: it is not without interest that in real life or in Racine's source, the sultana—Amurat's mother, not his concubine—agreed to share Bajazet with her rival, a slave, one day a week, and put him to death for exceeding the ration.[19] The background is carefully sketched in, and bears a family resemblance to that of Imperial Rome. As in *Britannicus*, governments are unstable, and palace revolutions frequent; and the janissaries make and unmake sultans, as the legions made and unmade emperors. As in *Britannicus*, human life is of little account: where in *Britannicus* Locuste tries her poisons out on a slave, Acomat in *Bajazet* remarks with careless indifference:

> Cet esclave n'est plus. Un ordre, cher Osmin,
> L'a fait précipiter dans le fond de l'Euxin,
>
> (I, 1, ll. 79–80)

Sultans mistrust their near relations and their ministers, and put them to death or suffer death at their hands: Amurat's intention of killing his half-brother, Bajazet, has plenty of precedents. Sultans are guided only by the interest of the state, and their word cannot be trusted. The claustrophobic atmosphere of Néron's palace is intensified in the seraglio, which is not only full of ever-vigilant spies, but from which outsiders are excluded on pain of death. If Néron's palace has its 'chemins écartés' (*Britannicus*, l. 1725), the seraglio has its 'chemins obscurs' and its 'détours' which one has to have been brought up in it to know (ll. 209, 1423). It is thickly populated by a venal and cowardly host of officials, women, slaves, and sinister mutes.

This is a fitting setting for a tragedy in which Bajazet is condemned to untruthfulness and dissimulation, since if he reveals his

[19] Mme de Sévigné complained that 'the manners of the Turks are ill observed in it; they do not make so much fuss about marrying' (March 16, 1672).

real feelings to Roxane, he condemns not only himself but Atalide to death. It is a fitting setting, too, for the intrigues of the fourth main character in the play, the vizier, Acomat. Like Narcisse, he is a Machiavellian character, shrewd and unscrupulous, who comes to grief because of his ignorance of an important factor in the situation—in this case, the love of Bajazet for Atalide; but he is a highly individual creation. He is crafty, cautious, well-versed in worldly wisdom, aware of the way of sultans with their viziers, and determined to preserve his life if he can. His measures include marriage with Atalide, but he makes no pretence of being in love with her, and is quite free from jealousy (ll. 1369–72).[20] He has many good qualities: he is good-humoured, takes what comes philosophically, is not without loyalty to his allies, displays courage in the face of adverse fortune, and is prepared to die bravely. His weaknesses are his ignorance of the human heart, and a habitual inaccuracy that seems in part to stem from that ignorance as well as from his inability to distinguish between facts and his own wishes, and in part to be deliberate. The account he gives to his confidant of the relationship between Bajazet and Roxane does not correspond to the reality:

> Bajazet est aimable. Il vit que son salut
> Dépendait de lui plaire, et bientôt il lui plut.
>
> (I, 1, ll. 155–6)

His description in the following scene of the state of affairs in Amurat's camp (ll. 215–17) bears little relation to what Osmin has just told him. It is therefore in character that he should give Atalide a misleading account of Bajazet's interview with Roxane:

> Enfin, avec des yeux qui découvraient son âme,
> L'une a tendu la main pour gage de sa flamme;
> L'autre, avec des regards éloquents, pleins d'amour,
> L'a de ses feux, Madame, assurée à son tour.
>
> (III, 2, ll. 885–8)

As Acomat observed all this from afar (l. 883), it is clear that this is wishful thinking or pure fancy. It is this false account that arouses

---

[20] Cf. Artabaze in Du Ryer's *Thémistocle* (1647–8):

> Pour moi je ne me sers de cette passion
> Qu'autant qu'elle est utile à mon ambition.
>
> (II, 5, ll. 692–3)

Atalide's jealousy, so that, in the last resort, Acomat himself brings about the ruin of his projects.

The action of the play is a dual one. Off the stage, at Bagdad, invisible but all-important, is Sultan Amurat. He is fighting the Persians; his janissaries are disaffected, but will rally to him if he is victorious, so that the outcome of the play depends on a battle that is to take place hundreds of miles away from Constantinople —that has, indeed, already been lost or won, though the result has not yet reached Constantinople. In fact, Amurat has won it and consolidated his position: Acomat, Bajazet, and Roxane are doomed to failure from the outset. The arrival of successive emissaries from Amurat keeps our attention fixed on him. In Constantinople, Acomat is plotting to replace Amurat by Bajazet, with the help of Roxane, Amurat's sultana, whom he has caused to fall in love with Bajazet. Roxane has orders from Amurat to put Bajazet to death on the least suspicion of disaffection, so that Bajazet must either marry her or lose his life at her hands; it is strictly true that, as she puts it, he breathes only as long as she loves him (l. 510). The turning point comes in Act IV, when, on the one hand, news of Amurat's victory arrives, and, on the other, Roxane finally establishes that Bajazet loves Atalide. The fate of the characters is now virtually sealed. In a dramatic scene, Roxane has a final interview with Bajazet; outside are the mutes, waiting to strangle Bajazet when he leaves ('S'il sort, il est mort', l. 1456). His last words, a plea for the life of Atalide, ending with the words, 'Et si jamais je vous fus cher . . .', make her mind up. Her decision is expressed by the single word: 'Sortez'. The second emissary of Amurat, the slave, Orcan, like a *deus ex machina*, after helping Roxane to put Bajazet to death, puts her to death in her turn. Atalide commits suicide.

Suspense is maintained until the very end of the play. It is, perhaps, the need for maintaining suspense that is responsible for two slight flaws. To reassure Atalide, Bajazet writes her a letter, which she conceals in her bosom, where it is found by Roxane's attendants after Roxane's threats against Bajazet's life have caused her to faint—a somewhat contrived and artificial episode. At the end of the play, Acomat tries to save Bajazet's life, but his troops arrive a few minutes too late. These two incidents introduce an element of chance into the dénouement, which for once is not inherent in the situation and inevitable.

4

From *Mithridate* to *Phèdre*

Of all Racine's works, *Mithridate* (January 1673) is the one most strongly influenced by Corneille. A historical tragedy, it is his second attempt to write a *Nicomède* (the first was *Alexandre*). Whether the starting point was Corneille's play or the history of Mithridates can only be conjectured; though, as the subject of *Mithridate* was very largely invented by Racine, the first alternative cannot be ruled out.

The historical Mithridates, who had made himself proof against poisons by dosing himself with them, was, at the end of his life, defeated by the Romans, planned to march against Rome, was prevented by the rebellion of his son, Pharnaces, and killed himself. Some years before, after a previous defeat, he had given orders that his wives and sisters should be put to death so that they should not fall into the hands of his enemies. One of his wives, the Greek Monime, attempted to strangle herself with her diadem, but it broke and she was despatched by Mithridates's eunuch. Shortly afterwards, Mithridates executed his son, Xiphares, whose mother had handed Mithridates's treasure over to the Romans.

Many of these historical facts—often transformed—have passed into Racine's tragedy. His Mithridate, too, is defeated by Rome, plans to attack Rome, is prevented by the rebellion of Pharnace, and commits suicide. His Mithridate, too, is impervious to poison. His Mithridate, like the historical one, attempted to seduce Monime before offering her marriage, and then sent her a diadem in earnest of his good intentions. His Monime, like the real one, tries—though not at Mithridate's behest—to strangle herself with her diadem, which breaks; and Mithridate sends her poison, a reminiscence of the historical episode (V, 2). Xipharès's devotion to his father is attributed to the fact that his mother handed Mithridate's treasure over to the Romans.

All this attention to detail, however, does not alter the fact that Racine has telescoped into twenty-four hours or so the unrelated events of as many years; that the real Monime was the wife—only one of the wives—of Mithridate, not his betrothed; that neither Xiphares nor Pharnaces was in love with her; that her death preceded the revolt of Pharnaces and the death of Mithridates by several years; that Xiphares was not a relentless enemy of Rome; and that the essential action of *Mithridate*, invented by Racine, owes more to Corneille than to history.

The two brothers, the pro-Roman Pharnace and the anti-Roman Xipharès, both in love with the anti-Roman Monime, reproduce the situation of *Nicomède*. The character and situation of Mithridate owes something both to Corneille's *Sertorius* and to his *Attila*. Like Sertorius, he is torn between love and political expediency, his rival (like Sertorius's) being his principal lieutenant; and, like Attila, he is a cruel, crafty, Oriental despot and the implacable enemy of Rome. Attila, moreover, ascertains the mutual love of Ildione (whom he loves) and Ardaric by a similar trick to that played by Mithridate on Monime: Attila offers to give Ildione to Ardaric, providing Ardaric is willing to marry her, and Ardaric half confesses that he is in love with her (*Attila*, IV, 4). Monime, attached to her first lover, Xipharès, though contracted to marry Mithridate, is reminiscent of Pauline in Corneille's *Polyeucte*, and her words

> De mes faibles efforts ma vertu se défie.
> Je sais qu'en vous voyant, un tendre souvenir
> Peut m'arracher du cœur quelque indigne soupir;
> Que je verrai mon âme, en secret déchirée,
> Revoler vers le bien dont elle est séparée,
>
> (II, 6, ll. 728–32)

echo Pauline's:

> Mon père, je suis femme, et je sais ma faiblesse,
> Je sens déjà mon cœur qui pour lui s'intéresse,

Et poussera sans doute, en dépit de ma foi,
Quelque soupir indigne et de vous et de moi.
(Polyeucte, I. 4, ll. 342–4)

One of the finest scenes of *Mithridate* is a council scene (II, 1),
a type of scene for which Corneille was renowned; and, although
the subject debated is of a different nature, this scene challenges
comparison with the famous scene in *Cinna.* In both, a
sovereign—Auguste in *Cinna,* Mithridate in Racine's play—makes a
proposal—Auguste, that he should abdicate, Mithridate, that he
should march on Rome; and in both the attitudes of his hearers to the
proposal are determined by secret motives. Pharnace, in love with
Monime and secretly allied with Rome, is unwilling to go and seek
the hand of a Parthian princess; and Xipharès, whom Monime has
just implored to keep away from her, is eager to lead the troops
against Rome in his father's stead. In *Mithridate,* as in *Cinna,* the
council scene contributes to the subsequent action: Pharnace refuses
to obey his father, is suspected of loving Monime, is placed under
arrest, and accuses his brother of being in love with her, too.

Like many of Corneille's tragedies, *Mithridate* is not altogether
tragic. Mithridate's death, like Bajazet's, is not inevitable; rescue is at
hand, but comes too late. More important, like many of Corneille's
tragedies, *Mithridate* has a happy ending, or, at least, an ending that
strikes many readers as being happy. True, the subject, as Racine says
in his preface, is the death of Mithridate; but, although Mithridate is
not without nobility and wins our sympathy by his heroism, his
jealousy, and his mental conflict, the fact remains that he is cruel,
ruthless, suspicious, wily, and the obstacle to the union of the two
young lovers, and that the play ends with Xipharès putting the
Romans to flight, and the dying Mithridate sparing Monime's life
and consenting to her marriage with Xipharès.

Mithridate also contains some verbal reminiscences of Corneille.
Not only does Monime echo Pauline's words, but her line,

Le ciel m'inspirera quel parti je dois prendre,
(IV, 2, l. 1263)

recalls that of Auguste:

Le ciel m'inspirera ce qu'ici je dois faire.
(Cinna, IV, 3, l. 1258)

Mithridate's phrases, 'une main qui m'est chère' (l. 1059) and 'des plus chères mains craignant les trahisons' (l. 1413), recall the words of the dying Séleucus in *Rodogune*:

> Une main qui nous fut bien chère
> Venge ainsi le refus d'un coup trop inhumain.
> (V, 4, ll. 1643–4)

Mithridate, too, contains two examples of a device of which Corneille was fond, but which is rare in Racine—the repetition by one character of the words of another. In Act I, scene 3, the antagonism between Pharnace and Xipharès is brought out by the different ways in which they both repeat Monime's words, 'déguisements' and 'secrets sentiments' (ll. 245–6, 285–6, 315, 318). Monime herself catches the trick and, in Act III, scene 5, refers to Xipharès in the words just used about him by his father, 'Ce fils victorieux', 'cet ennemi de Rome, et cet autre vous-même, ce Xipharès' (ll. 1105–8; cf. ll. 1061–70).

This does not prevent *Mithridate* from being characteristic in many respects of Racine. The false report at the beginning of Mithridate's death in a nocturnal battle foreshadows the battle in Act V in which he takes his own life. The frequent references to Monime's *bandeau* or *diadème* not only keep her position as Mithridate's betrothed, as an 'esclave couronnée' (l. 255) before our eyes, but prepare us for her attempt to strangle herself with it. The play is a curious anticipation of *Phèdre*: the reported death of Mithridate causes his fiancée, Monime, to seek the protection of his son, Xipharès, which leads to the avowal of their mutual love and to the jealousy of Mithridate when he returns—exactly as the reported death of Thésée brings his wife, Phèdre, to seek the alliance of his son, Hippolyte, which leads to her declaration of her love for him and to the jealousy of Thésée when he returns. There are differences: in *Mithridate, both* sons love Monime, as yet unmarried, and her love (unlike Phèdre's) is returned; but there is a family resemblance. The scene in which Mithridate reproaches Monime with having agreed to marry him although she loved his son, and she reproaches him with having surprised her secret by an unworthy trick, is moving because we feel sympathy for both; and the monologue that follows, in which Mithridate gives expression to his dilemma and his conflicting emotions is Racine at his best. One is inclined to regret that he allowed the love affair between Monime and the rather conventional seventeenth-century lover, Xipharès, to distract attention from Mithridate.

Iphigénie was first performed at Versailles on August 18, 1674, in the course of festivities celebrating Louis XIV's conquest of Franche-Comté. Two forgotten poets, Le Clerc and Coras, wrote a play on the same subject to compete with it when it was put on in Paris at the end of the year; but the government, presumably at Racine's request, forbade the actors to perform it until his tragedy had finished its run. It is an adaptation of Euripides's *Iphigenia in Aulis*, Racine's first treatment of a Greek subject since *Andromaque* and *Les Plaideurs*. It is possible that the popularity of the operas of Lulli and his librettist, Quinault, such as *Cadmus* (1673) and *Alceste* (January 1674), may have stimulated him to return to Greece; and a parallel between his *Bérénice* and the *Iphigenia* of Euripides in a defence of *Bérénice* by Subligny[1] may have drawn his attention to this particular tragedy. Racine has, of course, made a number of changes. Ulysse replaces

---

[1] The passage is not without interest:

'. . . M. Racine's *Bérénice* closely resembles this *Iphigenia*.

'The poor girl at first rejoices at her coming marriage with Achilles; as Bérénice rejoices at her coming wedding with Titus. Iphigenia is surprised, protests, and bursts into tears, when she learns that instead of marrying him, she must be sacrificed to the salvation of the Greeks by her own father; as Bérénice gives vent in laments and sighs, when she is told that she must be sacrificed to the laws of the Romans, and that she is abandoned by that same lover, whom she thought she was to marry. Agamemnon weeps on seeing his daughter weep; as Titus weeps on seeing his mistress weep. The Greek never allows himself to be so moved as to change his purpose; as the Roman, however deeply he is affected, never allows himself to be swayed. In the transport of their passion, they both say very similar things. One is reproached by his daughter and by his wife for his tears and his loyalty to the oracle and the satisfaction of the Greeks; as the other is by his mistress for his tears and his loyalty to the laws and the contentment of the Romans. And finally the catastrophe of *Iphigenia* is nothing else than the resolution of this generous maiden, who, wearying of weeping uselessly, suddenly overcomes her weakness, and herself exhorts her father to sacrifice her, as the dénouement of *Bérénice* consists only in the sudden change of this Queen, who, after having shed so many tears in vain, resolves to depart, and herself exhorts her lover to live in peace away from her.' (Subligny, *Réponse à la critique de la Bérénice de Racine*)

Agamemnon's brother, Menelaus; the infant Orestes is omitted; and the letter from Agamemnon to his wife, telling her to turn back, instead of being intercepted by Menelaus, fails to arrive, the messenger having lost his way. More important, Iphigénie and Achille are betrothed and in love; and, to eke out his material and to provide a different dénouement, Racine has invented the character of Eriphile, a captive princess in love with Achille. The usual situation of a pair of happy lovers and a third person in love with one of them is thus created. Suspense is provided by an ambiguous oracle, which seems to demand the sacrifice of Iphigénie, but finally turns out to refer to Eriphile, and a succession of *péripéties*.

The characters have been modified, too. Racine's Agamemnon is more complex and more convincing than Euripides's. His motives are mixed. His position of commander in chief of the Greek troops gives him a satisfaction that he is unwilling to lose (ll. 79–82); he has a sense of responsibility to the Greek heroes who have entrusted him with the command (ll. 209–10, 1358–68); he is afraid of what the army will do if he does not sacrifice Iphigénie (ll. 293–6, 1237–40); and he resents the interference of Achille in a scene of which the Greek play offers no equivalent (IV, 6). Nevertheless, he is genuinely fond of his daughter, and, in the last resort, his paternal love prevails: he tries to prevent her arrival in the camp, and, having failed, tries to send her away again.

Aristotle criticized the Iphigenia of Euripides for her inconsistency: 'Iphigenia as a suppliant is quite unlike what she is later'.[2] Whether or not Iphigenia's final, dignified acceptance of death in Euripides's play is inconsistent, Racine seems to have taken note of the criticism and has, as the seventeenth-century Greek scholar, Dacier, pointed out, made his Iphigénie 'consistently noble, without any unevenness'.[3] She will die with dignity if die she must, but there is no question of her accepting her fate voluntarily and refusing to be rescued. Apart from a fit of jealousy when she thinks that Achilles loves Eriphile (II, 5), she is uniformly soft-hearted and affectionate.

Eriphile, Racine's own creation, is an interesting character, who in some ways anticipates Phèdre. Of unknown parentage, brought up

[2] *Classical Literary Criticism*, translated by T. S. Dorsch, Penguin Classics, 1972 reprint, p. 52.

[3] Dacier, *La Poétique d'Aristote traduite en français*, 1692, quoted by Picard, *Supplément au Corpus racinianum*, 1961, p. 33.

without having known the affection of a mother or a father, she is envious of the family life of Iphigénie (ll. 417–26): one is a little reminded of Edmund in *King Lear*. She is doomed, an oracle—fulfilled at the end of the play—having foretold that, without perishing, she cannot know herself (l. 430). She is jealous of Iphigénie, and tries to prevent her marriage to Achille, even at the cost of bringing about her death. Moreover, her love for Achille, the conqueror of Lesbos, where she was taken captive, and the enemy of Troy, which she regards as her own country, is a guilty one:

> Cet Achille, l'auteur de tes maux et des miens,
> Dont la sanglante main m'enleva prisonnière,
> Qui m'arracha d'un coup ma naissance et ton père,
> De qui jusques au nom tout doit m'être odieux,
> Est de tous les mortels le plus cher à mes yeux.
>   (II, 1, ll. 472–6)

It is almost as if Andromaque had fallen in love with Pyrrhus.

The gods play an important part in *Iphigénie*; without them, indeed, there could be no play. The Greek fleet is becalmed by Diana, who can be appeased only by a human sacrifice; and when the victim is dead, the winds blow.

> A peine son sang coule et fait rougir la terre,
> Les Dieux font sur l'autel entendre le tonnerre,
> Les vents agitent l'air d'heureux frémissements,
> Et la mer leur répond par ses mugissements.
> La rive au loin gémit, blanchissante d'écume.
> La flamme du bûcher d'elle-même s'allume.
> Le ciel brille d'éclairs, s'entr'ouvre, et parmi nous
> Jette une sainte horreur qui nous rassure tous.
> Le soldat étonné dit que dans une nue
> Jusque sur le bûcher Diane est descendue,
> Et croit que s'élevant au travers de ses feux,
> Elle portait au ciel notre encens et nos vœux.
>   (V, 6, ll. 1777–88)

Even if we discount the secondhand report that the soldiers think they have seen Diana herself, there can be no doubt that the events that Ulysse is describing are supernatural. The words *dieu* or *dieux* occur seventy-eight times in this play—as against fifty-three in

Phèdre, some twenty-four in *Andromaque,* and under twenty in the other previous tragedies. The gods constantly harass Agamemnon in his dreams:

> Pour comble de malheur, les Dieux toutes les nuits,
> Dès qu'un léger sommeil suspendait mes ennuis,
> Vengeant de leurs autels le sanglant privilège,
> Me venaient reprocher ma pitié sacrilège,
> Et présentant la foudre à mon esprit confus,
> Le bras déjà levé, menaçaient mes refus.
>
> (I, 1, ll. 83–8)

The characters are related to the gods, too. Agamemnon's wife, Clytemnestre, is the daughter of Jupiter by Leda, so that Iphigénie is Jupiter's grand-daughter. Achille is the son of the goddess, Thetis, and Peleus. Agamemnon belongs to the ill-fated house of Atreus, who killed the three sons of his brother, Thyestes, and had them cooked and served up to him as a repast. Clytemnestre twice alludes to this episode:

> Vous ne démentez point une race funeste.
> Oui, vous êtes le sang d'Atrée et de Thyeste.
>
> (IV, 4, ll. 1249–50. Cf. ll. 1689–91)

When Iphigénie says,

> Vos yeux me reverront dans Oreste mon frère.
> Puisse-t-il être, hélas! moins funeste à sa mère!
>
> (V. 3, ll. 1661–2)

we are reminded that the legendary Orestes murdered his mother to avenge his father, killed on his return from the Trojan War by Clytemnestra and her lover Ægisthus.

The play, however, ends happily on the whole. Eriphile turns out to be the intended sacrificial victim; Iphigénie is saved; her father and her bridegroom are reconciled and 'prêts à confirmer leur auguste alliance' (l. 1794, i.e. her marriage is imminent). This happy ending to some extent jars with the rest of the play. The gods are not malignant; the oracle was ambiguous and wrongly interpreted. It is not clear why the gods should have sent Agamemnon bad dreams, since they do not want his daughter to be sacrificed; but no other explanation is suggested. Moreover, Agamemnon's family history becomes irrelevant: there is no similarity between his character and that of Atreus, or between the latter's treatment of his nephews and the fate of his daughter. And the happy ending makes it at least less likely that Oreste will have to kill his mother, the starting point of whose infidelity to her husband and subsequent murder of him was the sacrifice of her daughter.

The use of the gods in *Iphigénie* is thus not altogether satisfactory. A play in which the gods demand a human sacrifice and intervene directly in human affairs may disconcert a modern reader; but it is no less disconcerting to find at the end that the action of the play is based on a misunderstanding of the will of the gods, and that Iphigénie never was in any danger. In *Phèdre*, these defects are avoided.

In October 1674, Racine was presented with a sinecure—the post of *trésorier de France* in the tax office of Moulins—worth 2,400 livres a year. With this, in addition to his royal pension (1,500 livres since 1670), his earnings as a playwright, an ecclesiastical benefice, and the interest on his savings, he was now quite comfortably off, enjoying an income of six or seven thousand livres a year. On New Year's Day 1675, Mme de Thianges, the sister of Mme de Montespan, gave her nephew, the young duc du Maine, the illegitimate offspring of Louis XIV and Mme de Montespan, a kind of dolls' house or waxwork show, called the *Chambre du Sublime*. It was a room, in which the young duke was surrounded by La Rochefoucauld and his son, Bossuet, Mme Scarron (the duke's governess and the future Mme de Maintenon), Mme de Thianges, Mme de Lafayette, Boileau, Racine, and La Fontaine. This suggests that Racine was now an established dramatist and a favourite at court. Another sign of success is that, for an edition of his works published in 1676, he rewrote the prefaces of some of his plays, making them less polemical; these are the 'second prefaces' in editions of his works.

It was at this period that Racine wrote *Phèdre,* first performed at the Hôtel de Bourgogne on January 1, 1677. Pradon, a protégé of the duchesse de Bouillon (one of Mazarin's nieces), prepared a rival *Phèdre et Hippolyte*, performed two days later. According to Racine's friend, Valincour, this was at first the more successful of the two tragedies, *Phèdre* nearly failed, and Racine was in despair. If this was so, however, the superiority of Racine's play soon asserted itself.

What made Racine treat the subject of Phaedra and treat it as he did, we can only surmise; but there are some suggestive facts. Quinault's *Bellérophon* (1670 or 1671), in which the hero, falsely accused by Sténobée of a guilty passion for her, kills a monster that is ravaging the country, and she, at the false news of his death, commits suicide, is strikingly like *Phèdre* in the outlines of its plot; and one of Thomas Corneille's best plays, *Ariane* (1672), is about Phaedra's sister, Ariadne. Moreover, a number of writers attacked French tragedy for its preoccupation with love and the way it portrayed that passion. Nicole, in his *Traité de la Comédie*, published in 1667 and reprinted in 1675, complained that the theatre shows love in an honourable and attractive light; Rapin in his *Reflexions sur la Poétique* (1674) considered love beneath the dignity of tragedy; and Boileau in his *Art poétique* (1674) recommended that love, combated by remorse, should appear as a weakness and not a virtue. More important, in a dialogue, *Entretien sur les tragédies de ce temps*, written after *Iphigénie*, abbé Villiers urged Racine and Corneille to write tragedies without love, and pointed out that when the Greeks portrayed love, they portrayed it as a weakness, quoting Phaedra as an example:

> If they show a woman passionately in love, like Phaedra in the *Hippolytus* of Euripides, they immediately warn us that this love is an effect of the revenge of the gods, and not of the derangement of those who feel it; and, generally speaking, it can be said that they adduce nothing to authorize the disorders of our hearts.

Quinault and Thomas Corneille may have drawn Racine's attention to the subject; Nicole and Boileau may have predisposed him to treat love as a guilty passion; but the association of subject and treatment by Villiers may have finally determined Racine to write *Phèdre*, in which, as he says in the preface, the weaknesses of love are shown as genuine weaknesses and the havoc wreaked by the passions and the hideousness of vice are made clear.

The story of Phaedra had been treated in antiquity by Euripides in his *Hippolytus*, and by Seneca—to whom Racine owes more than to Euripides—in his *Phaedra*. Phaedra, in Seneca's play, is consumed by a guilty passion for Hippolytus, the son of her husband, Theseus, by a previous wife. During the absence of her husband on an expedition to Hades with his friend, Pirithous, she confesses her love, first to her nurse, and then to Hippolytus himself. Hippolytus, appalled, goes off, leaving his sword behind. Theseus returns, is told by Phaedra that Hippolytus has raped her, and calls on Neptune to kill Hippolytus. A monster from the sea causes Hippolytus's horses to take fright and drag him along the ground, entangled in the reins. After his death, Phaedra confesses her guilt and stabs herself. Seneca and Euripides also provided Racine with the outline of some of his scenes (l. 3; II, 5; IV, 2; V, 6), and the germ of some of his best passages: Phèdre recalling the sufferings of her mother and sister at the hands of Venus (ll. 249–54) and 'C'est toi qui l'as nommé' (l. 264) were suggested by Euripides, for instance, and the speech, 'Oui, Prince, je languis, je brûle pour Thésée' (ll. 634 ff.) by Seneca.

Racine's tragedy is remarkable, not only for what he changed and added, but for what he kept—the mythological and supernatural element, and Phèdre's adulterous and incestuous passion. Thésée, it is true, has not actually visited the underworld; his journey thither is merely a rumour. The dénouement, similarly, is to some extent rationalized—Hippolyte loses control of his horses (l. 1536) because, having fallen in love, he has neglected manly exercises (ll. 129–32, 550–2); nevertheless, it remains supernatural. Not only does a monster appear from the deep in answer to Thésée's prayer, but there is a suggestion that Neptune himself goaded the horses (ll. 1539–40). The sixteenth-century dramatist, Garnier, in his *Hippolyte*, retained Phèdre's incest and adultery; but the seventeenth-century writers who treated this or similar subjects (such as Quinault in *Bellérophon* or Racine himself in *Mithridate*) had turned the faithless wife into a fiancée. Racine's Phèdre is not, of course, incestuous in the strictest sense—there is no blood relationship between Hippolyte and her; but marriage between a man and his stepmother was forbidden by ancient law, as it is by the Church.

Some of Racine's alterations have the object, as he says in his preface, of making Phèdre 'less odious'. She is much less shameless than in Seneca, and a false report of Thésée's death makes her interview with Hippolyte necessary, and excuses her avowal of her love (l. 350), since Greek law admitted of marriage between stepmother and stepson after the death of the husband and father.[4] It is the nurse who accuses Hippolyte, not Phèdre; and she accuses him of intending to violate Phèdre, not of having carried out his intention.

[4] See J. E. White, Jr., 'Phèdre is not incestuous' in *Romance Notes,* Vol. IX, no. 1, Autumn 1967, pp. 92–4.

Moreover, Phèdre, after Œnone has accused Hippolyte, might have confessed the truth, but for a fit of jealousy caused by the news that he is in love with Aricie.

The invention of Aricie—mentioned in the *Æneid* as the birthplace or mother of Hippolytus's son—is Racine's main change, a characteristic one. It has many advantages. Without it, the material provided by Euripides and Seneca would have been insufficient for a modern, five-act play. It creates the usual Racinian situation, Hippolyte and Aricie mutually in love, and Phèdre hopelessly in love with Hippolyte. It enables Racine to make his motivation more complex, to modernize his psychology, and to make his play more dramatic. The ancient Hippolytus, the votary of Artemis, devoted to chastity and hunting, would be out of place in the modern world; Racine's Hippolyte, in love with Aricie, is not. Jealousy is added to the range of Phèdre's emotions. Hippolyte counters the accusation by an admission of his love for Aricie, whose later confirmation makes Thésée realize—too late—that his wrath against his son was unjustified. The invention of Aricie, too, enables Racine to introduce a political subplot.[5] Aricie, who has claims on the throne, is destined to celibacy not only by law (ll. 427–8), but also from choice (ll. 433–5). She is thus the counterpart of Hippolyte, the enemy of love; but, since his love for her is guilty (because it is illegal), he is also to some extent the counterpart of Phèdre, endowed with a tragic flaw. The subplot, the love of Hippolyte and Aricie, thus to some extent mirrors the main plot, the love of Phèdre for Hippolyte, as the story of Gloucester and his sons in *King Lear* mirrors that of Lear and his daughters.

It is difficult not to regard *Phèdre* as the culmination of Racine's previous work. The situation is a fusion of *Bajazet* (in which Amurat's concubine, Roxane, is in love with his half-brother, Bajazet, who loves and is loved by Atalide) and *Mithridate* (in which Mithridate's bride to be, Monime, loves and is loved by his son, Xipharès). Like Mithridate, Thésée is believed dead, but returns. *Phèdre* resembles *Iphigénie* in being an adaptation of a Greek play and in introducing the gods (though more successfully). Eriphile in *Iphigénie* is a foretaste of Phèdre herself. And in its characterization, its poetry, and its structure, *Phèdre* is Racine at his best.

The characterization is excellent. Hippolyte, though transformed,

5 See below, pp. 115–16.

still has some of the characteristics of his ancient model. The son of an Amazon, he is fond of hunting and seclusion, shocked by sexual immorality, and averse even from legitimate love (ll. 531–2). With all his virtues, he not only falls in love with Aricie in defiance of his father's commands, but plans rebellion against him, so that, like Phèdre, he has a guilty conscience. Above all, Phèdre, though guilty of an incestuous passion, responsible for the death of Hippolyte, and only saved from destroying her rival by lack of opportunity ('Il faut perdre Aricie', l. 1259), never forfeits the sympathy of audience or readers.

There are a number of reasons for this. For one thing, Phèdre is the victim of heredity, the daughter of Pasiphaë, who mated with a bull and gave birth to the minotaur. She has struggled against her passion, having Hippolyte sent away from Athens—in vain, since Thésée himself on his departure entrusted her to his care in Trézène; and she has been trying to starve herself to death, so that, when the tragedy opens, she is already a dying woman,

> Une femme mourante et qui cherche à mourir.
>
> (I, 1, l. 44)

She never ceases to condemn herself, and upbraids Œnone who urges her to give way to her passion.

Perhaps the chief reason is that Phèdre, as we see her in the play, acts involuntarily; the balance of her mind is disturbed, and she is not in control of herself. She is full of contradictions: how, she asks on her first appearance, comes her hair to be dressed, only to be told that she herself insisted on being adorned; and at the end we see her alternately embracing her children and driving them away again, writing letters and tearing them up. What makes her act, reluctantly, involuntarily, is her obsession.

> Dieux! que ne suis-je assise à l'ombre des forêts!
> Quand pourrai-je, au travers d'une noble poussière,
> Suivre de l'œil un char fuyant dans la carrière?
>
> (I, 3, ll. 176–8)

she asks abstractedly, and this involuntary remark—

> Où laissé-je égarer mes vœux et mon esprit?
>
> (l. 180)

—leads her to tell Œnone of her love. Her confession of her love to

Hippolyte is no less involuntary. Thésée being mentioned, she cannot help continuing:

> Il n'est point mort, puisqu'il respire en vous.
> Toujours devant mes yeux je crois voir mon époux.
> Je le vois, je lui parle, et mon cœur . . . Je m'égare,
> Seigneur; ma folle ardeur malgré moi se déclare.
>
> (II, 5, ll. 627–30)

—as it does in the very next speech, 'Oui, Prince, je languis, je brûle pour Thésée'. This passionate declaration of love is followed by the question,

> Cet aveu si honteux, le crois-tu volontaire?
>
> (l. 694)

In Act IV, she appears before Thésée with a confused idea of helping Hippolyte, but no clear plan. Then, however, she learns that he loves Aricie, and in a paroxysm of jealousy thinks of appealing to Thésée, suddenly realizing in a moment of lucidity the enormity of the idea:

> Que fais-je? Où ma raison se va-t-elle égarer?
> Moi jalouse! Et Thésée est celui que j'implore!
>
> (IV, 6, ll. 1264–5)

Phèdre is a woman with an obsession, moving in a hallucinatory state; if she is a criminal, her crime is due to mental disease. Sick in body and mind, Phèdre arouses our sympathies, because in her we recognize ourselves. Racine's claim that the character of Phèdre was the best thing he had put on the stage is fully justified.

The crux of the tragedy is the false accusation of Hippolyte, Thésée's belief in it, and Hippolyte's inability to establish his innocence; and it is interesting to see how Racine makes these things convincing. Thésée, the former profligate, is wholly devoted to Phèdre and trusts her implicitly. Hippolyte's indifference to women is suspicious to a man of Thésée's temperament, and the circumstantial evidence against him is strong: Phèdre's embarrassed reception of her husband, Hippolyte's frigid greeting, his request to leave Trézène without seeing Phèdre again, Phèdre's previous insistence that he should be banished from Athens, the fact that his sword is in Phèdre's possession, and her genuine tears (l. 1442) are enough to explain why an impetuous man like Thésée should believe the accusation without question, and condemn his son to exile and death.

Hippolyte's state of mind is particularly complex and interesting. Young and untried, he has the greatest admiration and respect for his father, and is deterred by filial piety from telling him the truth (ll. 1089–90, 1340–2). But this is not all. The influence of his Amazon mother and his revulsion from his father's profligacy have made love abhorrent to him. He has just become aware that what he feels for Aricie is love, and yielded to his passion for her, but not without a struggle and a sense of guilt. Phèdre's advances fill him with shame, disgust, and horror (ll. 718, 743–6), and he cannot bear to speak of them. 'Phèdre', he begins to tell Théramène, and then breaks off in horror:

> Mais non, grands Dieux! qu'en un profond oubli
> Cet horrible secret demeure enseveli.
>
> (II, 6, 11.720–1)

Only to Aricie can he bring himself to speak of his experience:

> Je n'ai pu vous cacher, jugez si je vous aime,
> Tout ce que je voulais me cacher à moi-même;
>
> (V, 1, ll. 1345–6)

and he insists that she should tell no one.

In *Phèdre*, as in *Iphigénie*, there are frequent references to the gods. The mainspring of the action is the destructive passion of love; but Phèdre regards herself as being persecuted by Venus like all her family. There are other suggestions that the gods represent not merely human passion, but some malignant force that delights in tormenting us. Hippolyte places his trust in them.

> Mais l'innocence enfin n'a rien à redouter.
>
> (III, 6, 1. 996)
> Sur l'équité des Dieux osons nous confier . . .
>
> (V, 1, 1. 1351)

It is misplaced. Thésée finds the friendship of Neptune no less injurious than the hostility of Venus is to his wife

> Je hais jusques au soin dont m'honorent les Dieux;
> Et je m'en vais pleurer leurs faveurs meurtrières . . .
>
> (V, 7, ll. 1612–13)

But the gods in *Phèdre* do not influence the action. We are not bound to believe in the objective reality of Venus; the tragedy loses none of its force if we regard her as a symbol of human passion and heredity. We must accept the existence of Neptune, who sends a monster to attack Hippolyte in response to Thésée's appeal; but Neptune merely represents Thésée's hot temper and injustice—he does nothing that Thésée could not have done by other means.

As in *Iphigénie,* the characters have direct relations with the gods. Thésée is a favourite of Neptune. Phèdre and her family have incurred the wrath of Venus, one consequence of which was the minotaur, the fruit of the unnatural union of Phèdre's mother with a bull, and therefore Phèdre's half-brother. Through her mother, Phèdre is descended from the sun, and her father, Minos, sits in judgement in the underworld:

> Misérable! et je vis? et je soutiens la vue
> De ce sacré Soleil dont je suis descendue?
> J'ai pour aïeul le père et le maître des Dieux;
> Le ciel, tout l'univers est plein de mes aïeux.
> Où me cacher? Fuyons dans la nuit infernale.
> Mais que dis-je? Mon père y tient l'urne fatale;
> Le Sort, dit-on, l'a mise en ses sévères mains:
> Minos juge aux enfers tous les pâles humains.
>
> (IV, 6, ll. 1273–80)

In *Phèdre,* the semi-divinity of the characters not merely contrasts with their despair, it enhances it. Such are what Racine calls 'the ornaments of fable, which contributes greatly to poetry'.

Racine's craftmanship in *Phèdre* is masterly. The similarity of the two plots is emphasized in the first two acts by the parallelism of the construction. [Act I is in two parts: in one, Hippolyte reluctantly tells his tutor, Théramène, of his love for Aricie (scene 1); in the other, Phèdre involuntarily tells her nurse, Œnone, of her love for Hippolyte (scene 3).]The exposition is completed in the first scene of the second act, when Aricie confesses her love for Hippolyte to her confidante. Hippolyte, in love with Aricie, has been shunning her (ll. 49–50), just as Phèdre, in love with Hippolyte, had him banished from Athens. On the other hand, Hippolyte, 'contre l'amour fièrement révolté' (l. 531) resembles Aricie, 'de tout temps à l'amour opposée' (l. 433). As Act I shows Hippolyte and Phèdre admitting to

their confidants that they are in love, and ends with the news that
Thésée is dead, so Act II shows Hippolyte and Phèdre confessing
their love to the objects of their affection, and ends with the news
that Thésée is alive. Apart from the scene between Aricie and her
confidante, Act II contains two main scenes: in one, Hippolyte offers
to support Aricie's claim to the throne of Athens, and tells her of his
love for her (scene 2); in the other, Phèdre asks Hippolyte to support
her son's claim to the throne of Athens, and tells him of her love for
him (scene 5).

Everything that happens is carefully prepared. Phèdre's declaration of love to Hippolyte, in which she says she loves Thésée in him,
is prepared by her remark:

> Mes yeux le retrouvaient dans les traits de son père.
>
> (I, 3, l. 290)

The audience is prepared for the return of Thésée by Aricie's scepti-
cism about the report of his death (ll. 389–91), by Hippolyte's
attempt to reassure Phèdre (ll. 618–22), and by a rumour that he is
alive (ll. 729–30). It is prepared for the manner of Hippolyte's death
by his neglect of his horsemanship. It is prepared for the dénouement
in another way by two lines of Hippolyte's comforting speech to
Phèdre:

> Neptune le protège, et ce Dieu tutélaire
> Ne sera pas en vain imploré par mon père,
>
> (II, 5, ll. 621–2)

in which he correctly forecasts the future without knowing how his
prophecy will be fulfilled.

Dramatic irony of this kind plays a considerable part in *Phèdre*.
Œnone tells Phèdre:

> Quoiqu'il vous reste à peine une faible lumière,
> Mon âme chez les morts descendra la première.
> Mille chemins ouverts y conduisent toujours,
> Et ma juste douleur choisira les plus courts.
> Cruelle, quand ma foi vous a-t-elle déçue?
>
> (I, 3. ll. 229–33)

In the event, Œnone's attempts to help will prove disastrous, Phèdre
will revile her, and she will drown herself in consequence; but,

without any idea of all this, she is merely marshalling arguments to prevail upon Phèdre to confide in her. Phèdre replies:

> Quand tu sauras mon crime, et le sort qui m'accable,
> Je n'en mourrai pas moins, j'en mourrai plus coupable.
>
> (ll. 241–2)

This again is exactly what is to happen; but Phèdre has no inkling at this stage of the full meaning of 'plus coupable'. Phèdre tells Hippolyte that if he had gone to Crete in place of his father:

> Par vous aurait péri le monstre de la Crète . . .
>
> (l. 649)

The phrase is applicable to Phèdre herself, and she is about to perish because of Hippolyte.

> Je ne me verrai point préférer de rivale,
>
> (III, 1, l. 790)

says Phèdre, only to have her confidence rudely shattered. 'Souffrez', Hippolyte implores Thésée,

> que d'un beau trépas la mémoire durable,
> Éternisant des jours si noblement finis,
> Prouve à tout l'avenir que j'étais votre fils.
>
> (III, 5, ll. 950–2)

His wish is granted, but not in the way he means: his father condemns him to death. Aricie's lie to Thésée—

> Seigneur, il me disait un éternel adieu—
>
> (V, 3, l. 1416)

turns out to be the literal truth.

A work of genius, says Empson, is 'a sort of miracle whose style carries its personality into every part of it, whose matter consists of microcosms of its form, and whose flesh has the character of the flesh of an organism'.[6] *Phèdre* is a work of this kind, closely knit, dense in texture, laden with significance. Neither dramatic irony nor the mirroring of the main plot by the subplot are the only means of achieving this result. The fate of Pirithoüs—'livré par ce barbare à des monstres cruels' (l. 963)—foreshadows that of Hippolyte. Words and phrases are repeated. Thésée tells Phèdre,

[6] W. Empson, *Seven Types of Ambiguity*, Penguin Books, 1965, p. 45.

Il soutient qu'Aricie a son cœur, a sa foi,
Qu'il aime.

(ll. 1187–8)

That the words have struck home, is shown by the fact that she broods upon them afterwards:

Hippolyte est sensible, et ne sent rien pour moi!
Aricie a son cœur! Aricie a sa foi!

(IV, 5, ll. 1203–4)

In the next scene, in her jealous fury, she says:

Mes homicides mains, promptes à me venger,
Dans le sang innocent brûlent de se plonger.

(IV, 6, ll. 1271–2)

This harks back to her words at the beginning of the play:

Grâces au ciel, mes mains ne sont point criminelles,

(I, 3, l. 221)

the contrast emphasizing her progressive degeneration in between. Thésée calls on Neptune to punish Hippolyte:

Souviens-toi que pour prix de mes efforts heureux,
Tu promis d'exaucer le premier de mes vœux.

(IV, 2, ll. 1067–8)

Aricie warns him later—

Craignez, Seigneur, craignez que le ciel rigoureux,
Ne vous haïsse assez pour exaucer vos vœux.

(V. 3, ll. 1435–6)

The repetition of certain words, too, reminds the reader of the main situations, themes, and conflicts of the play. The chief key-words or symbols of this kind are the word *poison* (equated with passion), words denoting light and darkness (equated with innocence and guilt), and the word *monstre*.

J'aime! Ne pense pas qu'au moment que je t'aime,
Innocente à mes yeux, je m'approuve moi-même
Ni que du fol amour qui trouble ma raison
Ma lâche complaisance ait nourri le poison,

(II, 5, ll. 673–6)

says Phèdre. Hippolyte echoes her:

> Dieux! que dira le Roi? Quel funeste poison
> L'amour a répandu sur toute sa maison!
>
> (III, 6, ll. 991–2)

Love has turned Trézène into

> un lieu funeste et profané,
> Où la vertu respire un air empoisonné . . .
>
> (V, 1, ll. 1359–60)

It is appropriate that Phèdre should kill herself by taking poison, instead of hanging herself as in Euripides, or stabbing herself as in Seneca.

Phèdre, the descendant of the sun, can no longer bear the light of day, and seeks darkness—from love,

> Dieux! que ne suis-je assise à l'ombre des forêts!
>
> (I, 3, l. 176)

or from guilt and shame:

> Je voulais en mourant prendre soin de ma gloire,
> Et dérober au jour une flamme si noire . . .
>
> (I, 3, ll. 309–10)

'Fuyons dans la nuit infernale', she says (l. 1277).

The word *monstre* occurs thirty times in Racine's plays, eighteen of them in *Phèdre*. Thésée has destroyed monsters, including the minotaur, the monster of Crete, and Hippolyte longs to emulate him. Thésée's amorous adventures are to some extent palliated by the monsters he has killed, whereas Hippolyte has no such excuse:

> . . . aucuns monstres par moi domptés jusqu'aujourd'hui
> Ne m'ont acquis le droit de faillir comme lui.
>
> (I, 1, ll. 99–100)

The word is also used figuratively. In her aberration, Phèdre calls Hippolyte a monster; so does Thésée, deluded by her. But she also sees herself as a monster:

> Digne fils du héros qui t'a donné le jour,
> Délivre l'univers d'un monstre qui t'irrite.

La veuve de Thésée ose aimer Hippolyte!
Crois-moi, ce monstre affreux ne doit point t'échapper.

(II, 5, ll. 700–3)

Hippolyte asks Thésée's leave to kill any monster that may have
escaped him (l. 948). Aricie, in a speech that recalls this one, tries to
show Thésée that he has, in fact, spared one—Phèdre:

Vos invincibles mains
Ont de monstres sans nombre affranchi les humains;
Mais tout n'est pas détruit, et vous en laissez vivre
Un . . .

(V, 3, ll. 1443–6)

Hippolyte does kill a monster, but meets his own death at the same
time. The sacrifice of his life is needed to bring about the death of
Phèdre, the Cretan monster.

At the end of the play, these themes come together. Phèdre takes
poison,

Et la mort, à mes yeux dérobant la clarté,
Rend au jour, qu'ils souillaient, toute sa pureté.

(V, 7, ll. 1643–4)

Phèdre, the monster who shunned light, has relegated herself to
eternal darkness, and the purity of the light of day has been restored.

The universal theme, the depiction of the human condition, of
human nature striving after virtue but unable to resist vice, the
impeccable construction, the inevitability of the tragic outcome, the
suggestive and emotive power of the verse may explain why Racine
liked *Phèdre* best of all his plays, and why his preference has been
shared by so many others.

5

Esther *and* Athalie

It was twelve years before Racine wrote another play. In 1677, he was supplanted in the good graces of Mlle Champmeslé by the comte de Clermont-Tonnerre, became reconciled with the Church and Port-Royal, abandoned the theatre, married (June), and was appointed historiographer royal along with Boileau (September). Although there is some uncertainty about the exact sequence of events, and although it has been argued that his genuine religious conversion came later and that his silence was exclusively due to his appointment as historiographer, there seems no good reason to doubt that some spiritual crisis led both to his retirement from the theatre and to the acceptance of the appointment. That the question cannot be settled does not much matter, since it has little bearing on his work—unless, of course, one believes, as some have done, that the coming conversion is already evident in *Bérénice* (in which the moral sense asserts itself) and in *Iphigénie* and *Phèdre* (in which the gods reappear).

Henceforth, Racine led the life of a conscientious historiographer, a successful courtier, a family man, and a pious Christian. His piety need not be doubted because it fell short of saintliness and allowed him to revise his works and to place his pen occasionally—and reluctantly—at the disposal of Louis XIV or Mme de Maintenon. It was at the behest of the latter that his last two plays were written. In the school she had founded at Saint-Cyr in 1686 for the daughters of impoverished gentlemen, play-acting was regarded as good for the girls; but as the plays written for the purpose by the headmistress,

Mme de Brinon, were bad, Mme de Maintenon suggested that the girls should perform tragedies of Corneille and Racine instead. *Cinna* and *Andromaque* were acted, but too successfully. 'Our little girls have just played *Andromaque*, and have acted it so well that they shall never act it again, or any of your plays,' she wrote to Racine, appealing to him to write something suitable for them. The result was *Esther*, first performed at Saint-Cyr on January 26, 1689, before an audience that included Louis XIV, Mme de Maintenon, and a few favoured courtiers. Several performances were given in the following weeks—Louis XIV was delighted, and Mme de Maintenon was no doubt not unwilling to give semi-publicity to a play which could be (and was) interpreted as celebrating Louis XIV and herself in the characters of Assuérus and Esther, and as depicting her former rival, Mme de Montespan, and her enemy, Louvois, in an unfavourable light as Vasti and Aman.[1]

Mme de Sévigné, who saw the play on February 19, put her impressions into a letter two days later:

> I cannot tell you how excessively pleasurable this play is: it is a thing that is not easy to perform, and that will never be imitated; there is such a perfect and such a complete harmony between the verse, the songs, the actresses, that one wishes for nothing more; the girls playing kings and persons of note are perfectly suited to their parts; one is wrapt, and has no other regret than that of seeing such a delightful play come to an end; everything in it is simple, everything in it is innocent, everything in it is sublime and touching; the fidelity to sacred history inspires respect; all the songs, matching the words (which are taken from the Psalms or the Book of Wisdom), and appropriate to the subject, are of a beauty that cannot be borne without tears: the measure of one's approbation of this play is that of one's taste and attentiveness. I was charmed by it . . .

Esther was perfectly adapted to the requirements of Mme de Maintenon and Saint-Cyr. It is a three-act play, based on the story of Esther as told in the Old Testament and the Apocrypha, and the style is full of biblical words and turns of phrase; each act takes place in a

[1] According to Louis Racine and Voltaire, Aman's words, 'il sait qu'il me doit tout' (l. 866), had been spoken by Louvois, in a moment of pique, of Louis XIV.

different part of the palace of Assuérus, allowing of a succession of splendid settings—Esther's apartments, Assuérus's throne-room, and Esther's gardens; and there is a chorus of female attendants, singing music by J. B. Moreau.

The biblical story is, on the whole, faithfully dramatized, with some modifications. To concentrate the action, the massacre of the Jews is timed to take place in ten days, instead of a year, and Esther's two banquets are reduced to one. To increase the interest, Mardochée enters the palace and sees Esther, instead of merely communicating with her through a messenger, and an additional *péripétie* is provided by giving Assuérus a dream, ambiguously interpreted by Chaldean soothsayers. Zarès appears only as the anxious wife of Aman, her rôle as his evil counsellor having been allotted to an invented character, Hydaspe. The principle of propriety imposed other changes. Aman does not bribe Assuérus to allow him to massacre the Jews; Esther becomes the niece—from being the cousin—of Mardochée; there is no question of her having spent a night with Assuérus before being selected to be his wife; and Aman embraces her feet, instead of flinging himself across the couch on which she is reclining. At the end, Aman is torn to pieces by the mob, instead of being hanged, and Assuérus countermands the order for the massacre, which his biblical counterpart cannot do. The counter-massacre by the Jews of their enemies is reduced to the statement that they shall be given 'le sang de tous leurs ennemis' (III, 7, l. 1183). Esther and her compatriots thus become more appealing, more virtuous, and less bloodthirsty than in the Bible.

Unlike Racine's previous plays, *Esther* shows divine providence at work. God causes Assuérus to choose Esther to be his wife (ll. 67–75); God sends Mardochée to her (ll. 231–2); God makes Assuérus receive Esther with indulgence and stretch out his sceptre to her (ll. 717–26); and God finally shows Aman to Assuérus in his true colours (ll. 1138, 1156–9, 1176–89).

Slight as *Esther* is, and even without the satisfaction of being one of a select, handpicked audience, or the additional appeal of recognizing contemporary personalities in it, anyone who has the good fortune to see it performed with its music is likely to succumb to its charm and to understand the enthusiasm of Mme de Sévigné and her contemporaries for it.

As early as February 1689, Mme de Sévigné reported that Racine was to write another play for the following winter. In March, she thinks that the subject is Absalom or Jephthah; but if Racine at first considered these subjects, he discarded them in favour of that of Athaliah, not improbably because of its topical interest: a play about a restoration could scarcely fail to interest a court that had given refuge to James II of England and his Queen, and that had sent an expeditionary force to Ireland with him. *Athalie*, however, was not given the same publicity as *Esther*. Many *dévots*, like the parish priest of Versailles, Hébert, who had refused to go and see *Esther*, held that the public performances of that play were training the girls in immodesty; and their remonstrances prevailed on Mme de Maintenon at the last moment, when everything was ready for the performance of *Athalie*. It was acted once or twice in 1691 at Versailles before the King, with the choruses, but with the girls wearing their ordinary dresses.

Athalie is a biblical tragedy with choruses, like *Esther*; but it is a more elaborate play in five acts, and, as the Bible provided merely the bare bones of the action,[2] Racine was able to give freer play to his imagination. Like *Britannicus*, it is a historical, political tragedy. The invention of Athalie's dream is a brilliant way of providing dramatic interest. At the same time as Joad prepares his coup d'état, Athalie's dream draws her attention to the temple and to Joas (if the dream is divinely inspired, this is not mere coincidence); as he prepares to proclaim Joas king, she plans to seize Joas and put him to death. The play is a race between Joad and Athalie, in which he completes his plans first, and both forestalls and outwits her.

The coup d'état is skilfully prepared and shows Racine's attention to detail. At the opening of the play, Joad has decided that the time has come to reveal the existence of Joas and proclaim him king (ll. 165–6), and he has secretly called together the Levites, increased their numbers, and made them take a solemn oath of fidelity to the legitimate heir who is to be revealed to them (ll. 209–13). He decides to advance the proclamation of Joas to steal a march on Athalie and Mathan (ll. 1096–7), and distributes a secret hoard of arms. The next step is to present Joas to the leaders of the Levites (IV, 3), after which he plans to march on Athalie's palace, counting on popular support,

[2] II Kings, xi; II Chronicles, xxii and xxiii.

first making the Levites swear to live, fight, and die for their king (ll. 1333–72). This plan being frustrated by Athalie's attack on the temple, Joad makes preparations to repel her (ll. 1445–52). As Athalie attacks, Joas is crowned—secretly—so that Athalie will be taken by surprise:

> Des enfants de Lévi la troupe partagée
> Dans un profond silence aux portes s'est rangée.
> Tous doivent à la fois précipiter leurs pas,
> Et crier pour signal: 'Vive le roi Joas!'
>
> (V, 1, ll. 1531–4)

Finally, Athalie is lured into the temple by a trick. Joad gives orders that as soon as she is inside, the trumpet shall sound to dismay her troops, while the news of the coronation of Joas shall be spread to rally his supporters (ll. 1681–8). Athalie herself is demoralized by the sudden drawing of a curtain, revealing Joas crowned and enthroned (V, 5). Her troops flee, and she herself is put to death (V, 6).

The success of the trick by which Athalie is lured into the temple without her army is carefully prepared. Joad promises to show her a concealed 'treasure'—understood literally by Athalie and Abner, but metaphorically by Joad. In the very first scene of the play, Abner had warned Joad that Mathan had persuaded Athalie that the temple was full of treasure:

> Tantôt, voyant pour l'or sa soif insatiable,
> Il lui feint qu'en un lieu que vous seul connaissez,
> Vous cachez des trésors par David amassés,
>
> (I, 1, ll. 48–50)

lines that are echoed in Act V, scene 2, when Joad says:

> Il est vrai, de David un trésor est resté.
>
> (l. 1649)

Athalie, in other words, falls into Joad's trap because of a conviction implanted in her by her own evil counsellor, who helps to bring about her—and his own—destruction.

Beside Joad's efficiency and resourcefulness, his success has two causes. One is his resolution, which springs from his faith in God, but which, if it did not, would be no less politic: nothing could put more heart into his followers than his fearlessness, his refusal to be dismayed, his determination, not merely not to give up Joas or to allow Josabet to escape with him, but to crown him forthwith (III, 6). A great leader without faith would not have acted otherwise. The other, of course, is divine providence. The action of the play proceeds logically from the circumstances, states of mind, and actions of the characters. At the same time, the events of the play are made to appear as God's handiwork, either because they correspond to Joad's faith that God will overthrow the impious (ll. 61–2, 1668), or because they appear to take place in answer to a prayer (ll. 292–4, 632, 1669–72), or because they are attributed by the characters of the play to God. Athalie, for instance, has been profoundly disturbed for two days by a dream, which has impaired her judgement.

> La peur d'un vain remords trouble cette grande âme:
> Elle flotte, elle hésite; en un mot, elle est femme.
>
> (III, 3, ll. 875–6)

No doubt her dream and her state of mind are susceptible of a natural explanation ('la peur d'un vain remords', 'elle est femme'). No doubt, too, her dreaming of Joas and her emotion on seeing him in the temple could be explained in a natural way by his resemblance to his father, her son, Ochosias:

> Je vois d'Ochosias et le port et le geste . . .
>
> (V, 6, l. 1771).

On the other hand, Athalie is convinced that her dream has a supernatural origin because it has occurred twice (ll. 515–20). In one way or another, all the events of the tragedy are attributed to God. It is he who leads Athalie to the temple:

> Dans le temple des Juifs un instinct m'a poussée,
> Et d'apaiser leur Dieu j'ai conçu la pensée . . .
>
> (II, 5, ll. 527–8)

It is God who causes her to be abashed in the temple by Joad's words:

> J'ignore si de Dieu l'ange se dévoilant
> Est venu lui montrer un glaive étincelant;
> Mais sa langue en sa bouche à l'instant s'est glacée,
> Et toute son audace a paru terrassée.
> Ses yeux, comme effrayés, n'osaient se détourner;
> Surtout Éliacin paraissait l'étonner.
>
> (II, 2, ll. 409–14)

(The suggestion of divine intervention is followed by a natural explanation). God inspires Joas's replies to her interrogation:

> Daigne mettre, grand Dieu, ta sagesse en sa bouche.
>
> (II, 7, l. 632)

God is responsible for the actions of Mathan:

> De Dieu que j'ai quitté l'importune mémoire
> Jette encore en mon âme un reste de terreur;
> Et c'est ce qui redouble et nourrit ma fureur.
>
> (III, 3, ll. 956–8)

God inspires Joad's prophecy, showing how the downfall of Athalie is part of the pattern of God's purpose for the world, a necessary prelude to the coming of Christ and the spread of Christianity among the Gentiles. God dissipates Athalie's army (l. 1748). Athalie herself explains how she has been defeated by God:

> Impitoyable Dieu, toi seul as tout conduit.
> C'est toi qui me flattant d'une vengeance aisée,
> M'as vingt fois en un jour à moi-même opposée,
> Tantôt pour un enfant excitant mes remords,
> Tantôt m'éblouissant de tes riches trésors,
> Que j'ai craint de livrer aux flammes, au pillage.
>
> (V, 6, ll. 1774–9)

Racine probably meant the spectator to see the action of *Athalie* as the work of God, to see God—as Sainte-Beuve puts it—as 'the chief, or rather the only, character in *Athalie*, from the first line to the last'.[3] But there is nothing to compel the spectator to think that the characters are right in attributing everything that happens to God, any more than he need accept Phèdre's faith in the objective reality of Venus. *Athalie* can be taken either as a straightforward account of a theocratic revolution, as *Britannicus* is of a palace revolution, or as an illustration of divine providence. This is one reason why the play has appealed through the ages to Christians and unbelievers alike.

Another is that it is one of Racine's best plays. The lesser characters—the time-serving, ambitious, unscrupulous, crafty Mathan, the high priest of Baal, a renegade, free-thinking but with a remnant of fear of the God he has deserted; Abner, loyal and God-fearing, but

[3] *Port-Royal*, Livre VI, ch. XI.

endowed with purely human prudence and with no appreciation of other forces than military might; the tender and timorous Josabet, who nevertheless trusts her husband, Joad; and the infant, Joas—are worthy to stand beside Joad, whose ruthless fanaticism is in no wise glossed over, and Athalie, the powerful and successful queen, brought low, bewildered, distressed, and unsure of herself. Racine was steeped in the Bible, and the biblical atmosphere is skilfully reproduced. It is true that Sainte-Beuve and Renan have found the temple more like a Greek temple than the one described in detail in the Old Testament, that the latter contrasts the great queen of Racine's play with her father, Ahab, in the Bible, who sulked because Naboth would not give him his vineyard,[4] and that Racine is guilty of one or two anachronisms, such as priests sprinkling the congregation with the blood of the sacrifice (1. 392) or swearing an oath on Holy Writ (ll. 1370, 1403). But most people, unaware of these things, are likely to be impressed by the many echoes of the Bible, by the skilful introduction of references to Jewish beliefs and customs, history and traditions, by the setting of the play in the temple, the organization and the place of which in Jewish national life are made clear, and by the characterization: even Renan considers Joad as an admirable depiction of a high-priest and a prophet.

Athalie, too, is a well-constructed and highly dramatic play. Everything is carefully prepared, and everything follows logically; but we cannot be sure what the outcome will be, nor can we know how it will be brought about, and suspense is maintained. Athalie visits the temple, listens to Abner and Mathan debating whether Joas should be spared or put to death, sends for him, and is disarmed by his replies (Act II). But danger is not averted. Mathan is sent to the temple to demand Joas; Joad refuses, decides to proclaim him king, and delivers his prophecy (Act III). Joad crowns Joas king, and prepares to attack Athalie; she, however, attacks the temple first (Act IV). Abner is sent to demand the treasure, and urges that any treasure should be handed over along with Joas, since resistance is hopeless; but Joad's careful preparations and his trick get the better of the queen.

If, with all this, one remembers that *Athalie* not only contains some of Racine's finest verse, but that the priestly robes, the numerous

[4] See Sainte-Beuve's essay on Racine in his *Portraits Littéraires*, and Ernest Renan, *Sur Corneille, Racine et Bossuet*, 1926, pp. 87–113.

cast, and the enthronement of Joas provide an element of spectacle, and that the first four acts end with choruses to which the
music of Moreau lends an additional charm, one can understand how
even such an enemy of the Catholic Church as Voltaire could call
Athalie 'the work coming nearest to perfection that was ever produced by the hand of men'.

   Athalie was Racine's last play, though he wrote two works in the
last years of his life that deserve to be mentioned—the *Cantiques
spirituels* of 1694, and the posthumously published *Abrégé de l'histoire
de Port-Royal*, an admirable piece of historical writing based on first-
hand knowledge. He died on April 21, 1699, and was buried at Port-
Royal des Champs. In 1711, when the monastery was razed to the
ground, his body was reinterred in the church of Saint-Etienne-du-
Mont in Paris.

6

Tragedy

Although the term 'tragi-comedy' was still occasionally used, Racine and his contemporaries virtually knew only two kinds of play, tragedy and comedy; and they were often distinguished by their subject matter and the social class of their characters, rather than by their essential nature. According to Corneille, for instance, a tragedy depicted royal characters in danger of losing their lives or their states or of being banished; whereas a comedy showed characters of lower rank exposed to lesser perils, such as the loss of a mistress or lover. That is why he called his *Tite et Bérénice* a heroic comedy, not a tragedy. This does not mean that seventeenth-century French drama is lacking in variety; but it does mean that plays that do not strike us as comic (Molière's *Dom Garcie*, for instance) may be labelled comedies, and that many tragedies do not seem to us to be tragic. As there is no general agreement nowadays about the precise meaning of the word 'tragic' or the essential characteristics of a tragedy, there may well be disagreement whether a play is tragic or not; but if by tragedy we mean a play like *Macbeth*, in which an otherwise noble character, through some weakness of character or some excess of passion, brings about his own destruction and that of others, it may safely be said that many seventeenth-century French tragedies are not tragic.

In reading seventeenth-century French drama, it is best not to judge plays by their labels, nor their authors by intentions or standards that were alien to them. Corneille, for instance, was inclined to regard Aristotle's theory of catharsis as nonsense, thought that it was enough to arouse either pity or terror, and was prepared to substitute admiration for both; and few of his plays, most of which end happily, are likely to strike a modern reader as tragic. This need not hinder appreciation of his work: he is a great dramatist, and no more to be condemned for calling his plays tragedies in the language of his time than Shakespeare for not having obeyed the rule of the unities. Racine, one of the few men of his age and his country who read Greek, is more respectful to Aristotle than Corneille, and maintains in the prefaces to *Iphigénie* and *Phèdre* that pity and terror are the aims of tragedy. But although a higher proportion of his tragedies are likely to strike us as tragic, this is not true of all of them; some have happy or partially happy endings. Since the question whether a tragedy can end happily has been debated at least since Aristotle, since it is not impossible for a play to appeal to the tragic emotions at least until the dénouement, since different conceptions of tragedy exist, and since the effect of a play will vary with each spectator or reader, it is unwise to be dogmatic. Nevertheless, several of Racine's tragedies have given the impression of ending happily, and of being tragedies only in the seventeenth-century French sense, or at least of having more in common with such tragedies than other plays of Racine.

Few, probably, would contest that *La Thébaïde, Andromaque, Britannicus,*[1] *Bajazet,* and *Phèdre* are tragic: they end unhappily, the death of one or more characters being brought about by the passions of the protagonist or protagonists. To that list, most people would probably be ready to add *Bérénice*; though as the catastrophe is due to the hopeless situation in which the characters find themselves rather than to the nature of their passions, as the play arouses pity rather than terror, and as it is somewhat exceptional for a tragedy to end with separation instead of death, it might be argued that it is pathetic rather than tragic.

Alexandre, on the other hand, ends happily, and it would be

---

[1] Professor R. C. Knight expresses reservations about *Britannicus* in his article, 'A Minimal Definition of Seventeenth-Century Tragedy', in *French Studies*, vol. X, 1956, pp. 302–3. So does Professor B. Weinberg: 'There is [. . .] a kind of fundamental dichotomy in the play: Néron is the hero and performs the central action, but such tragic effect as there is—and it is secondary—belongs to a secondary personage' (*The Art of Jean Racine*, 1963, p. 127).

difficult to maintain that it is in any way tragic; the death of Taxile, about whom no one cares, is a convenient means of bringing about a happy ending. *Esther* and *Athalie* show the triumph of the oppressed faithful over their ungodly oppressors; *Esther* ends with a song of triumph, and *Athalie* with Joad's comment (not unreminiscent of the final chorus in Mozart's *Don Giovanni*) that the downfall of the queen shows that

> les rois dans le ciel ont un juge sévère,
> L'innocence un vengeur, et l'orphelin un père.

$$\text{(V, 8, ll. 1815–16)}$$

It is true that Joas is destined to be a bad king and to kill Zacharie, but Joad's prophecy makes it clear that this is only one episode in the creation of the New Jerusalem. It has also been said that Athalie, thrown off her balance by a dream sent by God, is like Phèdre persecuted by Venus, and that she arouses more sympathy than the fanatical Joad and his cruel God. No one can gainsay the right of the reader to see *Athalie*, as Voltaire did, as an illustration of religious fanaticism; but it is unlikely that this was how Racine saw it. He would certainly not have equated the God of the Bible with Venus; Athalie is a murderess, a wicked, though efficient, queen, a usurper, an idolatress, and the daughter of Jezebel, whose fate is continually kept before our eyes; she appears in only two acts out of five; and the play ends with a sense of relief and triumph. One may be sure that, for Racine, *Athalie* ended happily, with the destruction of Athalie, not only an unrighteous character, but an obstacle to the coming of Christ, and with the triumph of the righteous.

Mithridate and *Iphigénie* are more problematical and seem to fall somewhere in between the two groups so far considered. Mithridate, the implacable antagonist of Rome, dies at the end of the play to which he gives his name; and there are moments when he enjoys the sympathy of the audience—when he displays his resilience in Act III, for example, or when he lays bare his distress, his irresolution, his utter disarray in the dilemma before him (IV, 5). His death, on the other hand, is not the inevitable result of his two passions, hostility to Rome and love of Monime. Pharnace has sent for the Romans *before* Mithridate's return, believing him to be dead; and Mithridate, thinking himself defeated, kills himself, and Xipharès arrives just too late to save him. Moreover, the sympathies of the audience are at the very least divided between Mithridate and the two lovers, Xipharès and Monime, and probably go preponderantly to the latter, rather than to the unscrupulous, cruel, crafty old king. For most people, probably, *Mithridate*, in which Mithridate, the obstacle to the union of the lovers, is not only removed by death, but gives his consent to their marriage, is a play with a happy ending.

Iphigénie ends rather similarly with the death of a character (Eriphile) who does not enjoy the sympathies of the audience, with Agamemnon agreeing to the marriage of Achille and Iphigénie, and with the Greek fleet about to set out for Troy. It has been argued that the audience knows from Homer that the reconciliation of Achille and Agamemnon is only temporary; but, even if one could assume that everyone in Racine's audience was familiar with the *Iliad*, the liberties he has taken with the story of Iphigenia seem to require us to dismiss Greek legend from our minds. More important, the prophecy that Achille is to die in the Trojan War is mentioned several times in the play, and there is a reference to the future death of Clytemnestre at the hands of her son. The tone of the last scene, however, is far from tragic, and it is difficult to regard *Iphigénie* as a play giving rise to pity and terror, or at least as a play after which the audience leaves the theatre with these emotions.

Of Racine's eleven tragedies, five, then, either are not tragic or cannot be considered tragic without reservations. This does not necessarily mean that they are negligible or inferior.

The source of tragedy in Racine's plays is primarily human. He accepts Aristotle's doctrine that the characters of tragedy, those, that is to say, 'whose misfortune forms the catastrophe of the tragedy', should be neither wholly bad, nor wholly good, but should owe their misfortune to some flaw that arouses pity, not hatred (first preface to *Andromaque*). Despite this, and even though he says that he could not kill such a virtuous and amiable person as Iphigénie and had to spare her life, several of his characters die who are either innocent or have faults that do not justify the fate that overtakes them, and who are the victims of the faults or passions of others, rather than of their own. Antigone and Hémon are guiltless; Britannicus is merely immature and a little imprudent; Bajazet and Atalide do nothing more than conceal their love, and in self-defence aid and abet Roxane's self-deception; and Hippolyte's worst crime is to disobey his father in falling in love with Aricie. Bérénice and Titus are guilty of nothing worse than a certain lack of foresight, and are the victims of the situation in which they find themselves, not of themselves or anyone else. With these reservations, it can be said that the tragic dénouement springs from some passion or flaw of character: hatred and ambition in *La Thébaïde*; love and jealousy in *Andromaque*, *Bajazet*, and *Phèdre*; ambition and lust in *Britannicus*.

The tragic emotions are intensified by the rank and stature of the characters. They must be heroic, says Racine in the preface to *Bérénice*; and he insists, in the preface to *Bajazet*, that they must seem different from the people we meet every day, and remote, since respect increases with distance. The mythological background of some of the plays is a means of conferring remoteness, heroic stature, and dignity on characters who are not only legendary, but often descended from gods or in contact with them. When they are not semi-divine, they are at least royal; and in two of his tragedies at least, Racine lays stress on the pomp and circumstance surrounding them. Agrippine has the unusual honour of being preceded by laurel-crowned fasces; and she was the 'âme toute-puissante' of the senate, until the day when Néron was himself

> ébloui de sa gloire,
> Quand les ambassadeurs de tant de rois divers
> Vinrent le reconnaître au nom de l'univers.
> *(Britannicus*, I, 1, ll. 100–2)

Titus is described at the ceremony held to deify his father, enthroned in imperial pomp, and surrounded by kings, consuls, and senators, all with their eyes fixed upon him.

Whatever the external trappings, however, the hero, the king, or the princess is but a man or a woman, endowed with the passions and weaknesses of ordinary men, suffering as acutely, as easily hurt, as vulnerable as the rest of us. Indeed, royal rank brings with it additional problems. Etéocle and Polynice, twin brothers, fight for the throne; Agrippine and Néron, mother and son, struggle for power; Britannicus, Bajazet, and Joas are in danger of death because of their claims on the throne; Aricie is condemned to celibacy for the same reason; Titus is the prisoner of his rank, and cannot marry whom he chooses; Mithridate is torn between love of his bride and his need for his son's help in the war against Rome; and Agamemnon, as supreme commander, is required to sacrifice his daughter. The contrast between the dignity and rank of the protagonists and their fundamental humanity increases the poignancy of their situation, the emotion that we feel at the sight of Oreste raving mad, of the physical disarray of Néron or Britannicus, or of Mithridate's change of expression betraying his innermost feelings ('vous changez de visage', l. 1112), or at the description of Phèdre as a 'femme mourante et qui cherche à mourir' (l. 44). Racine is as much aware as Montaigne, though he would probably have expressed it differently, that 'when seated upon the most elevated throne in the world, we are but seated upon our breech'.

Although men and women in Racine are the victims of human passions, their own or another's, there is also some sense of forces outside that intervene to make matters worse. Chance, ill luck, play a part in the tragic dénouement: Acomat's men arrive just too late to save Bajazet's life, as Xipharès is too late to save Mithridate. More frequently, an action produces unforeseen results, which are the opposite of those intended or expected; fate has its paradoxes and ironies. Hermione draws the attention of the Greeks to Astyanax's existence with the object of preventing Pyrrhus from marrying Andromaque; in fact, she drives Pyrrhus into Andromaque's arms, and brings about his death as well as her own. Of Oreste, who comes to Epirus in the hope of winning Hermione, and loses her, Cléone observes:

> Le coup qui l'a perdu n'est parti que de lui.
>
> (III, 3, l. 836)

The assassination of Britannicus, intended amongst other things to ensure Néron's possession of Junie, deprives him of her for ever, as Eriphile's attempt to prevent Iphigénie's escape leads to her own undoing. These actions are caused by jealousy; but it is Bérénice's virtue that prevents her marriage with Titus, since he owes his sense of responsibility to her. Aricie persuades Hippolyte to go and see Phèdre out of pity (II, 3); it is that interview that causes Phèdre to declare her love for him, and leads to the final catastrophe.

Some of Racine's characters speak of an external malignant force that intervenes in human life—fate or gods. Jocaste accuses the gods both of causing her to commit the original crime for which she and her family are being punished, her involuntary, incestuous marriage with her son, Œdipus,—

> Voilà de ces grands Dieux la suprême justice!
> Jusques au bord du crime ils conduisent nos pas;
> Ils nous le font commettre, et ne l'excusent pas!
> (*La Thébaïde*, III, 2, ll. 608–10)

—and of tormenting her in the present, of alternately raising and dashing her hopes. One thinks of Gloucester in *King Lear*;

> As Flies to wanton Boyes, are we to th'Gods,
> They kill us for their sport.

In fact, nothing happens in *La Thébaïde*, any more than in *King Lear*, that cannot be attributed to human nature; but it pleases Jocaste, as it pleases Gloucester, to blame the gods.

In *Andromaque*, it is Oreste above all who accuses fate or the gods. After overcoming, as he thought, his passion for Hermione, he attended the council of Greek chieftains, hoping to find consolation in war, but fate ('le sort') had sent him into the very trap he was trying to avoid: they were assembled to discuss Pyrrhus's apparent intention of marrying Andromaque, and appointed Oreste Greek ambassador to Pyrrhus.

> Puisqu'après tant d'efforts ma résistance est vaine,
> Je me livre en aveugle au destin qui m'entraîne.
> (I, 1, ll. 97–8)

Oreste, indeed, is a curious anticipation of the Byronic hero, doomed to wretchedness, dogged by misfortune, seeking death in vain, casting a blight on all who approach him, filled with self-hatred, predisposed to crime, and persecuted by the gods, who are unjust:

> Je ne sais de tout temps quelle injuste puissance
> Laisse le crime en paix et poursuit l'innocence.
> De quelque part sur moi que je tourne les yeux,
> Je ne vois que malheurs qui condamnent les Dieux.
> (III, 1, ll. 773–6)

> Grâce aux Dieux! Mon malheur passe mon espérance:
> Oui, je te loue, ô Ciel, de ta persévérance.

Appliqué sans relâche au soin de me punir,
Au comble des douleurs tu m'as fait parvenir.
Ta haine a pris plaisir à former ma misère;
J'étais né pour servir d'exemple à ta colère,
Pour être du malheur un modèle accompli.

(V, 5, ll. 1613–19)

This might be Childe Harold speaking. Presumably, although Oreste in *Andromaque* has not killed his mother, Racine had in mind the fact that Orestes, according to the passage of Virgil quoted in his preface, when he killed Pyrrhus, had already murdered his mother, and was pursued by the avenging furies. Once again, although nothing that happens in the play need be attributed to any agency other than human nature, the gods have objective reality for a character in it and are blamed by him.

Apart from insignificant mentions, the gods are absent from the plays between *Andromaque* and *Iphigénie*. There is an echo of Oreste in Xipharès—

Je suis un malheureux que le destin poursuit . . .

(*Mithridate*, IV, 2, l. 1218)

—but, in fact, fate is kind to him. In *Iphigénie*, however, there is no doubt of the objective reality of the gods, who becalm the Greek fleet and can be appeased only by the sacrifice of Eriphile. An orphan, persecuted by the gods, and doomed to perish, she resembles Oreste. In *Phèdre*, the gods play a less positive, more acceptable part. Phèdre regards herself as being, like her mother and sister, the victim of the gods, and Œnone tells her:

Vous aimez. On ne peut vaincre sa destinée.
Par un charme fatal vous fûtes entraînée.

(IV, 6, ll. 1297–8)

Since Racine says in the preface that Phèdre is 'involved by her destiny and by the wrath of the gods in an illegitimate passion, which she is the first to abominate', he presumably shares this point of view. Phèdre wants to hide from Apollo and the other gods from whom she is descended, and she is loath to go down into the underworld where her father, Minos, sits in judgment. Thésée calls upon Neptune to avenge him, and Neptune in response sends a monster from the deep to attack Hippolyte. For the characters, then, the gods exist and intervene in human affairs; but there is nothing to stop the spectator from regarding Venus as the projection of Phèdre's passions, and Apollo and Minos as projections of her conscience. The only god whose independent existence has to be accepted is Neptune; but Neptune accomplishes nothing that could not have happened otherwise. Thésée could have punished his son by other, less picturesque, less poetically satisfying, means. The same is true of *Esther* and *Athalie*. Divine providence is at work, but, whatever Racine himself may have believed, it is open to the spectator to explain everything in terms of human psychology.

Racine, in other words, does not compel us to believe in the intervention of external forces in human life, except in *Iphigénie*. In some of his plays, however, he raises the question whether there are in the universe external forces, good or evil, that influence human life. The fact that the question is raised without any answer's being imposed enriches his tragedies.

Although the tragedy in Racine springs primarily from human nature, his work is based on no single conception of human nature; no single type of character is found throughout. The kind of love and the kind of characters portrayed in *Andromaque* recur, but are not universal in Racine. Like Hermione, Roxane deceives herself; and her passion is governed by no considerations of gratitude:

> Les bienfaits dans un cœur balancent-ils l'amour?
> Et sans chercher plus loin, quand l'ingrat me sut plaire,
> Ai-je mieux reconnu les bontés de son frère?
> (*Bajazet*, III, 7, ll. 1088–90)

Roxane resembles Hermione not only in her violence, but in her weakness; she threatens to kill Bajazet because he will not promise to marry her, but hesitates, and confesses her love:

> Je te donne, cruel, des armes contre moi,
> Sans doute, et je devrais retenir ma faiblesse:
> Tu vas en triompher. Oui, je te le confesse,
> J'affectais à tes yeux une fausse fierté.
> De toi dépend ma joie et ma félicité.
> (II, 1, ll. 552–6)

Love and hatred are close together in Roxane and Phèdre, who, like
Hermione, destroy their lovers on discovering that they love other
women, and are equally vindictive towards their rivals. But
although Roxane and Phèdre and to a lesser extent Eriphile continue
Hermione, the atmosphere of the plays in which they are found is
very different. In *Andromaque*, Pyrrhus and Oreste have similar
passions to Hermione, and they are offset only by Andromaque.
Roxane, Eriphile, and Phèdre are alone in the plays in which they
occur; and Phèdre is very different from her predecessors in having a
moral sense. She does not merely swing between love and hatred like
them; she is also the victim of a love that she abhors and condemns.

On the whole, the lovers in other plays are different from these.
Néron, jealous and vindictive, is vicious, sadistic, and ambitious for
power as well; and he is not—except, perhaps, at the end—unbalanced and distraught. The love of Junie and Britannicus is a tender
love, like that of Bérénice:

> Elle passe ses jours, Paulin, sans rien prétendre
> Que quelque heure à me voir, et le reste à m'attendre.
>
> (II, 2, ll. 535–6)

> Un soupir, un regard, un mot de votre bouche,
> Voilà l'ambition d'un cœur comme le mien.
>
> (II, 4, ll. 576–7)

Like Hermione, Bérénice deceives herself—though not about Titus's
love, which is not in doubt, but about the prospects of marrying him.
She is also harsh to Antiochus when he tells her on Titus's behalf that
she must leave Rome (IV, 3), and her despair is unconcealed:

> Elle n'entend ni pleurs, ni conseil, ni raison;
> Elle implore à grands cris le fer et le poison.
>
> (IV, 7, ll. 1229–30)

But this is far from the violence, the lethal frenzy of Hermione or
Roxane. Titus and Antiochus are both devoted lovers; so are Bajazet,
Xipharès, Achille, and Hippolyte. Atalide, Monime, and Iphigénie
are their feminine counterparts. Both Atalide and Iphigénie know
jealousy; but Iphigénie sheds tears for her rival, and even Atalide's
jealousy, though it helps to bring about the death of her lover, is very
subdued:

Tant que j'ai respiré, vos yeux me sont témoins
Que votre seul péril occupait tous mes soins;
Et puisqu'il ne pouvait finir qu'avec ma vie,
C'est sans regret aussi que je la sacrifie.
Il est vrai, si le ciel eût écouté mes vœux,
Qu'il pouvait m'accorder un trépas plus heureux.
Vous n'en auriez pas moins épousé ma rivale:
Vous pouviez l'assurer de la foi conjugale,
Mais vous n'auriez pas joint à ce titre d'époux
Tous ces gages d'amour qu'elle a reçus de vous.

(III, 4, ll. 959–68)

Mithridate, jealous of Monime's love for his son, thinks of killing him, but hesitates, since Xipharès is his mainstay in his struggle against Rome, and in the end, dying, consents to the marriage of Xipharès and Monime. Aricie loves Hippolyte with a rational love, based on his genuine worth.

Non que par les yeux seuls lâchement enchantée,
J'aime en lui sa beauté, sa grâce tant vantée,
Présents dont la nature a voulu l'honorer,
Qu'il méprise lui-même, et qu'il semble ignorer.
J'aime, je prise en lui de plus nobles richesses,
Les vertus de son père, et non point les faiblesses.

(*Phèdre*, II, 1, ll. 437–42)

Nor is sexual love the only passion depicted by Racine. It is absent from *Esther* and *Athalie*. Maternal love is represented in different ways by Jocaste, Andromaque, Clytemnestre, and (one might add) Josabet. From *La Thébaïde* onwards, ambition plays a large part. Agrippine, Acomat, Aman, and Mathan are ambitious; Néron is eager for power as well as for Junie; Mithridate is torn between love and the ambition to conquer Rome, as Agamemnon is torn between ambition and paternal affection; and even Hippolyte has political ambitions, though they do not conflict with his love for Aricie. Piety and religious fervour appear in *Esther* and *Athalie*.

It should not be overlooked, either, how many of Racine's characters are neither passionate, nor vicious, nor weak. Acomat and Mathan are not conspicuously virtuous, but they are neither passionate nor unbalanced; and Acomat is a loyal ally. Mithridate,

Mardochée, and Joad are not lacking in resolution. A long list of noble and virtuous characters could be drawn up—Antigone and Hémon; Porus, Cléofile, and Alexandre; Andromaque; Junie, Britannicus, and Burrhus; Titus, Bérénice, and Antiochus; Bajazet and Atalide; Xipharès and Monime; Achille and the tender-hearted Iphigénie; Aricie and Hippolyte; Esther and Mardochée; Joad, Josabet, and Abner. In view of the fact that playwrights were normally responsible for casting their plays, it is perhaps significant that Racine's favourite actresses, Mlle Duparc and Mlle Champmeslé, played Andromaque, Atalide, and Iphigénie—not Hermione, Roxane, and Eriphile.[2]

The diversity of Racine's portrayal of human nature is a good reason for doubting whether his plays are, as has so often been asserted, imbued with Jansenism. That Racine owed a great deal to his upbringing at Port-Royal, including a sound knowledge of Greek, a hatred for the meretricious, and an ideal of Christian piety, and that, without Port-Royal, his plays, particularly the four last, would not have been what they are, is certain. That his tragedies often depict human weakness and subjection to passion is also true; but whether this is due to Jansenism is another matter. For one thing, students of the movement stress the difficulty of defining its views, point to the wide divergence of opinion within it, and add that the Jansenists never refused to condemn the five propositions—they merely refused to admit that they could be found in Jansenius's volume. For another, it is not certain that the *solitaires* inculcated their theological views in their pupils—Racine's fellow-pupil, Thomas du Fossé, denies that they did—, or that Racine would have been receptive if they had. In later life, although he made no secret of his partiality for Port-Royal, he always denied that he was a Jansenist; and there seems no reason to disbelieve him. The more pessimistic conception of human nature prevalent in the second half of the century, not only in Racine's works, may have been influenced by Jansenism; but Jansenism was certainly not its only cause.

Nor is it easy to detect Jansenism in Racine's tragedies. The view that *Phèdre*, in particular, is a Jansenist play seems doubtful, not only because the most apparently Jansenist passages in it have their counterparts in the corresponding plays of Euripides and Seneca, but

[2] See above, p. 4, and G. May, 'Comment Racine distribuait ses rôles', in *French Studies*, vol. IV, 1950, pp. 306–12.

because the idea that Phèdre is the victim of the gods is difficult to square with Christianity. And although some of Racine's most interesting creations are passionate, unbalanced, uncontrolled, distraught beings like Oreste, Pyrrhus, Hermione, Roxane, and Phèdre, they should not blind us to the variety of his characterization and the breadth of his vision. Men and women like these exist in life, as well as in literature; we are all of us, perhaps, potentially at least, Oreste or Phèdre at some time in our lives. But Oreste and Phèdre are not the whole of human nature, nor are they the whole of Racine.

7

Craftsmanship

Racine inherited the form of tragedy described in Chapter 1; and though he handles it with originality and independence, he accepts its limitations, and does not try to pour more into the vessel than it can conveniently contain. This is particularly evident in his attitude to the principle of verisimilitude and the unities. By verisimilitude, he does not mean probability in the ordinary sense—a tragedy like *Phèdre*, in which Phèdre falls in love with her stepson, Thésée calls on Neptune to avenge him, and Hippolyte's death is caused by the appearance of a sea monster, is clearly not probable. He means, as he makes clear in the prefaces to *Alexandre, Britannicus,* and *Bérénice*, simplicity: a play, the action of which takes place in twelve hours or so, must contain few incidents and little matter. The events of a longer period of time must not be crammed into it; nor must it contain anything extraneous or inessential:

> One cannot be too careful to show nothing on the stage that is not essential. And the finest scenes are in danger of becoming tedious, as soon as they can be separated from the action, and interrupt it instead of leading it to its termination. (Preface to *Mithridate*.)

Racine, indeed, eliminated one or two scenes he regarded as superfluous from later editions of his plays, notably *Britannicus*.

Racine's plays, though not all as simple as *Alexandre* and *Bérénice*, are all relatively simple. They depict a crisis, and they deal with a unified action. This does not mean that there is only one plot—there are always two at least; but they are closely linked. In *Britannicus*, for instance, the struggle for power between Agrippine and Néron and the rivalry in love between Néron and Britannicus are inextricably linked, because Britannicus is not only in love with Junie, but is also, with his claims on the throne, a pawn in the game between Agrippine and her son. Eriphile is an invention of Racine's, but her fate is intertwined with that of Iphigénie, not only because she is the victim intended by the oracle, but because she is in love with Achille and jealous of Iphigénie. Hippolyte's love for Aricie explains his indifference to Phèdre's advances, arouses her jealousy, and stops her intervening to save his life.

The unities of time and place, it has often been observed, are not so much limitations to Racine as challenges, invitations to introduce into his plays through the medium of language the time and space that could not be included in the action and shown on the stage. Racine, of course, is not the only seventeenth-century French dramatist to allude to places outside the stage or to events preceding the action of the play or taking place off the stage; but no other dramatist, it may safely be said, made such liberal use of time and space, used them so systematically and so evocatively, so effectively created an atmosphere with them, and made them so integral a part of the play.

Most of Racine's plays contain references to the sea—which, so far as we know, Racine had never seen. Pylade, in *Andromaque*, plans to escape by sea:

Nos vaisseaux sont tout prêts, et le vent nous appelle.
Je sais de ce palais tous les détours obscurs;
Vous voyez que la mer en vient battre les murs . . .
(III, 1, ll. 790–2)

Bérénice imagines the wastes of sea ('tant de mers', l. 1114) that will lie between Titus and her when she has gone back to the East. The walls of the seraglio in *Bajazet* are washed by the sea; Acomat throws Amurat's untimely messenger into the Black Sea, and has ships in the harbour in readiness for a quick escape. *Mithridate* takes place in a seaport in the Crimea, on the Cimmerian Bosporus (Kerch Straits). The news of Mithridate's return is brought by light vessels, after which his fleet heaves into sight, covering the sea (l. 328), and he sails into the harbour. Mithridate kills himself on the shore, surrounded by Romans who have come in from the sea.

The setting of *Iphigénie* is a camp by the seashore, where the Greek fleet, becalmed, is waiting for a wind to take it to Troy. There are many references to the sea, to the ships, and to the state of the weather.

> Les vents nous auraient-ils exaucés cette nuit?
> Mais tout dort, et l'armée, et les vents, et Neptune,
>
>   (I, 1, ll. 8–9)

says Arcas at the beginning of the play; and, at the end, when Eriphile kills herself,

> Les Dieux font sur l'autel entendre le tonnerre,
> Les vents agitent l'air d'heureux frémissements,
> Et la mer leur répond par ses mugissements.
> La rive au loin gémit, blanchissante d'écume.
>
>   (V, 6, ll. 1778–81)

In between, there are several allusions to the ships stopping when the wind dropped—

> Il fallut s'arrêter, et la rame inutile
> Fatigua vainement une mer immobile[1]
>
>   (I, 1. ll. 49–50)

—, to the motionless ships, and to the prospect of movement offered by the sacrifice of Iphigénie:

> Voyez tout l'Hellespont blanchissant sous nos rames . . .
>
>   (I, 5, l. 381)

> Déjà dans les vaisseaux la voile se déploie;
> Déjà sur sa parole ils se tournent vers Troie.
>
>   (III, 3, ll. 841–2)

In *Phèdre*, we see Hippolyte's ships on the point of departure—

> Déjà de ses vaisseaux la pointe était tournée,
> Et la voile flottait aux vents abandonnée;
>
>   (III, 1, ll. 797–8)

[1] Victor Hugo condemned this couplet on the grounds that oars are not useless when ships are becalmed. Probably Racine means us to understand that some supernatural power is preventing the oars from propelling the ships.

Œnone throws herself into the sea and vanishes from sight; and the encounter between Hippolyte and the monster, brought from the deep in an enormous wave, takes place on the seashore.

The importance of Rome and the East in *Bérénice* has been mentioned.[2] The action of *Bajazet* takes place in the seraglio, but is influenced by reports, messengers, and orders from the distant camp of Amurat. If Alexandre Hardy or Shakespeare had written *Bajazet*, they would probably have made the scene shift between Constantinople and Bagdad. It would be idle to discuss the comparative merits of the two kinds of play, or to claim that the unities are in themselves good; but it is probable that *Bajazet* gains because so much of its action is determined in an unseen, remote place, by an invisible and sinister figure.

Mithridate again has an Oriental setting, the Crimea, on the confines of Europe and Asia. On the other hand, Mithridate's lifelong enemy is Rome, and Monime is Greek. East and West come together in Act III, when Mithridate outlines his plans for attacking Rome itself. In *Iphigénie*, besides the sea and, beyond it, Troy, there is Lesbos, conquered by Achille, and, above all, just out of sight the altar, where Iphigénie is to be married or sacrificed. In *Phèdre*, besides the sea, we hear of the forests, where Hippolyte hunts, of Crete, far away, where Thésée slew the minotaur with the aid of Phèdre's sister, Ariane, and of Hades, whither rumour has it that Thésée has gone, and where Phèdre's father sits in judgment. In *Athalie*, what lies outside the temple is revealed by Athalie, who speaks of her relations with the surrounding nations (ll. 471–84), and by Josabet:

> Je sais une secrète issue
> Par où, sans qu'on le voie, et sans être aperçue,
> De Cédron avec lui traversant le torrent,
> J'irai dans le désert . . .
>
> (III, 6, ll. 1059–62)

As for time, the importance of the Trojan War in *Andromaque* has been mentioned.[3] Particularly characteristic of *Bérénice* is the sense of duration, not only of the years that have rolled by since Titus and Bérénice met, but of the waste of time that lies ahead. Both past and future are introduced into *Iphigénie*—the past history of the house of Atreus, to which Agamemnon and Iphigénie belong, and of the

[2] See above, p. 53.   [3] See above, pp. 38–40.

events leading up to the Trojan War, including the career of Helen,
the sister of Clytemnestre and the mother of Eriphile; the future fall
of Troy—

> la perfide Troie abandonnée aux flammes,
> Ses peuples dans vos fers, Priam à vos genoux,
> Hélène par vos mains rendue à son époux.
> Voyez de vos vaisseaux les poupes couronnées
> Dans cette même Aulide avec vous retournées . . .
>
> (I, 5, ll. 382–6)

There are allusions to the prediction that Achille will fall in the
Trojan War, and a suggestion of Oreste's future matricide. In *Phèdre*,
Thésée's exploits and the history of Phèdre's ill-fated family are
recalled; there is no future. In *Athalie,* time past is represented by the
previous history of the Jews, particularly that of Ahab, Jezebel, and
Athalie herself; time to come is revealed by the prophecy of Joad,
foretelling the future murder of Zacharie by Joas and the coming of
Christ and the New Jerusalem—one thinks of the procession of
future kings in *Macbeth*.

Several of Racine's plays end with a vista of future time, which has
been compared to the unbounded horizon in the background of the
paintings of some of his contemporaries. *Andromaque.* ends with
Oreste raving on the stage; his future is left to the imagination of the
spectator. *Britannicus* closes with a suggestion of Néron's criminal
future:

> Plût aux Dieux que ce fût le dernier de ses crimes!
>
> (V, 8, l. 1768)

Bérénice with the word 'Hélas!'

Even the simple, unchanging stage set may have symbolic significance. *Britannicus* opens with Agrippine waiting outside Néron's
door, trying in vain to see him; he has eluded her by going out
through 'une porte au public moins connue' (l. 135). The scene of
Bérénice is a closet between Titus's suite and that of Bérénice:

> Souvent ce cabinet superbe et solitaire
> Des secrets de Titus est le dépositaire.
> C'est ici quelquefois qu'il se cache à sa cour,
> Lorsqu'il vient à la Reine expliquer son amour.

De son appartement cette porte est prochaine,
Et cette autre conduit dans celui de la Reine.

(I, 1, ll. 3–8)

Act V of *Bajazet*, set in the seraglio, is made dramatic by the fact that Orcan and the mutes are waiting outside for Bajazet.

Je puis le retenir. Mais s'il sort, il est mort,

says Roxane (l. 1456). This gives point to the last word of the scene, Roxane's command to Bajazet, 'Sortez' (l. 1564). *Iphigénie* takes place in Agamemnon's tent, within sight of the sea; *Athalie* in the temple of Jerusalem, 'dans un vestibule de l'appartement du grand prêtre'.

Racine's independence shows itself in other ways. *Phèdre* is unique amongst seventeenth-century French treatments of the subject because, in defiance of propriety, Phèdre is Thésée's wife, so that her love for Hippolyte, her stepson, is incestuous. Racine also endows his confidants, some of them at least, with characters and gives them parts to play. Paulin in *Bérénice* represents the Roman people. Arcas, Agamemnon's confidant, takes it upon himself to try to save Iphigénie by informing Clytemnestre that her husband is about to offer her up at the altar. Œnone, devoted and well–meaning, is cursed by Phèdre for her pernicious counsels and casts herself into the sea. The most interesting are Burrhus and Narcisse, who represent the virtuous and the vicious aspects of Néron's character, but who exist in their own right. The one, honourable and public-spirited, does his best to counter Néron's evil propensities, and is driven to side with Agrippine against her son; the other, ambitious and unscrupulous, in the confidence of both Britannicus and Néron and betraying the former to the latter, mistaken in his estimate of Junie's readiness to surrender to Néron and of the servility of the Roman populace, ends by being murdered by the mob.

Nor did Racine consider that unity of tone precluded occasional comic touches. There is nothing, of course, like the grave-diggers' scene in *Hamlet* or the porter's scene in *Macbeth*, and the comic element is less pronounced than in Corneille; but it is there—particularly, perhaps, in *Andromaque*. Pyrrhus's irony, in his reception of Oreste (ll. 173–80) or his bland remark to Hermione,

Je rends grâces au ciel que votre indifférence
De mes heureux soupirs m'apprenne l'innocence,

(IV, 5, ll. 1345–6)

verges on the comic. One is reminded of Molière's *dépit amoureux* scenes by the characters of *Andromaque*, convinced that they are not in love, but betraying by their words and actions that they are —Hermione finding pretexts for remaining in Epirus (ll. 436 ff.) or Pyrrhus unable to leave Andromaque's presence (III, 6). One scene particularly struck Racine's contemporaries as comic: Act II, scene 5, in which Pyrrhus, resolved to break with Andromaque, cannot stop talking of her, and ends by going off to see her. Boileau told Brossette that the audience always smiled at this scene, and Dubos says that the pit laughed almost as loudly as it would have done at a comedy.

Just as Narcisse is telling Britannicus that Junie is listening favourably to Néron's protestations of love, she bursts in (III, 6), exactly as Alcippe in Corneille's *Menteur* appears just as Dorante has finished describing how he killed him in a duel. Bajazet arrives as Atalide expresses her determination not to see him again:

> Il ne me verra plus. —Madame, le voici.
>
> (III, 3, l. 940)

Acomat is amusing with his shrewd common sense—

> Je sais rendre aux sultans de fidèles services;
> Mais je laisse au vulgaire adorer leurs caprices,
> Et ne me pique point du scrupule insensé
> De bénir mon trépas quand ils l'ont prononcé
>
> (I, 1, ll. 197–200)

—or preparing to make a hurried escape when Roxane and Bajazet fall out, grumbling at love and lovers, and loading a ship with his possessions (ll. 869–74). Agamemnon bluntly asks Achille:

> Pourquoi le demander, puisque vous le savez?
>
> (IV, 6, l. 1340)

and Clytemnestre harangues Agamemnon a little in the manner of Mrs. Caudle:

> *Vous savez, et Calchas mille fois vous l'a dit,*
> Qu'un hymen clandestin mit ce prince en son lit,
> Et qu'il en eut pour gage une jeune princesse,
> Que sa mère a cachée au reste de la Grèce.

Mais non, l'amour d'un frère et son honneur blessé
Sont les moindres des soins dont vous êtes pressé.

(IV, 4, ll. 1283–8)

('How often have you been told . . . but would you listen?')[4]

Racine's plays are very carefully constructed. According to his son, Louis, he began by writing out a plan in prose, act by act and scene by scene, and was wont to say, 'My tragedy is done', considering the main work over. One might be inclined to think that Louis Racine was merely attributing to his father the widespread anecdote about Menander,[5] were it not that his statement is confirmed by Mme de Caylus in her memoirs, and that there exists a prose summary of the first act of an *Iphigénie en Tauride*.

In *Britannicus*—to take an example—, each act advances the action a stage further, each containing one great scene (I, 1; II, 6, the eavesdropping scene; III, 8, the quarrel; IV, 2, the interview between mother and son; V, 5, the narrative of the death of Britannicus), each reaching at least one climax, and each (except the last) ending on a note of doubt or uncertainty. Act I, the exposition, contains a series of conversations about Néron, causing us to speculate about his true nature: is he grateful or ungrateful, good or bad? It ends with Britannicus promising to meet Agrippine at the house of Pallas. In Act II, Néron first appears, and his vicious propensities are revealed. The two high points of the act are the discovery of his love for Junie and consequent jealousy of Britannicus, and the revelation of his cruelty, when he orders Junie to make Britannicus believe that she no longer loves him, and listens from a place of concealment to make sure that he is obeyed. The act ends with Néron's determination to be revenged on Britannicus, and Narcisse's threat to destroy both Junie and Britannicus. In Act III, Burrhus is worried by Néron's love for Junie and intention of divorcing Octavie, and Agrippine is angered by the exile of Pallas. Britannicus's fortunes take a turn for

---

[4] See below, p. 147 ('Il est donc juif').

[5] See, for instance, Montaigne, *Essais*, ed. P. Villey and V.-L. Saulnier, 1965, Book I, chapter 26, pp. 170–1; Balzac, *Œuvres*, ed. L. Moreau, 1854, vol. I, p. 191; Chapelain, *Opuscules critiques*, ed. A. C. Hunter, 1936, p. 289. The eighteenth-century Italian dramatist, Alfieri, described his method of working as 'ideare, stendere, verseggiare'.

the better, when Agrippine promises to help him (III, 5), and he is reconciled with Junie (III, 7). Then, however, he quarrels with Néron, he and Agrippine are arrested, and Néron rebukes Burrhus. In Act IV, Britannicus's fate is in the balance. There are three high points in this act. First, Agrippine has her interview with Néron. This is, in fact, the climax of the whole tragedy. It achieves nothing, however; her recital of her crimes and her demand for his gratitude, i.e. submission, alarm him, and, immediately afterwards, we learn that he is bent on putting Britannicus to death. The second high point is the interview of Néron with Burrhus, whose remonstrances prove more effective than Agrippine's diatribe. The third interview of this tripartite act is with Narcisse, who combats the good influence of Burrhus. The act ends on a note of uncertainty, with Néron's ambiguous remark:

> Viens, Narcisse. Allons voir ce que nous devons faire.
>
> (IV, 4, l. 1480)

Suspense is continued into the fifth act, in which three scenes contrast the optimism of Agrippine and Britannicus with the forebodings of Junie. Then Burrhus reports that Britannicus has been murdered, and Junie is proved right.

Like the acts, each scene has one or more climaxes or dramatic moments. There are two in Act II, scene 2, in which we learn, first of Néron's love and jealousy, then, however, that this is counteracted by some remaining scruples and his fear of Agrippine; in Act II, scene 3, in which he first tells Junie that he means to marry her—the climax is the two words, 'Moi, Madame' (l. 572),—and then threatens to kill Britannicus if she betrays her love; in Act III, scene 5, a short scene, in which Britannicus first says that his friends will come to his aid, then, in a sudden collapse, admits that he has none, and finally Agrippine promises her help; in Act IV, scene 3, in which Néron first discloses his intention of killing Britannicus, and then changes his mind in response to Burrhus's arguments; and in Act IV, scene 4, in which Narcisse combats Néron's decision to spare Britannicus's life, Néron remains firm, Narcisse returns to the charge, and Néron gives a brief, enigmatic reply. There is a single climax in Act III, scene 1, in which Burrhus's pleading elicits Néron's reply, 'le mal est sans remède' (l. 776); in Act III, scene 7, in which Junie prevails upon Britannicus to forgive her apparent indifference; in the following scene, in which the quarrel between Britannicus and Néron culminates in the arrest of the former; and in Act IV, scene 2, in which Agrippine's long speech is followed by Néron's apparent capitulation.

The exposition is good. Agrippine, anxiously waiting to see Néron, may appropriately review her relations with her son; and it is natural enough that her confidante, Albine, should be ignorant of the concealed tensions in their relationship. Entrances and exits are carefully justified. In the first scene, Agrippine explains why she is trying to see her son; Burrhus comes out with a message from the emperor, and tells her that Néron has left by another door. Burrhus leaves her when Britannicus appears, accompanied by Narcisse:

> Voici Britannicus. Je lui cède ma place.
>
> (I, 2, l. 283)

Britannicus explains that he has come in search of Junie, who has been arrested and brought to the palace. Agrippine leaves for Pallas's house, telling Britannicus to follow her thither, which he duly does, after giving instructions to Narcisse to find out what he can about Junie. It would be tedious to continue; but this act, at least, justifies the claim made by Racine in the preface to *Alexandre* that his scenes are 'necessarily linked to one another' and that his actors 'do not come on to the stage without the reason that brings them there being apparent'.

The reversals of the situation are all psychological in *Britannicus*, brought about by decisions of Agrippine or Néron, or attempts to influence them. The tragedy begins just after the arrest of Junie. In it, Néron compels Junie to receive Britannicus frigidly, decides to get rid of Britannicus, and exiles Pallas. Agrippine promises to help Britannicus, and Junie and Britannicus are reconciled; but Néron and Britannicus quarrel, and Britannicus is arrested. Agrippine, Burrhus, and Narcisse in turn try to influence Néron, who finally poisons Britannicus.

Hope and fear alternate in this way in all Racine's plays. Jocaste and Antiochus respectively summarize the vicissitudes of *La Thé-baïde* and *Bérénice*. In *Alexandre*, Axiane tries to win over Taxile to her side, fails, tries to make his army revolt, and is made prisoner, along with Porus. Alexandre gives Porus's kingdom to Taxile, and promises him the hand of Axiane. Axiane believes Porus to be dead; then he is reported alive, and Taxile goes off to fight him. In the last act, Axiane fears that Porus has been defeated; then we learn that he is alive and Taxile dead, and all ends happily. In *Andromaque*, everything depends on Andromaque and Pyrrhus. Whenever Pyrrhus seems about to marry Andromaque, Oreste hopes afresh and Hermione despairs, until finally the wedding is fixed and she commands Oreste to kill him. The alternations of hope and fear in *Bajazet* are due to Roxane; if her suspicions are allayed, all is well, but if they revive, danger presses. Both *Mithridate* and *Phèdre* begin with a false rumour of the death of Mithridate and Thésée respectively, and their unexpected return precipitates a crisis. Otherwise the reversals of the situation in these plays spring from the emotions of the characters. Mithridate's suspicions and jealousy of his two sons, and his implacable hatred of Rome and need for Xipharès are the motive force in *Mithridate*. In *Phèdre*, the report of Thésée's death leads Phèdre to confess her love; she is repulsed, but hopes that Hippolyte may yet be won. Thésée returns, and Hippolyte is accused of attempting to rape Phèdre. He defends himself and hints at the truth; Thésée, however, does not believe him. Phèdre comes to save Hippolyte, but, in her jealousy on learning that he loves Aricie, desists. Thésée is finally persuaded of his son's innocence, but it is too late. External events are more important in *Iphigénie* than in the other plays. Agamemnon tries to prevent Clytemnestre and Iphigénie from coming to the camp, but they lose their way and do not receive his letter; Achille returns from Lesbos in time to provide another obstacle to the sacrifice of Iphigénie; and she is saved at the end by the discovery that Eriphile is the daughter of Helen and the intended victim.[6]

The details of Racine's plots are carefully worked out, particularly those of the political subplots and the connection between love and politics. In *Britannicus*, Agrippine is contending for power with Néron. She has the support of Pallas, backs Néron's half-brother, Britannicus, who has a claim to the throne, and encourages him to marry Junie. Néron counter-attacks by carrying Junie off, banishing Pallas, and poisoning Britannicus.

In *Bajazet*, Sultan Amurat, an heir having been born to him at last, wants to put his half-brother, Bajazet, to death (ll. 73–6, 113–4), and in his absence, his sultana, Roxane, has orders to kill Bajazet on the least suspicion of revolt (ll. 129–32, 302). His vizier, Acomat, aware that Amurat intends to get rid of him (ll. 85–6), has been plotting

[6] For *Athalie*, see above, p. 89.

against the absent sultan, enlisting Roxane's sympathy for Bajazet, and causing her to fall in love with him. Careful plans have been made for a revolution. Roxane controls the seraglio, and Acomat the city of Constantinople. He has won over the priesthood (ll. 233–6), and has the people on his side, partly through the priesthood, and partly because he has spread a false rumour that Amurat intends to move the seat of government elsewhere (ll. 243–6). The arrangements for the coup d'état are complete in Act III, scene 2:

> Et tandis qu'elle [the sultana] montre au peuple épouvanté
> Du prophète divin l'étendard redouté,
> Qu'à marcher sur mes pas Bajazet se dispose,
> Je vais de ce signal faire entendre la cause,
> Remplir tous les esprits d'une juste terreur,
> Et proclamer enfin le nouvel empereur.
>
> (ll. 847–52)

In Act IV, scene 6, Acomat reports that practically the whole of Constantinople is assembled, waiting for the promised signal. Acomat's reward is to be the hand of Bajazet's cousin, Atalide, who would prove a useful safeguard later on against Bajazet (ll. 182–94); his ideas and Agrippine's are similar.

Hippolyte in *Phèdre*[7] is heir to Trézène, but—as the son of a foreign mother—not to Athens; though it is not impossible that he may usurp the throne of Athens (ll. 201–2, 210–12). Phèdre is Thésée's wife, and her son is the legitimate heir to the Athenian throne. Aricie is the daughter of a king, and the sister of brothers who have rebelled against Thésée; and Thésée has condemned her to celibacy, so that their claims may not be revived by her husband. When Thésée is reported dead, Hippolyte succeeds automatically to Trézène, but the succession of Phèdre's son to the throne of Athens is more doubtful. Three parties form in the city, one in favour of Phèdre's son, one in favour of Hippolyte, and one in favour of Aricie (ll. 325–30, 485–508). It is clearly politic that two of the parties should combine against the third. Hippolyte proposes an alliance with Aricie in an interview which turns into a declaration of love; she accepts—her interests accord with the promptings of her heart (ll. 572–6). Phèdre's proposal of an alliance with Hippolyte comes too late. Athens, however, declares for Phèdre's son (ll. 722–4). Hippolyte is

---

[7] For the coup d'état in *Athalie*, see above, pp. 85–6.

on the verge of setting out for Athens to establish Aricie's authority
and his own (ll. 735–6), while Phèdre is thinking of buying Hippolyte's hand with the crown of Athens (ll. 795–802), when Thésée
returns. Hippolyte, banished by Thésée, resolves to depart and seek
allies:

> De puissants defénseurs prendront notre querelle;
> Argos nous tend les bras, et Sparte nous appelle.
> A nos amis communs portons nos justes cris;
> Ne souffrons pas que Phèdre, assemblant nos débris,
> Du trône paternel nous chasse l'un et l'autre,
> Et promette à son fils ma dépouille et la vôtre.
> L'occasion est belle, il la faut embrasser.
>
> (V, 1, ll. 1365–71)

Racine's superb craftsmanship can be seen, too, in the careful
preparation of the *péripéties* and the dénouement of his plays, a
precaution often omitted by lesser dramatists. The death of Pyrrhus
at the hands of Oreste is forecast by Oreste's remark:

> Il épouse, dit–il, Hermione demain;
> Il veut, pour m'honorer, la tenir de ma main.
> Ah! plutôt cette main dans le sang du barbare . . .
>
> (*Andromaque*, III, 1, ll. 731–3)

The manner of Pyrrhus's death is prepared, too. He promises
Andromaque that he will protect her son—

> Je défendrai sa vie aux dépens de mes jours
>
> (I, 4, l. 288)

—and falls an easy prey to Oreste's companions precisely because he
has sent his guard to look after Astyanax (ll. 1453–7). The abortive
interview in *Britannicus* reflects Néron's earlier statement:—

> Éloigné de ses yeux, j'ordonne, je menace,
> J'écoute vos conseils, j'ose les approuver;
> Je m'excite contre elle, et tâche à la braver.
> Mais (je t'expose ici mon âme toute nue)
> Sitôt que mon malheur me ramène à sa vue,
>
> Mon Génie étonné tremble devant le sien.
>
> (II, 2, ll. 496–500, 506)

During the interview, he listens submissively to his mother, but, as soon as she has gone, acts in defiance of her wishes. This result confirms Burrhus's warnings that threats and a show of displeasure would be ineffective (ll. 831, 1104–6). Junie thinks of entering the temple of Vesta long before the end of the tragedy:

> Ma fuite arrêtera vos discordes fatales;
> Seigneur, j'irai remplir le nombre des Vestales.
>
> (III, 8, ll. 1075–6)

The death of Britannicus is hinted at:—

> Britannicus le gêne, Albine . . .
>
> (I, 1, l. 13)
>
> Néron impunément ne sera pas jaloux.
>
> (II, 2, l. 445)
>
> tu peux concevoir
> Que je lui vendrai cher le plaisir de la voir.
>
> (II, 2. ll. 521–2)
>
> Et sa perte sera l'infaillible salaire
> D'un geste ou d'un soupir échappé pour lui plaire.
>
> (II, 3, ll. 683–4)

Néron's distraction after Junie's escape is foreshadowed by 'ces sombres regards errants à l'aventure' (l. 380) and the remark, 'Je souffre trop, éloigné de Junie' (l. 799).

We are prepared for Bajazet's death by constant reminders that he lives only so long as Roxane is convinced of his love. Roxane's own death is foretold by her promise:

> De ma sanglante mort ta mort sera suivie
>
> (II, 1, l. 557)

—an example of dramatic irony, since she is thinking of suicide, and is in fact murdered after Bajazet's death. Atalide's uncontrollable jealousy, to which the catastrophe is largely due, is carefully unfolded. In the first act, she tells her confidante:

> D'un mouvement jaloux je ne fus pas maîtresse,
>
> (I. 4, l. 378)

and

Peut-être Bajazet, secondant ton envie,
Plus que tu ne voudras aura soin de sa vie.

(I, 4, ll. 405–6)

In Act III, she again expresses her jealousy to her confidante (scenes 1 and 3), before allowing Bajazet to see it (scene 4). We are warned of the trick by which Mithridate lures Monime into confessing her love for Xipharès by Pharnace's remark that

Le Roi, toujours fertile en dangereux détours,
S'armera contre nous de nos moindres discours.

(I, 5, ll. 369–70)

Mithridate's sending poison to Monime is also carefully prepared:

Ne vous assurez point sur l'amour qu'il vous porte:
Sa jalouse fureur n'en sera que plus forte.

(I, 5, ll.355–6)

Qu'elle ne pousse point cette même tendresse,
Que sais-je? à des fureurs dont mon cœur outragé
Ne se repentirait qu'après s'être vengé.

(II, 5, ll. 632–4)

Vous dépendez ici d'une main violente,
Que le sang le plus cher rarement épouvante;
Et je n'ose vous dire à quelle cruauté
Mithridate jaloux s'est souvent emporté.

(IV, 2, ll. 1203–6)

The audience is prepared for the revolt of the army in Act V of *Iphigénie* by references to the unrest of the troops (ll. 293–4, 1237–40), and for the sacrifice of Eriphile by the mystery of Eriphile's identity and by hints that Helen had a daughter and that oracles are prone to mislead (ll. 237–42, 427–34, 1110–11, 1265–6, 1283–6). In *Athalie*, Joas's identity is revealed, and Joad prophesies that he will turn into an ungodly king, and kill Joad's son, Zacharie. The first is foreshadowed by the lines:

Comme si dans le fond de ce vaste édifice
Dieu cachait un vengeur armé pour son supplice

(I, 1. ll. 55–6)

and

> O jour heureux pour moi!
> De quelle ardeur j'irais reconnaître mon roi!
>
> (I, 1, ll. 145–6)

the second by Josabet's fears that Joas will turn out like his family (ll. 237–40), by Joad's prayer to God to put an end to Joas's life if her fears are justified (ll. 283–6), and by Mathan's suggestion that some 'monstre naissant' (l. 603) is being reared in the temple. Joad's prophecy is recalled when Joas and Zacharie embrace, and Joad, with dramatic irony, says,

> Enfants, ainsi toujours puissiez-vous être unis!
>
> (IV, 4, l. 1416)

and when, at the end of the play, Athalie curses Joas (ll. 1783–90).[8]

Vocabulary and imagery are also used to keep the themes and the situations of the tragedy constantly in the spectator's mind, and to foreshadow the dénouement. The use of the word *sang* in *La Thébaïde* and of the words *diadème* or *bandeau* in *Mithridate* has been mentioned. The word *nœuds* is similarly used in *Bajazet*, now in its figurative sense of the marriage bond, now in its literal sense of the noose with which mutes strangle their victims, now—with dramatic irony—in both senses at once:

> Loin de vous séparer, je prétends aujourd'hui
> Par des nœuds éternels vous unir avec lui.
>
> (V, 6, ll. 1623–4)

> Moi seule, j'ai tissu le lien malheureux
> Dont tu viens d'éprouver les détestables nœuds.
>
> (V, 12, ll. 1731–2)

Words for light and darkness, eyes and glances recur in *Britannicus*. The description of Junie's arrival in the palace condenses into a single tableau the essence of the tragedy. She is illuminated by torchlight, her eyes wet with tears and upturned towards heaven; Néron watches her from the shadows. Junie is a creature of shadow, night, obscurity (ll. 415, 613, 615) forced by Néron into the brilliance of himself and his court—the words, *éclat, clarté, gloire, splendeur* are all used (ll. 450, 455, 617, 624, 630, 973, 1550). *Britannicus* is a good illustration of the close scrutiny to which Racine's characters subject

[8] See also above, p. 86.

one another. Britannicus refers to Narcisse's eyes 'sur ma conduite incessamment ouverts' (l. 345). This is dramatic irony: he believes Narcisse to be his guide and friend; in fact, Narcisse is watching his actions and reporting them to Néron. Britannicus in his turn orders Narcisse:

> Examine leurs yeux, observe leurs discours . . .
>
> (I, 4, l. 349)

This is not the only association of sight and sound; where scrutiny is close, thoughts must be expressed silently, and silence itself must be interpreted.

> J'entendrai des regards que vous croirez muets,
>
> (II, 3, l. 682)

says Néron. Junie in the scene that follows warns Britannicus that walls have eyes (l. 713), and he reproaches her:

> Quoi! même vos regards ont appris à se taire?
> Que vois-je? Vous craignez de rencontrer mes yeux?
>
> (II, 6, ll. 736–7)

His supporters, he tells her, approve his opposition to Néron with their eyes:

> Chacun semble des yeux approuver mon courroux . . .
>
> (II, 6, l. 721)

Eyes, then, reveal as well as scrutinize. Junie's eyes, associated several times with tears and described as sad, are upturned towards heaven again in the last act:

> vos yeux, vos tristes yeux
> Avec de longs regards se tournent vers les cieux,
>
> (V, 1, ll. 1501–2)

another way of preparing us for her retreat into the temple of Vesta. Néron is a hypocrite, but not a consummate hypocrite. Agrippine relates how, on the occasion when he first showed signs of independence, he:

> Laissa sur son visage éclater son dépit,
>
> (I, 1, l. 106)

but then simulated respect to cover up his insult (l. 108). When he has seen Junie, Narcisse notices his 'sombres regards errants à l'aventure' (l. 380). Néron can watch Britannicus's death with impassivity, with 'yeux indifférents' (l. 1711); but the loss of Junie is less easily borne:

ses yeux mal assurés
N'osent lever au ciel leurs regards égarés . . .
(ll. 1757–8)

His restless eyes recall that earlier line (380). Unlike Junie, Néron cannot raise his eyes to heaven, nor does he weep—weeping, in *Britannicus*, is reserved for Junie and Britannicus.

Eyes are also dangerous. Both Agrippine and Junie advise Britannicus to avoid Néron's eyes (ll. 926, 1017); he pays no heed and meets his death. Junie finds refuge from Néron's eyes in the temple of Vesta (l. 1074). Agrippine's eyes are imperious; Néron cannot withstand them, though he can act freely when he is out of their sight.[9]

Careful preparation and suspense or curiosity are not mutually exclusive. The preparation may be more apparent to the reader than to the spectator—as few of us see a play of Racine's nowadays without having read it, it is not easy to judge; and in any case the preparatory hints may be ambiguous—dramatic irony is not uncommon—or may only be understood afterwards. It is not until one has seen or read the whole play that the significance of Junie's upturned eyes, or of Neptune's affection for Thésée, or of Hippolyte's neglect of manly exercises, or of Athalie's conviction that the temple contains hidden treasure becomes evident.

It is sometimes said that Racine's indifference to suspense or curiosity is shown by the fact that he treated subjects familiar to his audience. The presence of *péripéties* in all his tragedies and the delayed appearance of many of his main characters—Néron, Titus, Bajazet, Mithridate, Aricie, and Athalie first appear in the second act, Thésée in the third—seem to contradict this view. It is difficult, too, to know how familiar his subjects were to his audience—the amount of information he gives in the preface to *Athalie* may indicate that

[9] See J. Starobinski, 'The Poetics of the Glance in Racine', in *Racine, Modern Judgments*, ed. R. C. Knight, 1969, pp. 88–100; J. Brody, ' "Les yeux de César". The Language of Vision in *Britannicus*', in *Studies in Seventeenth Century Literature presented to Morris Bishop*, ed. J.-J. Demorest, 1962, pp. 185–201; and E. M. Zimmermann, 'La Lumière et la Voix. Etude sur l'unité de *Britannicus*', in *Revue des Sciences Humaines*, vol. XXXIII, 1968, pp. 169–83.

that subject was not as familiar as one might have supposed; but even if the subjects were familiar, the audience cannot have known beforehand how they were going to be treated. No one acquainted with Euripides or Sophocles would have expected *La Thébaïde* to end with the death of Antigone—who cannot, therefore, bury Polynice and incur her uncle's wrath. No one acquainted with Euripides would have expected Iphigénie to return home with her mother at the end of the play. However familiar the audience may have been with the history of Mithridates, it can scarcely have expected Monime and Xipharès to be in love, still less Monime—not yet Mithridate's wife—to have survived Mithridate. Moreover, since Racine did sometimes treat his sources with great freedom, since contemporary dramatists treated sources with equal or greater freedom, how could the theatre-goer, seeing a play for the first time, know what to expect? If Magnon in his *Tite* (1660) could bring Bérénice to Rome disguised as a man and make her marry Tite at the end of the play, and if Racine could kill off Antigone, how could the public be sure that Titus would not marry Bérénice at the end of his play? D'Aubignac insists that the incidents and the dénouement of a play must be prepared but not foreseen; Racine's plays give the impression that he had taken this advice to heart.

Since a tragedy is not a work of history, historical accuracy might seem superfluous, even in a historical tragedy, were it not that Racine lays claim to it. In the first preface to *Andromaque,* he says that he has portrayed his characters in exactly the same way as the ancient poets, not considering himself free to make any change. He insists on the accuracy of his portrayal of Nero and Mithridates, adding that the details of Mithridate's plan of invading Italy come from the ancient historians. In the first preface to *Bajazet*, he declares: 'The chief thing after which I have striven was to change nothing in either the manners or the customs of the nation.'

Racine was under no obligation to aim at historical accuracy. The seventeenth-century French dramatist had a pretty free hand. Dramatic theory, it is true, recommended that kings should talk like kings, and that historical (or legendary) characters should have the characteristics generally associated with them; but the principles of verisimilitude and propriety allowed or required great changes. It was, for instance, neither probable nor proper that a king should travel alone (like Laius in Sophocles's *Œdipus*), or that a princess should become a concubine (like Andromache); and the public expected the hero or the heroine to be in love. The plays themselves offer great variety, some treating historical subjects quite faithfully, such as Corneille's *Horace*, others at the other extreme, such as Corneille's *Héraclius* or Quinault's *Astrate*, having little or nothing historical about them except the names of the characters.

Racine's claims to historical accuracy cannot be accepted without reservations; too much weight must not be given to his professions. He was not primarily concerned with historical truth; and although, for example, he says in the preface to *Iphigénie* that 'the taste of Paris has shown itself to be identical with that of Athens', his own play is very different from that of Euripides, and its success by no means illustrates the unchanging nature of taste. Then again, Racine's practice varies considerably. Just as *Horace* is more historical than *Héraclius*, so *Britannicus* and *Athalie* are more historical than *Alexandre*, *Bajazet*, or even *Mithridate*.

Racine does, in fact, make changes in the interests of propriety, in other words in order to adapt his characters and subjects to the taste of his audience. This, of course, would be done to some extent by any dramatist in any age—historical characters thinking and talking on the stage as they would have done in real life would be wellnigh unintelligible; but the seventeenth-century public was probably less sensitive to the differences between civilizations than later generations schooled by Sir Walter Scott, Chateaubriand, and the Romantic historians and novelists. Racine's characters use the language of the polite society of seventeenth-century France, address each other as 'Madame' and 'Seigneur', and talk of their *gloire* or *honneur*, their *feux* or their *flammes*. The early nineteenth-century Irish novelist and traveller, Lady Morgan, may be wrong in saying that Agrippine in the first act of *Britannicus* has 'the air and character of one of the literary *précieuses* of the hôtel Rambouillet', but certainly some of Racine's characters, as we have seen, are as well versed in the psychology of love, as sensitive to nuances of behaviour, as if they had been there; and she is not altogether wrong in commenting on the unfailing politeness with which Junie asks Agrippine's leave to go and see to her expiring lover:[10]

[10] Lady Morgan, *France* (1816). See Elizabeth Suddaby and P. J. Yarrow, *Lady Morgan in France*, 1971, pp. 90–1.

> Pardonnez, Madame, à ce transport.
> Je vais le secourir, si je puis, ou le suivre.
>
> (V, 4, ll. 1614–15)

Racine's characters belong in many ways to their age and country. As love tragedies, his plays are largely anachronistic, and his heroes and heroines love in the manner of seventeenth-century Frenchmen and Frenchwomen. Of Alexandre, Boileau wrote: 'His physiognomy is neither Greek, nor barbaric. He is a foppish warrior'.[11] Créon, Néron, Titus, Mithridate, Achille, and Hippolyte are also lovers. Bajazet and Atalide are strangely monogamous: Corneille is reported to have remarked, after a performance of the play:

> There is not one character who has the sentiments that he ought to have and that they have in Constantinople; they all have, under a Turkish habit, the sentiment that people have in the middle of France

—harsh, but with a grain of truth. Racine's royal characters, too, have the dignity of Louis XIV, rather than the simplicity of rulers of city states or petty kingdoms. Renan pointed out how unlike Racine's Athalie is to her Biblical counterpart, whose father sulked when Naboth refused to sell him his vineyard: 'he laid him down upon his bed, and turned away his face, and would eat no bread'.[12] Similarly, Oreste, it has been observed, is a seventeenth-century ambassador.

Racine also modifies his characters considerably. He admits that he 'somewhat softens the ferocity of Pyrrhus',[13] that his Andromaque is the widow of Hector, not the concubine of Pyrrhus, and that her son is Astyanax, the son she had by Hector, not Molossus, her son by Pyrrhus: 'I thought it right to conform in that respect to the idea that we now have of that princess.'[14] His Hermione, Pyrrhus's betrothed, is jealous of Andromaque who has won his love; her classical counterpart, married, but barren, envies her rival's fertility. His Oreste has not killed his mother. His Junie is more modest than the historical one; there is nothing, he says, to stop a dramatist from improving the morals of a character, especially of

---

[11] *Dialogue des héros de romans.*   [12] 1 Kings, xxi, 4.
[13] First preface to *Andromaque.*   [14] Second preface to *Andromaque.*

one that is not well known.'[15] His Néron, maintains Pieter Geyl, is a perfect diplomat, gracefully courteous to Junie:

> His falseness and wickedness only transpire in glints from behind the mask of the man of the world. In short, the blood-thirsty and insane despot has been transposed into the terms of Racine's own, all-too-narrow sphere of life.[16]

His Bérénice is transformed from a middle-aged, experienced mistress into a young and virginal fiancée. Pieter Geyl again complains that there is 'nothing specifically Roman in Titus, nothing Oriental in either Antiochus or Bérénice', and that Mithridate makes one feel that

> the poet has remained blind to the barbaric—that is, to the really distinctive element on which true historic perception would have fastened.[17]

Racine's Hippolyte is not a devotee of Artemis; instead of giving us, says Dryden,

> the picture of a rough young man, of the Amazonian strain, a jolly huntsman, and both by his profession and his early rising a mortal enemy to love, he has chosen to give him the tone of gallantry, sent him to travel from Athens to Paris, taught him to make love, and transform the Hippolitus of Euripides into Monsieur Hippolite.[18]

Racine puts the accusation against Hippolyte into the mouth of Œnone, because it is below the dignity of a queen like Phèdre. Esther and Assuérus are less barbaric in *Esther* than in the Bible.

Nevertheless, despite all these reservations and strictures, one is left with the impression that there is in many of Racine's characters a substantial residuum of historical truth; that Néron and Agrippine, Acomat and Roxane, Mithridate and Phèdre, Joad, Mardochée, and Athalie are not only convincing and dramatically effective characters in their own right, but have some traits that attach them firmly to their age or country or source.

Much the same can be said of the situations and events in Racine's

[15] First preface to *Britannicus*.
[16] *Encounters in History*, Fontana Library, 1967, p. 78.
[17] Op. cit., pp. 76 and 79.   [18] Preface to *All for Love*.

tragedies as of the characters. Whatever he finds in his sources he usually changes into the typical situation: a pair of lovers, one of whom is loved without return by someone else. In writing *Andromaque*, he clearly wanted a seventeenth-century chain of lovers, and did not want a concubine and a jealous wife. He prolongs the life of Britannicus, creates Junie, and makes possible the rivalry in love of Néron and Britannicus. He not only changes the relationship of Titus and Bérénice, as we have seen, but adds the character of Antiochus so as to provide Bérénice with a second lover. The invention of Eriphile and Aricie fulfils a similar purpose. The characters of *Mithridate* are historical, but their relationship is a fabrication. Moreover, there are some anachronisms in Racine's tragedies. Greek weddings did not take place before an altar, as they do in *Andromaque* and *Iphigénie*; and Hermione's situation as an unmarried bride at Pyrrhus's court might have been possible in seventeenth-century Europe, but was not in ancient Greece. Alfred de Vigny complains that Racine, in *Bajazet*, to comply with the demands of the alexandrine, called Bagdad Babylon and Istambul (or Constantinople) Byzance.[19] The entry of Junie into the Vestal Virgins in *Britannicus*, the reference to Roman *mânes* in Greek plays,[20] and the note despatched by Agamemnon to Clytemnestre in *Iphigénie* are other examples.

Nevertheless, Racine does take great pains with his historical or legendary backgrounds. He does not, of course, fill his plays with local colour in the Romantic sense, interlard them with disquisitions on coinage or costumes or contemporary events, like Alexandre Dumas or Victor Hugo; but he does incorporate into them references to the institutions of the society in which the action of his play takes place, to the history of the country, or to the deeds of the ancestors of his characters. The Roman atmosphere is important in *Britannicus* and in *Bérénice*. In the first of these plays, there are references to such characteristic Roman institutions as the senate, tribunes, the fasces borne by lictors, and the eagles:

> Néron devant sa mère a permis le premier
> Qu'on portât les faisceaux couronnés de laurier.

(I, 1, ll. 85–6)

---

[19] Lettre à Lord * * *, prefixed to *Le More de Venise*.
[20] *Andromaque*, l. 986; *Phèdre*, ll. 378 and 1652.

Vous avez vu cent fois nos soldats en courroux
Porter en murmurant leurs aigles devant vous . . .

(IV, 2, ll. 1245–6)

Allusions to Roman history range from the golden age of the consuls (ll. 27–9) to the various emperors, Augustus, Caligula, and Claudius, as well as to their habit of repudiating their wives and of adopting or repudiating heirs. Agrippine's speech in Act IV, scene 2, is not only an outline of her career (and Néron's) but a graphic evocation of the manners of Imperial Rome. In Act IV, scene 4, Narcisse tells how the famous distiller of poisons, Locuste, tested the rapidity of her poison by trying it out on a slave, and mentions the fondness of Rome and of Néron for chariot races and the theatre:

Pour toute ambition, pour vertu singulière,
Il [Néron] excelle à conduire un char dans la carrière,
A disputer des prix indignes de ses mains,
A se donner lui-même en spectacle aux Romains,
A venir prodiguer sa voix sur un théâtre,
A réciter des chants qu'il veut qu'on idolâtre . . .

(ll. 1471–6)

In *Bérénice*, the senate plays an important part, with its hostility towards queens; there are references to the custom of adorning the statues of emperors with flowers or laurels (ll. 299–300, 1223–4), and to Roman history including the Jewish Wars, and a magnificent description of Titus enthroned, presiding over the ceremony at which his dead father, Vespasian, is deified.[21]

Bajazet portrays an Oriental despotism, with its mistrust, its uneasy and impermanent relations between sultan and grand vizier or sultan and brother, and its dependence on the janissaries. Mistrust means death, and death means strangulation by mutes. Like the history of the Roman emperors in *Britannicus*, the history of the Ottoman empire is sketched, particularly the reign of Suliman the Great (ll. 455–80). Mithridate is another Oriental despot, 'fertile en dangereux détours' (l. 369), and as prone as Amurat to put wives or sons to death. His speech in Act III, conveys a good impression of the state of the Roman empire at the time. *Esther* and *Athalie* take us into Hebrew antiquity, toned down a little, but in the main faithfully

[21] See below, p. 148.

depicted. We are not told why Vasthi was disgraced (in the Bible, she refused to appear before Ahasuerus and display her beauty to the people); we hear nothing of the twelve months' preparation undergone by women chosen to appear before Ahasurerus; and there is no question of Esther's being his concubine before being chosen to be his queen. But with minor exceptions such as these Racine, in his last two plays, faithfully reproduces the biblical atmosphere, largely by the use of biblical vocabulary and turns of phrase.[22]

The historical background, together with the evocation of events before and after the action and of places outside the stage, gives every one of Racine's tragedies, except the first two, an atmosphere of its own. The creation of this atmosphere is a unique feature of his tragedies. Corneille, in his best plays, also takes pains with his historical backgrounds, but in a different way; he is more interested in the complexity of political relationships, in questions of policy and the balance of power, than in atmosphere. Although his *Tite et Bérénice* is not one of his best plays, it is not unfair to compare it with Racine's *Bérénice* from this point of view. Corneille is more concerned with political considerations. When the senate meets, it is to alleviate the suffering caused by the eruption of Vesuvius. He dwells on the threat to Tite represented by his brother, Domitian, and by Domitie, who also has political ambitions, a threat that their marriage would increase. He discusses the nature of the senate, its composition, and the little weight that can be given in its degenerate state to its decisions. Racine simplifies all this and reduces it to a straightforward conflict between Titus's love and Rome's hatred of queens. On the other hand, Titus's imperial state is graphically described to show that he is a prisoner of it. Lesser dramatists usually neglect to give the setting of their plays any reality at all. Quinault's *Pausanias* was written in imitation of *Andromaque*, and his *Bellérophon* is, in some ways, a foretaste of *Phèdre*. The two plays of Thomas Corneille that survived longest were *Ariane*, a play about Phèdre's sister, and *Le Comte d'Essex*, which, like *Bajazet*, deals with a comparatively recent period of history. In all these plays, the authentic setting and the atmosphere of Racine's are completely lacking.

The historical truth in the characterization, the background, and

[22] For *Athalie*, see above, p. 89. See also L.-C. Delfour, *La Bible dans Racine*, 1891; J. Lichtenstein, *Racine poète biblique*, 1934; and G. Spillebout, *Le Vocabulaire biblique dans les tragédies sacrées de Racine*, 1968.

the atmosphere of Racine's tragedies, however relative, distinguishes him from his lesser contemporaries, is further evidence of his seriousness and careful craftsmanship, and is an integral part of his work. It is a means of creating complex and convincing characters, of endowing them with the necessary tragic dignity, of placing them in an appropriate background, and thereby giving solidity and depth to his plays. That the historical truth is only relative is not a weakness, but a strength. Racine is not a historian; he is a writer of poetic tragedy, the aim of which is neither realism nor escape, but something betwixt and between. Racine is trying to portray characters with whom we can identify ourselves in a setting that confers heroic stature upon them. Their world is neither that of seventeenth-century France nor the ancient world; it is a fusion of seventeenth-century Paris and ancient Greece or Rome, partaking of the characteristics of both, suspended between the two. The universality of Racine's tragedies is enhanced by the impression of timelessness thus achieved.

8

Style

If Racine's characters are both remote from ordinary humanity by virtue of their birth, their rank, and their exploits, and intensely human in their weaknesses, their passions, and their vulnerability, the language in which they express themselves must be sometimes dignified, majestic, and restrained, and sometimes natural, passionate, and sincere.

Many things help to give an impression of nobility. However distressed, however passionate Racine's characters are, however great their disarray, their speeches are usually logically composed and beautifully proportioned. To take just one example, Hermione's passionate outburst in Act 4, scene 5 of *Andromaque* (ll. 1356–86) can be summarized thus:

(1) *Thesis*
   (a)   an enumeration of indications of her love for him in the past (10 lines);
   (b)   a statement that she still loves him (3 lines).
(2) *Antithesis*
   (a)   a plea to Pyrrhus, if he wishes to marry Andromaque, to wait a day (6 lines);
   (b)   a complaint that he does not answer, and regrets every moment spent away from Andromaque (5 lines).
(3) *Synthesis*
      Let him go and marry Andromaque, but fear Hermione (7 lines).

Racine's characters speak in alexandrines—intended to be declaimed or intoned, not spoken realistically.[1] They use a small, select vocabulary of some 2,000 words,[2] general or abstract on the whole, rather than particular or concrete, never—except in *Les Plaideurs*—humdrum or vulgar. They make great use of inversion, which not only differentiates their language from that of everyday life, but strengthens the rhythm by more clearly separating groups of words than the normal order would do:

Toujours de ma fureur interrompre le cours . . .
    (*Andromaque*, I, 1, l. 47)

Periphrasis also marks their speech out as poetic, and gives an impression of dignity, as when Phèdre, telling her confidante how she was bringing up her husband's (and her) children, says:

De son fatal hymen je cultivais les fruits,
    (*Phèdre*, I, 3, l. 300)

or Abner relates how he expected Athalie to put him to death:

J'attendais que . . .
Elle vînt m'affranchir d'une importune vie,
Et retrancher des jours qu'aurait dû mille fois
Terminer la douleur de survivre à mes rois.
    (*Athalie*, V, 2, ll. 1570, 1572–4)

An effect of dignity and detachment is produced by the characters' habit of using the royal 'we', of referring to themselves or to one another as 'on', of speaking of themselves in the third person:

Captive, toujours triste, importune à moi–même,
Pouvez-vous souhaiter qu'Andromaque vous aime?
    (*Andromaque*, I, 4, ll. 301–2)

---

[1] See above, pp. 1–2, 31.

[2] According to Bryant C. Freeman and Alan Batson, *Concordance du théâtre et des poésies de Jean Racine*, 2 vols, 1968, the total vocabulary used by Racine in his verse comprises 4,088 words. This is the vocabulary of *Les Plaideurs* and his miscellaneous poems as well as his tragedies, and includes proper names.

of using the indefinite article instead of the definite article or a possessive adjective:

> Quels charmes ont pour vous *des* yeux infortunés
> Qu'à des pleurs éternels vous avez condamnés?
> Non, non, d'*un* ennemi respecter la misère,
> Sauver *des* malheureux, rendre *un* fils à sa mère . . .
> Seigneur, voilà des soins dignes du fils d'Achille,
>   (*Andromaque*, I, 4, ll. 303–6, 310)

of using *ce qui* or *ce que* for persons:

> Épouser ce qu'il hait, et punir ce qu'il aime,
>   (*Andromaque*, I, 1, l. 122)

of using plural instead of singular nouns:

> Pardonnez, Acomat: je plains avec sujet
> Des cœurs dont les bontés trop mal récompensées
> M'avaient pris pour objet de toutes leurs pensées
>   (*Bajazet*, II, 3, ll. 616–18)

(Bajazet is being deliberately vague; he means Atalide), and of apostrophizing their states of mind:

> Funeste aveuglement! Perfide jalousie!
> Récit menteur! Soupçons que je n'ai pu celer!
> Fallait-il vous entendre ou fallait-il parler?
>   (*Bajazet*, IV, 1, ll. 1150–2)

The formal patterns common in Racine's verse, although they serve other purposes (besides being satisfying in themselves), also serve this one. Many speeches are composed of series of quatrains (the opening speeches of *Andromaque*, for instance). Stichomythia—two speakers combating one another's arguments in alternate hemistiches, lines, or couplets—, though used more sparingly by Racine than by his contemporaries or predecessors, is not absent (*Britannicus*, ll. 1051–65, *Iphigénie*, ll. 569–75, for instance). Symmetry, on the other hand, is a constantly recurring feature:

> Bajazet interdit! Atalide étonnée!
>   (*Bajazet*, III, 7, l. 1069)

Je l'aimais à Lesbos, et je l'aime en Aulide.

> (*Iphigénie*, II, 1, l. 502)

Observons Bajazet; étonnons Atalide;
Et couronnons l'amant, ou perdons le perfide.

> (*Bajazet*, III, 8, ll. 1121–2)

Hippolyte est sensible, et ne sent rien pour moi!
Aricie a son cœur! Aricie a sa foi!

> (*Phèdre*, IV, 5, ll. 1203–4)

In the last two examples, it will be noticed, one line falling into two halves that express the same or a similar idea is accompanied by another, the two halves of which are antithetical. Symmetrical lines of this kind emphasize an idea or an emotion, and give the impression that the speaker is dwelling or brooding on it.

Just as one hemistich may echo another, so one line may echo another, expressing either the same idea or a contrary one. Sometimes similarity of structure reinforces similarity of idea:

Oui, comme *ses* exploits nous admirons *vos* coups:
Hector tomba sous *lui*, Troie expira sous *vous* . . .

> (*Andromaque*, I, 2, ll. 147–8)

Hécube / près d'Ulysse / acheva sa misère;
Cassandre / dans Argos / a suivi votre père . . .

> (*Andromaque*, I, 2, ll. 189–90)

Amant avec transport, mais *jaloux* sans retour,
Sa *haine* va toujours plus loin que son *amour*.

> (*Mithridate*, I, 5, ll. 353–4)

Each line of this last couplet expresses the opposition between two aspects of Mithridate's character (passionate love and extreme jealousy), *jaloux* corresponding to *haine*, and *amant* to *amour*, the order of the two aspects being reversed in the second line. Nor need repetition of ideas be confined to a couplet. Hippolyte addresses two quatrains to his father, each expressing the same idea that he is in love:

Non, mon père, ce cœur (c'est trop vous le celer)
N'a point d'un chaste amour dédaigné de brûler.
Je confesse à vos pieds ma véritable offense:
J'aime, j'aime, il est vrai, malgré votre défense.

Aricie à ses lois tient mes vœux asservis:
La fille de Pallante a vaincu votre fils.
Je l'adore, et mon âme, à vos ordres rebelle,
Ne peut ni soupirer ni brûler que pour elle.

(*Phèdre*, IV, 2, ll. 1119–26)

Both quatrains say the same thing, the second merely adding the name of his beloved; and both are similarly constructed—periphrasis leading up to the direct statement ('j'aime', 'j'adore'), followed in its turn by a confession of his disobedience to his father's orders.

Verbal repetition also gives an impression of stylization. Sometimes a word is used twice within a hemistich:[3]

Créon même, Créon pour la paix se déclare!

(*La Thébaïde*, III, 6, l. 824)

Songe, songe, Céphise, à cette nuit cruelle . . .

(*Andromaque*, III, 8, l. 997)

J'aimais, Seigneur, j'aimais: je voulais être aimée.

(*Bérénice*, V, 7, l. 1479)

This kind of repetition is sometimes an easy way of padding out half a line ('Hé bien, Madame, hé bien'), but it can be highly expressive. In the first example, it emphasizes the speaker's astonishment at Créon's unexpected attitude; in the second, it conveys the horror with which Andromaque recalls the fall of Troy; and in the third, it expresses the singlemindedness of Bérénice's devotion and the pathos of her situation. The repetition of a word, often in a slightly different form, in each of the two halves of a line or in two successive lines is also common:

L'Épire *sauvera* ce que Troie *a sauvé*.

(*Andromaque*, I, 2, l. 220)

Avant qu'il me *trahît*, vous m'*avez* tous *trahie*.

(*Andromaque*, II, 3, l. 470)

Tout m'afflige *et* me *nuit, et* conspire à me *nuire*.

(*Phèdre*, I, 3, l. 161)

Hippolyte est *sensible*, et ne *sent* rien pour moi!

(*Phèdre*, IV, 5, l. 1203)

---

[3] See above, p. 10.

C'est lui qui de *Pyrrhus* fait agir le courroux.
S'il faut fléchir *Pyrrhus*, qui le peut mieux que vous?
(*Andromaque*, III, 4, ll. 883–4)

Je mourrai; mais au moins ma mort me vengera.
Je ne mourrai pas seule, et quelqu'un me suivra.
(*Andromaque*, V, 2, ll. 1491–2)

Les déserts, autrefois *peuplés* de sénateurs,
Ne sont plus *habités* que par leurs délateurs.
(*Britannicus*, I, 2, ll. 209–10)

(In this last example, a synonym is substituted for the original word.)
Like his contemporaries,[4] Racine often uses pairs of lines beginning in the same way and expressing the same idea:

Faut-il que mes soupirs vous demandent sa vie?
Faut-il qu'en sa faveur j'embrasse vos genoux?
(*Andromaque*, III, 7, ll. 958–9)

Hippolyte demande à me voir en ce lieu?
Hippolyte me cherche, et veut me dire adieu?
(*Phèdre*, II, 1, ll. 367–8)

A whole series of lines may begin with the same word in this way:

un roi victorieux
Qui vous fait remonter au rang de vos aïeux,
Qui foule aux pieds pour vous vos vainqueurs en colère,
Qui ne se souvient plus qu'Achille était son père,
Qui dément ses exploits et les rend superflus?
(*Andromaque*, III, 8, ll. 987–91)

Agamemnon.
Vous êtes dans un camp . . .
Clytemnestre.
Où tout vous est soumis,
Où le sort de l'Asie en vos mains est remis,
Où je vois sous vos lois marcher la Grèce entière,
Où le fils de Thétis va m'appeler sa mère.
(*Iphigénie*, III, 1, ll. 803–6)

This kind of repetition is more frequent in *Andromaque* than in later

---

[4] See above, pp. 9–10.

plays, and Racine usually disguises it more than in the examples just
quoted. If a word or expression is used more than twice, it may
change its place in the line, or a synonym may take its place:

> *Maintenant que* je puis couronner tant d'attraits,
> *Maintenant que* je l'aime encor plus que jamais,
> *Lorsqu'un* heureux hymen, joignant nos destinées . . .
>   (*Bérénice*, II, 2, ll. 441–3)

Often there is a complex pattern of repetition:

> *Je m'en fie* aux transports qu'elle m'a fait paraître;
> *Je m'en fie* à Burrhus; *j'en crois* même son maître:
> *Je crois* qu'à mon exemple impuissant à trahir,
> Il *hait* à cœur ouvert, ou cesse de *haïr*.
>   (*Britannicus*, V, 1, ll. 1515–18)

Here, a line and a hemistich beginning with 'Je m'en fie' are followed
by a hemistich and a line beginning with 'Je crois', after which a line
made up of two antithetical halves, each containing the verb *haïr*,
provides an effective conclusion.

> *Quelle* fureur les borne au milieu de leur course?
> *Quel* charme ou quel poison en a tari la source?
> Les ombres par *trois fois* ont obscurci les cieux
> *Depuis que* le sommeil n'est entré dans vos yeux;
> Et le jour a *trois fois* chassé la nuit obscure
> *Depuis que* votre corps languit sans nourriture.
> A *quel* affreux dessein vous laissez-*vous* tenter?
> De *quel* droit sur vous-même osez-*vous* attenter?
> *Vous* offensez les Dieux auteurs de votre vie;
> *Vous trahissez* l'époux à qui la foi vous lie;
> *Vous trahissez* enfin vos enfants malheureux,
> Que *vous* précipitez sous un joug rigoureux.
> Songez qu'un même jour leur ravira leur mère,
> Et rendra l'espérance au fils de l'étrangère,
> A *ce* fier ennemi de vous, de votre sang,
> *Ce* fils qu'une Amazone a porté dans son flanc,
> *Cet* Hippolyte . . .
>   (*Phèdre*, I, 3, ll. 189–205)

This is a good example of the complex way in which Racine

handles this device. Four questions beginning with 'quel(le)' are interrupted by a quatrain consisting of two couplets each containing the expression 'trois fois' and a clause introduced by 'depuis que'. The last two of the questions introduced by 'quel' are in the second person plural, and lead up to four lines beginning with the word 'vous' (twice followed by the verb 'trahissez'). Then comes a sentence ending with three lines beginning with 'ce', and all referring to Hippolyte.

Sometimes instead of lines, couplets may begin in the same way; or lines beginning with the same word may occur at diminishing or increasing intervals. There is an instance of the former in *Bérénice*:

Phénice ne vient point? Moments trop rigoureux,
Que vous paraissez lents à mes rapides vœux!
Je m'agite, je cours, languissante, abattue;
La force m'abandonne, et le repos me tue.
Phénice ne vient point? Ah! que cette longueur
D'un présage funeste épouvante mon cœur!
Phénice n'aura point de réponse à me rendre.

(Bérénice, IV, 1, ll. 953–59)

The repetition at decreasing intervals enhances the impression conveyed by the words, that of the slow passage of time as Bérénice waits, of her growing impatience, and of her increasing conviction that the message when it comes will be unfavourable. In *Athalie*, there is an example of the opposite. The constant repetition of the name Jéhu in Act III, scene 6 leads up to a speech of Joad, in which the name Jéhu successively introduces a line, a couplet, a sentence of three lines, and finally a quatrain.

Repetition of one character's words by another, though relatively rare in Racine, is occasionally found. In *Britannicus*, Albine tells Agrippine that Néron owes her his love.

Il me le doit, Albine:
Tout, s'il est généreux, lui prescrit cette loi;
Mais tout, s'il est ingrat, lui parle contre moi.

(Britannicus, I, 1, ll. 20–2)

Here the repetition brings out a contrast, as it does in *Iphigénie*, Act III, scene 6. Achille refers to Agamemnon as 'un barbare', 'sanguinaire, parjure', 'le cruel' (ll. 964–92); Iphigénie takes up his words:

Car enfin ce cruel, que vous allez braver,
Cet ennemi barbare, injuste, sanguinaire,
Songez, quoi qu'il ait fait, songez qu'il est mon père.
(ll. 996–8)

In Act II, on the other hand, it is used in a different way, to show what a deep impression someone's words have made. Clytemnestre warns Iphigénie that they must depart, tells her

Pour votre hymen Achille a changé de pensée,
(II, 4, l. 634)

and says to Eriphile,

De vos desseins secrets on est trop éclairci,
Et ce n'est pas Calchas que vous cherchez ici.
(ll. 655–6)

In the next scene, left alone with Eriphile, Iphigénie broods on her mother's words:

Pour mon hymen Achille a changé de pensée;
Il me faut sans honneur retourner sur mes pas;
Et vous cherchez ici quelque autre que Calchas?
(II, 5, ll. 658–60)

When Britannicus tells Agrippine that 'Sylla, Pison, Plautus' are on his side, and she repeats the names (III, 5, l. 907), the repetition seems rather to indicate surprise and incredulity.[5]

Figures of speech help to make the speech of Racine's characters seem stylized and poetic, the product of conscious artistry; though they also, of course, give it force and vividness. Similes are rare,[6] but metaphor and metonymy—the substitution of one thing for another (e.g. the symbol for the thing represented, 'throne' for power, 'blood' for kinship, 'Racine' for Racine's tragedies, 'Rome' for the Roman people, and so forth)—are common. Racine often uses words in their literal and figurative meanings together—the use of *sang*, *nœuds*, *poison*, and *monstre* in this way has been mentioned.[7]

[5] See above, pp. 64, 78–9, for *Mithridate* and *Phèdre*.

[6] Excluding the choruses of *Esther*, the only extended simile in Racine's tragedies occurs in *La Thébaïde* (ll. 218–20).

[7] See above, pp. 29, 79–81, 119. The word *poison* is also used in *Mithridate* both literally and figuratively (as a symbol of love).

Sometimes Racine—like Corneille and other contemporaries—places a dead metaphor in a context that brings it to life again:

L'amour n'est pas un feu qu'on renferme en une âme:
Tout nous trahit, la voix, le silence, les yeux;
Et les feux mal couverts n'en éclatent que mieux.
(*Andromaque*, II, 2, ll. 574–6)

Et dérober au jour une flamme si noire.
(*Phèdre*, I, 3, l. 310)

(There is a good deal of disagreement whether for Racine these words conjured up the image of a black flame, or whether for him they merely meant 'shameful love').

Assez dans ses sillons votre sang englouti
A fait fumer le champ dont il était sorti.
(*Phèdre*, II, 2, ll. 503–4)

Great use is made of a particular kind of metonymy, synecdoche or the substitution of a part for the whole, often of a part of the body for the whole person. Occasionally this is so much a matter of convention that it leads to an unfortunate or nonsensical juxtaposition of words:

Il vous *rapporte un cœur* qu'il n'a pu vous *ôter*.
(*Andromaque*, II, 1, l. 404)

Ton *cœur*, impatient de *revoir* ta Troyenne . . .
(*Andromaque*, IV, 5, l. 1377)

Often, however, synecdoche isolates one aspect of the character, or creates a vivid image:

Quels charmes ont pour vous des yeux infortunés
Qu'à des pleurs éternels vous avez condamnés?
(*Andromaque*, I, 4, ll. 303–4)

Je fuis des yeux distraits,
Qui me voyant toujours, ne me voyaient jamais.
(*Bérénice*, I, 4, ll. 277–8)

Another figure of speech common in Racine is personification, often associated with synecdoche:

Et votre bouche encor, muette à tant d'ennui,
N'a pas daigné s'ouvrir pour se plaindre de lui?
                                   (*Andromaque*, IV, 2, ll. 1139–40)

Personification occasionally results in a graphic image—

Depuis ce coup fatal, le pouvoir d'Agrippine
Vers sa chute, à grands pas, chaque jour s'achemine
                                   (*Britannicus*, I, 1, ll. 111–12)

—, but is usually used in more subdued way. A more typical
example is:

Semble de son amant dédaigner l'inconstance,
Et croit que trop heureux de fléchir sa rigueur . . .
                                   (*Andromaque*, I, 1, 11. 126–7)

A few other figures of speech deserve to be mentioned. Understatement can be highly suggestive:

Crois qu'il m'en a coûté, pour vaincre tant d'amour,
Des combats dont mon cœur saignera plus d'un jour.
                                   (*Bérénice*, II, 2, ll. 453–4)

Racine, like his contemporaries, is fond of associating apparently
contradictory nouns and adjectives—

Favorables périls! Espérance inutile!
                                   (*Iphigénie*, IV, 1, l. 1093)

More characteristic of him is the association of other contradictory
expressions—verbs, or verbs and nouns:

Sa réponse est dictée, et même son silence.
                                   (*Britannicus*, I, 1, l. 120)
M'avez-vous, sans pitié, relégué dans ma cour?
                                   (*Britannicus*, II, 3, l. 546)
Madame, sans mourir, elle est morte pour lui.
                                   (*Britannicus*, V, 8, l. 1722)
Mon règne ne sera qu'un long bannissement . . .
                                   (*Bérénice*, III, 1, l. 754)
Mourrai-je tant de fois sans sortir de la vie?
                                   (*Iphigénie*, V, 4, l. 1673)

Enumeration is very commonly used for many purposes. It may evoke a scene—

> Mais tout dort, et l'armée, et les vents, et Neptune
> > (*Iphigénie*, I, 1, l. 9)

—or express passion:

> Mais fidèle, mais fier, et même un peu farouche,
> Charmant, jeune, traînant tous les cœurs après soi . . .
> > (*Phèdre*, II, 5, ll. 638–9)

Perhaps the best example of enumeration to evoke a scene and at the same time reveal the emotions of the speaker is Bérénice's description of Titus at the apotheosis of Vespasian.[8] Phèdre expresses her jealousy and despair in a long series of questions and statements (IV, 6). Enumeration is often used in narrative, where it may take the form of a series of nouns and participles, conjuring up a more vivid picture than the corresponding verbal nouns would have done.[9]

One other feature of Racine's verse, that shows his artistry and makes it expressive, is its musical quality. Onomatopœia is rare,[10] but alliteration and assonance are found almost everywhere, in both cases related sounds (*b* and *p*, *v* and *f*, *s* and *z*, *ou* and *u*)—not only identical sounds—being associated. There is strict assonance, for instance, in the line:

> Tout m'afflige et me nuit, et conspire à me nuire.
> > (*Phèdre*, I, 3, l. 161)

In the line,

> Le jour n'est pas plus pur que le fond de mon cœur,
> > (*Phèdre*, IV, 2, l. 1112)

strict assonance is confined to the *u* of *plus* and *pur* and the *on* of *fond*

---

[8] See below, p. 148.

[9] E.g. *Andromaque*, ll. 1333–40, and *Iphigénie*, ll. 382–6, quoted respectively on pp. 39 and 108 above. See also *Phèdre*, ll. 77–90. This use of participles is, of course, not confined to enumerations, e.g. 'Britannicus mourant (for 'la mort de Britannicus') excitera le zèle / De ses amis' (*Britannicus*, ll. 1347–8).

[10] E.g. Pour qui sont ces serpents qui sifflent sur vos têtes?
> (*Andromaque*, l. 1638)

and *mon*; but the *ou* of *jour*, the *œu* of *cœur* (foreshadowed by the mute *e*'s of *le*, *que*, and *de*) are related to the *u*, and prepare or prolong it. Alliteration is present in both the lines as well. In fact, the more one reads Racine, the more one finds that he seldom uses sounds in isolation, but that—consonants or vowels—they are usually taken up and woven into a complex pattern.

> Oui, Prince, je languis, je brûle pour Thésée.
> Je l'aime, non point tel que l'ont vu les enfers,
> Volage adorateur de mille objets divers,
> Qui va au Dieu des morts déshonorer la couche;
> Mais fidèle, mais fier, et même un peu farouche,
> Charmant, jeune, traînant tous les cœurs après soi,
> Tel qu'on dépeint nos Dieux, ou tel que je vous voi.
>
> (*Phèdre*, II, 5, ll. 634–40)

This is Racine at his best. The sound pattern—made up of *l*'s, *m*'s and *n*'s, of *j* and *ch* sounds, of *v*'s and *f*'s, *t*'s and *d*'s, *c*'s, *p*'s, *b*'s and *r*'s, of *è* and *é* sounds, of *a*'s and *o*'s, and of *ou*, *u*, *i*, and *eu* sounds,—reaches a climax in the fifth line with its *f*'s and *m*'s, its *i*'s and *è* sounds. Sound and sense combine to give an impression of Phèdre's almost trance-like state.

So far we have considered the nobility, the dignity, the stylization, the conscious artistry of Racine's verse. It is time to consider the other aspect of it—the impression of simplicity, of naturalness, of spontaneity, of uninhibited passion it gives. It is this, no doubt, that Sainte-Beuve had in mind when he said that Racine comes close to prose ('rase la prose')—corrected by Jules Lemaitre to: 'rase la prose, mais avec des ailes' ('skims over the surface of prose, but on wings'). The impression of naturalness and spontaneity is, of course, no less the product of art than the other. It results to some extent from some of the features we have examined already—symmetry, formal patterns, alliteration and assonance, understatement, enumeration, and so forth may well be used to suggest emotion. It results, too, from the discretion and flexibility with which Racine handles some of the devices used more mechanically by his contemporaries—series of parallel lines, for instance.

Racine's use of double-entendre is a good example of his discretion. In his contemporaries, it is often associated with disguise and confusion of identity, a character's speeches having two meanings, one to suit the person he is believed to be and the other the person he really is. In Racine, it is used to conceal the intentions of a character, as when Taxile, about to abandon Porus and join forces with Alexandre, ambiguously says:

Porus fait son devoir, et je ferai le mien.
(*Alexandre*, II, 4, l. 619)

or Néron, unable to refuse point-blank to comply with Agrippine's demands, tells her:

Oui, Madame, je veux que ma reconnaissance
Désormais dans les cœurs grave votre puissance . . .
(*Britannicus*, IV, 2, ll. 1295–6)

or Roxane tells Atalide:

Loin de vous séparer, je prétends aujourd'hui
Par des nœuds éternels vous unir avec lui
(*Bajazet*, V, 6, ll. 1623–4)

—which suggests the bonds of marriage, but really means death. Double-entendre thus creates suspense. It may also be used for dramatic irony, as when Iphigénie asks Agamemnon if she may be present at the sacrifice, unaware that she is to be the victim, and he replies, 'Vous y serez, ma fille' (l. 578).

Features that specifically give an impression of naturalness are the flexibility of Racine's verse, the varied length of his sentences, and the simplicity of his syntax.

In French, the last syllable of a word pronounced in isolation or of a group of words run together is accented. Where words or groups of words are clearly differentiated by the sense, the rhythm is strongly marked.

Bajazet / à vos soins / / tôt ou tard / plus sensi / -ble . . .
(*Bajazet*, V, 6, l. 1593)

is a good example of a line with a strongly marked rhythm, with the main stress falling regularly on the sixth syllable, and with a subsidiary stress in each of the two halves. Racine, however, often writes lines in which there is little or no break in the sense after the sixth syllable, with the result that the accent on that syllable is weak or disappears entirely, and that the main stress falls elsewhere.

J'ai trahi l'un./ / Mais l'au- / tre est peut-ê- / tre un ingrat.
Le temps pres- / / se. Que fai- / re en ce dou- / te funes- / te?
Allons: / / employons bien / le moment / qui nous res- / te.
(Bajazet, III, 8, ll. 1116–18)

Sometimes Racine uses ternary lines like those of the Romantic poets:

Toujours punir, / / toujours trembler / / dans vos projets . . .
(Britannicus, IV, 3, l. 1353)

Et ce vainqueur, / / suivant de près / sa renommée . . .
(Iphigénie, I, 1, l. 109)

The combination of different types of lines gives great flexibility to his verse. So does enjambement, the most daring example of which occurs in *Phèdre:*

Mais tout n'est pas détruit, et vous en laissez vivre
Un . . . Votre fils, Seigneur, me défend de poursuivre.
(Phèdre, V, 3, ll. 1445–6)

There seems to be no stress in the second half of the first line, and the main stress in the second is clearly on the word 'un'.[11]

The varied length of the sentences also makes for naturalness and flexibility. A hemistich, a line, or a couplet may all constitute a complete sentence. Long passages may be composed of quatrains; and though a quatrain is not necessarily filled by a single sentence, it often is. Quatrains may be linked by the repetition of the same rhyme or by assonanced rhymes (e.g. *irs, ille, is* in *Andromaque,* ll. 39–44).

Je ne vois que des tours que la cendre a couvertes,
Un fleuve teint de sang, des campagnes désertes,
Un enfant dans les fers; et je ne puis songer
Que Troie en cet état aspire à se venger.
Ah! si du fils d'Hector la perte était jurée,
Pourquoi d'un an entier l'avons-nous différée?
Dans le sein de Priam n'a-t-on pu l'immoler?
Sous tant de morts, sous Troie il fallait l'accabler.
(Andromaque, I, 2, ll. 201–8)

---

[11] See also below, p. 150.

The division between these two quatrains of a speech of Pyrrhus's is blurred, partly because one consists of a single sentence of four lines, and the other of three sentences (two questions, one of two lines, and two of one line), and partly because three of the four couplets have the same rhyme in *é* (*er* or *ée*).

Sentences, of course, are often longer than four lines in length; but the division of a speech into sentences may cut across the division into lines, another way of giving an impression of flexibility and naturalness, and the structure of Racine's sentences is usually simple, based largely on apposition and enumeration.

> Je jure par le ciel, qui me voit confondue,
> Par ces grands Ottomans dont je suis descendue,
> Et qui tous avec moi vous parlent à genoux
> Pour le plus pur du sang qu'ils ont transmis en nous:
> Bajazet à vos soins tôt ou tard plus sensible,
> Madame, à tant d'attraits n'était pas invincible.
>
> (*Bajazet*, V, 6, ll. 1589–94)

This sentence of six lines is essentially simple: 'I swear: Bajazet was not indifferent to you.' It is filled out, first by the things by which Atalide swears, and second, by her saying what she has to say twice over.[12]

The structure of the sentences is not only simple, but often ungrammatical. Ellipsis makes for concision, as in the second last line of the passage just quoted, where the sense strictly requires: 'Bajazet, *qui aurait été* tôt ou tard . . .' or in:

> Je t'aimais inconstant, qu'aurais-je fait fidèle?
>
> (*Andromaque*, IV, 5, l. 1365)
>
> Trop présente à mes yeux, je croyais lui parler . . .
>
> (*Britannicus*, II, 2, l. 401)
>
> Présente, je vous fuis; absente, je vous trouve . . .
>
> (*Phèdre*, II, 2, l. 542)

Racine often uses the figure of speech known as aposiopesis to give an impression of naturalness: the speaker, overcome by emotion, is unable to continue and breaks off:

[12] See also below, p. 150.

Bérénice.   Parlez.
Titus.   Rome . . . L'Empire . . .
Bérénice.   Hé bien?
Titus.   Sortons, Paulin; je ne lui puis rien dire.
                          (*Bérénice*, II, 4, ll. 623–4)

Je brûle, je l'adore; et loin de la bannir . . .
Ah! c'est un crime encor dont je la veux punir.
                      (*Mithridate*, IV, 5, ll. 1405–6)

The two aspects of Racine's style are, of course, neither inconsistent, nor separate. On the one hand, the same artistry is at work in both; on the other, the shift from one to the other is a means of conveying complex states of mind, of allowing the inner instability to be seen beneath the outer dignity and restraint.

A de moindres faveurs *des* malheureux prétendent,
Seigneur: c'est un exil que *mes* pleurs vous demandent.
                      (*Andromaque*, I, 4, ll. 337–8)

The pretence of detachment gives way to the direct appeal in the second line.

Tu veux que *je* le fuie. Hé bien! rien ne *m*'arrête:
Allons. N'*envions* plus son indigne conquête;
Que sur lui sa captive étende son pouvoir.
Fuyons . . . Mais si l'ingrat rentrait dans son devoir!
Si la foi dans son cœur retrouvait quelque place!
S'il venait à *mes* pieds *me* demander sa grâce!
Si sous *mes* lois, Amour, tu pouvais l'engager.
S'il voulait! . . . Mais l'ingrat ne veut que m'outrager.
Demeurons toutefois pour troubler leur fortune;
Prenons quelque plaisir à leur être importune;
Ou le forçant de rompre un nœud si solennel,
Aux yeux de tous les Grecs *rendons*-le criminel.
J'ai déjà sur le fils attiré leur colère;
Je veux qu'on vienne encor lui demander la mère.
Rendons-lui les tourments qu'elle *me* fait souffrir:
Qu'elle le perde, ou bien qu'il la fasse périr.
                      (*Andromaque*, II, 1, ll. 433–48)

In the grip of her jealousy, Hermione speaks naturally in the first person singular; the royal plural returns when pride reasserts itself, or she thinks of trying to save her face. Similarly, in her diatribe in Act IV, scene 5, she addresses Pyrrhus as *tu* in the first and third sections,[13] when passion is uppermost, but as *vous* in the comparatively serene middle section.

Direct statement may also be all the more effective for the periphrastic passages that precede or follow it, and the juxtaposition of the two may illuminate states of mind. Sometimes periphrasis is the mark of a character who hesitates to tell the truth, and then comes to the point in a burst of frankness, like Antiochus confessing his love to Bérénice:

> Si, dans ce haut degré de gloire et de puissance,
> Il vous souvient des lieux où vous prîtes naissance,
> Madame, il vous souvient que mon cœur en ces lieux
> Reçut le premier trait qui partit de vos yeux.
> J'aimai . . .
>
> (*Bérénice*, I, 4, ll. 187–91)

or Hippolyte telling his father that he loves Aricie.[14]

> *Asaph.*　　　　Seigneur, puisqu'il faut vous le dire,
> 　　　　C'est un de ces captifs à périr destinés,
> 　　　　Des rives du Jourdain sur l'Euphrate amenés.
> *Assuérus.*　Il est donc Juif?
>
> (*Esther*, II, 3, ll. 566–9)

Asaph is afraid to speak, and Assuérus expresses—with almost comic bluntness—what it is that he is hesitating to put into words. Hermione in the following exchange lets the truth slip out and then tries to cover up her embarrassment:

> *Hermione.*　Mais, Seigneur, cependant s'il épouse Andromaque?
> *Oreste.*　　Hé! Madame.
> *Hermione.*　　　　　Songez quelle honte pour nous
> 　　　　Si d'une Phrygienne il devenait l'époux!
> 　　　　(*Andromaque*, II, 2, ll. 570–2)

In the last resort, what makes Racine a great poet and a great dramatic poet is not only the variety of his rhythms, the flexibility of

---

[13] See above, p. 130.　　[14] See above, pp. 133–4.

his verse, its musicality, and the juxtaposition of different styles, but
also the fact that he has something to express. Content and style
cannot be separated, as the examination of a passage may show.

> Le temps n'est plus, Phénice, où je pouvais trembler.
> Titus m'aime, il peut tout, il n'a plus qu'à parler.
> Il verra le sénat m'apporter ses hommages,
> Et le peuple, de fleurs couronner ses images.
>   De cette nuit, Phénice, as-tu vu la splendeur?   5
> Tes yeux ne sont-ils pas tout pleins de sa grandeur?
> Ces flambeaux, ce bûcher, cette nuit enflammée,
> Ces aigles, ces faisceaux, ce peuple, cette armée,
> Cette foule de rois, ces consuls, ce sénat,
> Qui tous, de mon amant empruntaient leur éclat;   10
> Cette pourpre, cet or, que rehaussait sa gloire,
> Et ces lauriers encor témoins de sa victoire;
> Tous ces yeux qu'on voyait venir de toutes parts
> Confondre sur lui seul leurs avides regards;
> Ce port majestueux, cette douce présence.   15
> Ciel! avec quel respect et quelle complaisance
> Tous les cœurs en secret l'assuraient de leur foi!
> Parle: peut-on le voir sans penser comme moi
> Qu'en quelque obscurité que le sort l'eût fait naître,
> Le monde, en le voyant, eût reconnu son maître?   20
> Mais, Phénice, où m'emporte un souvenir charmant?
>   Cependant Rome entière, en ce même moment,
> Fait des vœux pour Titus, et par des sacrifices
> De son règne naissant célèbre les prémices.
> Que tardons-nous? Allons, pour son empire heureux,   25
> Au ciel, qui le protège, offrir aussi nos vœux.
> Aussitôt, sans l'attendre, et sans être attendue,
> Je reviens le chercher, et dans cette entrevue
> Dire tout ce qu'aux cœurs l'un de l'autre contents
> Inspirent des transports retenus si longtemps.   30
>   *(Bérénice*, I, 5, ll. 297–326)

This speech of Bérénice that concludes the first act of the tragedy is
at once lyrical and dramatic. Her confidante's doubts whether Titus
will marry her, she answers by this passionate affirmation. Her own
devotion to Titus is revealed by the tone of her description and by

her conviction that it is her lover who sheds lustre on the whole scene; but at the same time what she says confirms the doubts expressed by Phénice. This it does in two ways: Bérénice admits at the end (l. 27) that she is not in touch with Titus; and the very description in which she pours out her own love also makes clear the obstacles to their union and condenses into a graphic tableau the essential situation of the tragedy. And this, again, it does in two ways. The speech is an evocation of Imperial Rome—the ceremony described is the apotheosis of a Roman Emperor, Titus's father,—and the references to the eagles, the fasces, the purple, the senate, the consuls, the subject kings (Bérénice's peers), the Roman habit of decorating the statues of Emperors with flowers, all remind us that this is Rome, with institutions inherited from Republican days, and an inveterate hatred of kings and queens. Moreover, this is a good example of the significance of the eye in Racine: the word *voir* occurs four times, and the word *yeux* twice, and lines 13 and 14 depict Titus with the eyes of the world fixed upon him. Although Bérénice has yet to realize it, he is not his own master, not free to obey his desires. The act thus ends on a note of uncertainty.

The description is impressionistic and vivid, the contrast between the torches and the blazing pyre on the one hand, and the surrounding darkness on the other, summed up in the bold phrase, 'cette nuit enflammée', recalls the sharp contrast of light and darkness in some of the paintings of the period. The description of Titus (ll. 15–20) was no doubt intended as a compliment to Louis XIV, marked out as a king from all other men, according to Saint-Simon, by his stature, his majestic bearing, and his noble looks.

The passage gives the impression of being a passionate outburst, of being natural and sincere. For once, there is no logical argument, but an emotional progression. The speech falls into three parts: (1) an affirmation that Titus loves Bérénice and is all-powerful (ll. 1–4); (2) a description of Titus, subdivided into the description of the scene and the spectators (ll. 5–14) and that of Titus himself (ll. 15–21); and (3) a statement of Bérénice's intention of joining Rome in celebrating his accession and of going to see him.

The impression of spontaneity is due to many things. There is great variety in the length of the sentences of which the speech is made up. Two sentences of one line, one of two lines, and two questions of one line each precede a long sentence of nine lines. Then

come four sentences varying between one and three lines in length
and the terse question, 'Que tardons-nous', and the speech ends with
a sentence of just under six lines. The syntax is simple, with enumeration playing a great part: the central paragraph consists of three
questions, separated by a long series of nouns—giving the impression that Bérénice is launched, that emotion has taken over, that she
is beyond the reach of reason. This impression is strengthened by the
fact that the syntax is not only simple, but also incorrect. Racine
effectively uses the two rhetorical devices of aposiopesis and
anacoluthon. With modern punctuation, the full stop at the end of
line 15 would be a dash or a three-dot pause. The sentence is incom-
plete; it has no verb; Bérénice, overcome by emotion, cannot finish
it, and breaks off. The last four lines are muddled: '*Je* reviens . . . dire
tout ce qu'*aux cœurs l'un de l'autre contents*'. Once again, emotion has
got the better of reason; Bérénice seems to have passed from 'I' to 'we'.
But perhaps there is a deeper significance in her confusion than that.
It looks as if she were unwittingly letting the cat out of the bag,
betraying the fact that it is she who is speaking for them both, that
she is attributing her own feelings to Titus (as, in the body of the
speech, in lines 6, 13–14, 16–17, and 18–20, she attributes her own
feelings to Phénice and the spectators of the scene). The anacoluthon
increases the uncertainty in the minds of the audience.

The alexandrines in the first twenty-one lines have on the whole a
strong, regular beat, particularly in the enumeration. This ceases
when the climax is reached, signalled by the long, unbroken, slow
distiches (ll. 13–14, 16–17) and the irregular rhythm of lines 16 and
18, in both of which the main stress falls on the first syllable. All this
reinforces the impression of an incantation or a hallucination. In the
last eight lines, the rhythm becomes less marked, and the sense is
carried over from one line to the next.

Alliteration and assonance contribute greatly, not only to the
harmony of the passage, but to its emotional, hypnotic character.
There is not space for a detailed analysis of the sound patterns of the
whole passage; two lines must suffice. Lines 16 and 17 can be
transcribed in phonetic symbols thus:

$$\text{s} \quad \text{l} \;/\; \text{v} \;\; \text{k} \;/\; \text{k} \;\; \text{l} \;/\; \text{r} \;\; \text{sp} \quad /\; \text{k} \;\; \text{l} \;/\; \text{k} \quad \text{pl} \quad \text{z} \;\; \text{s}$$
$$\quad \text{j} \;\; \varepsilon \;/\; \text{a} \;\; \varepsilon \;/\; \quad \varepsilon \;/\; \quad \varepsilon \;\; \varepsilon \;/\; \text{e} \;/\; \quad \varepsilon \;/\; \quad \tilde{\text{ɔ}} \quad \varepsilon \quad \tilde{\text{a}}$$

t | l | k rz | | s kr | l s r | d | l r | f
u| ɛ| œ | ɑ̃| ə ɛ | a y ɛ| ə œ | wa

It will be noticed that in the first line, the sound *è* (ɛ) occurs seven times and the closely related *é* (e) once; and that, in the second, a similar pattern of vowels occurs in each of the two hemistiches: u—ɛ—œ—ɑ̃/y—ɛ—œ—wa. The *a* and *è* (ɛ) sounds and nasals of the second line take up the *a* and the nasal and the *è* (ɛ) sounds of the first. As regards consonants, *l*'s, *r*'s, and *k*, *s* and *z* sounds predominate. The *v* of line 16 and the *f* of line 17 hark back to the alliteration of *v*'s and *f*'s in lines 12–14.

This is not the only sign that there is conscious artistry at work, that this speech is deliberately poetic. Others are the progression of line 7 ('flambeaux'—'bûcher'—'nuit enflammée'); the passage from the inanimate to the human components of the scene, leading up to the close-up of Titus himself (one is reminded of the cinema); the contrast between the succession of nouns beginning with 'ce', 'cette', or 'ces' and the single, emphatic 'mon amant'; the contrast between the lengthy enumeration and the occasional simple, direct lines (2, 27–8); the inversion of lines 4, 5, 10, 14, 17, 24, and 29–30; the personification, associated with synecdoche in lines 13–14 and 17, and with metonymy in line 22 ('Rome entière'); and the symmetry and the chiasmus of line 15 ('Ce port majestueux, cette douce présence'). Other examples of balance and symmetry are the two parallel questions of lines 5 and 6, expressing the same idea, though with a significant difference, the first stressing the past, the second the living memory, and line 27 ('sans l'attendre, et sans être attendue'), in which the similarity of the two halves is emphasized by the repetition of the verb. After the personal nature of the body of the speech ('*mon* amant', l. 10; 'comme *moi*', l. 18; '*je* reviens', l. 28), the personification of the last two lines ('des transports' that 'inspirent') and the generalization ('tout ce qu'aux cœurs') bring it to a close with a touch of detachment and nobility.

9

Conclusion

Racine is a 'classic' in T. S. Eliot's sense, that is to say a careful craftsman with a long tradition behind him, who invents neither his matter nor his manner, but uses a dramatic form, a dramatic style already existing, and draws on materials present in the work of his predecessors. Without Corneille, without Thomas Corneille and Quinault, without Euripides and Seneca, without Sophocles and Virgil and Homer, Racine's plays would have been very different. Everything that he owed to his predecessors, however, was assimilated, and, passing through his mind, was transfigured, transformed into something different and original. The world of Racine's tragedies is *his* world, and unique.

All his technical skill and his verbal mastery are directed towards creating 'a simple action, sustained by the violence of the passions, the beauty of the sentiments, and the elegance of the expression' (preface to *Britannicus*), towards arousing our emotions by depicting, in basic human situations, unhappy, suffering, distressed, tormented characters, who move us, in the last resort, by their truth to nature. In Racine, there is little grandiloquence; no characters say the opposite of what we expect, or act apparently out of character. When Hermione says to her confidante:

> De tout ce que tu vois tâche de ne rien croire;
> Crois que je n'aime plus, vante-moi ma victoire;
> Crois que dans son dépit mon cœur est endurci,
> Hélas! et s'il se peut, fais-le-moi croire aussi,
>
> (*Andromaque*, II, 1, ll. 429–32)

the last words strike home because they reveal, not only that she is deluding herself, but that she knows that she is deluding herself. Quinault's Stratonice also repeats the word 'croire' in an expression of disappointed love;[1] but the repetition is overdone, and it is her interlocutor who comments, 'Ah, c'est un peu trop croire'. Hermione herself makes the comment; and we are moved by her realization of her vulnerability.

After the confession of her love to Hippolyte, Phèdre and Œnone see Thésée approaching with Hippolyte. 'On vient; je vois Thésée', says Œnone. 'Ah! je vois Hippolyte', says Phèdre (l. 909). There is an essential rightness about this remark, though exactly what it expresses is open to everyone of us to interpret—a passionate woman's preoccupation with her lover, shame, fear of betrayal, or a mixture of all three? There is nothing intrinsically poetic in the words, 'Je vois Hippolyte'; they are moving because of their context, because they reveal the workings of the unconscious—not the rational—mind. They say little; they are expressive because of what they suggest. This is equally true of such lines as:

> Parle-lui tous les jours des vertus de son père,
> Et quelquefois aussi parle-lui de sa mère.
> (*Andromaque*, IV, 1, ll. 1117–8)

> Titus vous chérissait, vous admiriez Titus.
> Cent fois je me suis fait une douceur extrême
> D'entretenir Titus dans un autre lui-même.
> (*Bérénice*, I, 4, ll. 270–2)

When, on the other hand, Roxane says:

> Avec quelle insolence et quelle cruauté
> Ils se jouaient tous deux de ma crédulité!
> (*Bajazet*, IV, 5, ll. 1295–6)

we are moved less by what the lines say or suggest, than by the fact that they are not a reply to what Zatime has just said, which Roxane, intent upon her own thoughts, does not heed, or has not heard.

The more obviously poetical passages in Racine, such as Néron's account of the abduction of Junie or Bérénice's description of Titus in his splendour, may be intrinsically magnificent, but they are doubly moving for what they reveal of the speaker's feelings.

---

[1] See above, p. 9.

Songe, songe, Céphise, à cette nuit cruelle
Qui fut pour tout un peuple une nuit éternelle.
Figure-toi Pyrrhus, les yeux étincelants,
Entrant à la lueur de nos palais brûlants,
Sur tous mes frères morts se faisant un passage,
Et de sang tout couvert échauffant le carnage.
Songe aux cris des vainqueurs, songe aux cris des mourants,
Dans la flamme étouffés, sous le fer expirants.
Peins-toi dans ces horreurs Andromaque éperdue:
Voilà comme Pyrrhus vint s'offrir à ma vue . . .
                    (*Andromaque*, III, 8, ll. 997–1006)

This is a splendid evocation of the scene: the darkness of the night contrasting with the flames of burning Troy, Pyrrhus and his men slaughtering, Andromaque cowering, a horrified eye–witness. But it is not just an objective description; it reveals and explains Andromaque's revulsion from Pyrrhus. The passage is lyrical as well as descriptive, because it is coloured by Andromaque's feelings; and it is dramatic because of its bearing on the relationship of the characters of the tragedy.

The truth to nature of Racine's tragedies is not only a matter of detail, but an essential feature of all his characterization. There are plenty of criminals in Racine; but there are few villains. Pyrrhus forces Andromaque to marry him by the unscrupulous abuse of his power; Hermione incites Oreste to murder Pyrrhus; and Oreste obeys. But we are aware that they are people like ourselves, driven beyond endurance by passions common to us all; we watch with horror, but also with sympathy. The supreme instance in Racine of a guilty character for whom we feel sympathy is Phèdre; but she is not the only one. Unprepossessing as Mithridate is in many ways, we can admire his courage, and feel for him in his inward conflict and distress. The once efficient Athalie is pathetic in her disturbed state of mind. When the sight of the child, Joas, arouses her pity, the latent, long unsatisfied need for an object on which to lavish her affection, one is reminded of the formidable Lady Macbeth, unable to kill Duncan because he reminded her of her father as he slept; the same touch of nature is there in both. Néron's nature has no better side, but even he to some extent arouses our sympathy in his desire to shake off the yoke of a possessive and tyrannical mother and in his distraction after the loss of Junie. Above all, Racine makes us aware that he is the helpless victim both of heredity and environment.

Whatever doubts one may feel in a general way about Keats's somewhat facile equation of beauty and truth, there is a sense in which it is applicable to Racine. The beauty of his tragedies, their impact, is in the last resort due to their human truth.

Translation of
Quotations

Note: Some of the quotations in Chapter 9, illustrating points of style, have been translated more literally than the rest. A few, illustrating word patterns or sound effects, have been left untranslated.

P. 7, 1. 28. You are dismayed, madam, and your countenance is discomposed.

1. 30. Come hither, Nero, and take your seat.

1. 32. I hear the thunder rumbling, and feel the earth quaking.

P. 8, 1. 19. I am robbed of her heart, I am robbed of her love.

1. 21. Either the sister's hand, or the brother's head.

1. 23. And betraying you now is being true to you.

1. 26. To have too much virtue is to be criminal.

1. 28. Rome is no longer in Rome, she is all where I am.

1. 31. He obeys orders in his party, you give them in yours; you are head of one, and he a subject in the other.

P. 9, 1. 3. Sophonisba, in short, although a captive and in tears, triumphs over Eryxa, although a queen and victorious.

1. 9. I took him from you valiant, noble, full of honour, and I give him back to you cowardly, ungrateful, and a poisoner; I took him from you honourable, and I give him back faithless; I give him back a poltroon,

and took him fearless; I took him as the greatest of African princes, and I give him back, in a word, as the slave of the Romans.

l. 18.   *Stratonice.* I do not doubt it, and my astonished heart believes far more than you have said. I believe that the Prince is so unfair as always to try to make you think ill of me; I believe that he cannot look on my marriage without regret; I believe that my happiness is his secret torment; I believe that he wants to deprive me of the greatness I am acquiring; I believe that he is influencing you against me.
Seleucus. You believe a little too much.

l. 30.   In Sertorius, I love that great skill in warfare that enables an outlaw to defy the whole world; in him, I love that laurel-crowned head, that brow that makes the bravest warriors tremble, that arm that seems to have victory as its birthright.

P. 10, l. 5   This heart, this craven heart dared to grant too much.

l. 7.   Cast, cast your eyes, my son, on this object; seek, seek in him a father's murderer.

l. 13.   You will tell the Queen . . .—Well, I shall tell her?—Nothing, Sire, nothing yet; to-morrow I shall think about it.

l. 21.   My father is trying to make me hate him; but he himself once ordered me to love him. If I love unjustly, I loved at first without crime. I received a lawful command from his mouth, and usually it is far easier to obey when one is asked to love than when one is told to hate. I loved him from duty, I loved him from habit; and once one has allowed a first love to be awakened, Julia, one finds that it is so sweet to love that one cannot easily lose the habit.

n. 6.   My heart, my craven heart feels pity for him?

P. 11, l. 1.   *Elpidia.* You are losing a lover, and I a son.
Aristida. What, you are losing a son, and I a lover?

l. 8.   He owes it to you, madam.—He owes it to me, Barcea, but what use is a hand constrained by duty?

l. 13.   Whatever happens, Syrtis will welcome you; in that retreat you will hold out, and for a long time. Meanwhile my father is making good his defeat; Hanno has brought help from Spain; and Hannibal himself will be here in a day or two.

l. 21.   Did you promise me them, when, on my defeat, you proposed Syrtis to me as a safe retreat, and when, in addition to your general's help, you held out hopes of that of Hanno and Hannibal?

n. 7.   He owes you his love.—He owes it to me, Albina . . .

P. 13, l. 11.   I hearken to my love, and hear nothing besides.

l. 21.   Always everything for you, and nothing ever for myself.

l. 29.   You have ordained that the murderer shall perish, and since I am he, I must obey; your wishes are my laws, and since you desire my death, I should have betrayed you, had I not given myself up.

P. 14, l. 4.   I prefer suffering near her to pleasure elsewhere.

l. 21.   I am not the man to help my rival.

l. 31.   To love at will is beyond our power. . . One often loves when one least wants to.

n. 11.   One does not always love the one whom one would like to love.

You whom I have pitied, in short whom I should like to love.—I understand you. Such is my unhappy lot: the heart is for Pyrrhus, and the good will for Orestes.

P. 15, l. 2.   I want to stop loving you, and lack the strength.

l. 8.   It is unseemly for a great queen to show love and to see dislike.

l. 16.   I shall never believe that there is a delight equal to that of seeing one's rival sacrificed to oneself.

l. 26.   If this ingrate perishes, I must die. I feel rage and affection, hatred and love by turns uppermost in my heart; I am his enemy, and I love him. When my displeasure grows, my passion increases; and although he is worthy of love, and although he has betrayed me, I cannot love him, and I cannot hate him.

P. 16, l. 5.   Goes as far as hatred, and yet, alas! I should hate you but little, if I did not love you.

l. 15.   What do you want, madam? I cannot tell.—What I want, alas! How should you know, if I do not?

l. 21.   Alas! I deluded myself, when I thought I hated him.

l. 29.   A criminal who has our heart is always innocent.

n. 13.   I am afraid to know myself in my present state.

n. 14.   Who told you to?

P. 17, l. 1.   His destruction is now my sole desire. I feel that I should witness his death with pleasure.

l. 5.   What, you have deprived me of one so charming, and you think you can escape my resentment?

l. 17.   Absence has produced its usual effect on me. Cleona whom I loved, is at last ceasing to rule my heart. . . I have seen Leonida again, and the sight of her fanned the embers of my love into a blaze.

l. 23.   The nearer a loved one is, the more powerful she is.

n. 15.   Love is not a fire that one shuts up in a soul: everything betrays us, the voice, silence, the eyes; and ill-banked fires merely blaze the more fiercely.

It is feared that the daring flame [i.e. love] of the sister may one day revive the ashes of her brothers.

P. 18, l. 4.   He loves me; not that he has dared to tell me; he has spared no effort to conceal his love; silence has always reigned over his mouth; but has a heart only one way of expressing itself? Does one say nothing with one's eyes, when the mouth is mute? The lover who most fears to reveal his feelings always says but too much to her who is willing to hear him; one vainly makes every effort to hold oneself in check; everything speaks in love, even silence itself.

l. 19.   My love is a mistake; but this mistake is dear to me. Your faithful advice is mistimed; love has not yet given way to my reason.

l. 27.   But what inflames you against Seleucus, madam? He has shown nothing but esteem for you.—Zenona, that is true, but the Prince his son has hitherto shown nothing but contempt for me.—The King spares no

effort to please you.—Prince Antiochus does not behave in the same way.—The King will love you; ask
for nothing more.—But the Prince his son will never
love me.—You so often name this son, opposed to
your wishes, that it looks as if he touches you more
nearly than his father.

n. 16. Everything betrays us, the voice, silence, the eyes. . .

I shall hear glances that you think mute.

P. 19, l. 13. As soon as my eyes encountered his, new emotions
were kindled in my heart. At the time I took them to
be hatred; and believing that my hatred had increased, I began to love. I at first attributed my unrest
to my hatred; I did not resist it, I accepted it without
difficulty; and when I perceived the error of my feelings, I tried to resist them, but too late.

l. 27. How can I accept the privileges of the diadem, if I
have not learned to govern myself? and by what unbridled thirst for the vain title of king, exert an
authority over others that I lack over myself?

n. 17. I, reign? I, bring a state under my sway, when my
weak reason no longer rules me! When I have abandoned control of my feelings.

P. 20, l. 13. I dearly loved the throne, and yet not so much as you;
only with you could life have appealed to me; but
without the throne and without you, what use is
life?

l. 18. Your son is no more, I cannot delude myself; nature
says so, and I dare not doubt it; but this doubt is so
sweet that murmuring love would like, if it dared, to
give the lie to nature.

l. 25. Everything injures me; everything destroys me; and
everything drives me to despair.

n. 18. Everything distresses and injures me, and conspires
to injure me.

P. 27, n. 5. *Stella.* The people, to whom God has vouchsafed the
right to interpret [the will of] the gods and to make
kings, must have taught you by its disturbances that
it revokes the decree that you caused to be pro-

claimed, that your efforts only serve to make you hated, and that I alone am to be obeyed.

Aurora. Know that if the people opposes my rule, its commotions show the justice of my cause; it is a monster with no discernment, which blindly seeks disorder, and which, such is its audacity, always turns against the sovereigns to whom it should be subject; in short, its wrath is not such as to alarm me; I can disarm it with a single glance.

Taxile. The people loves kings who know how to spare it.

Porus. It esteems even more those who know how to govern.

P. 28, l.   1.   He has the people on his side.—And I have the gods on mine.

l.   5.   One has the people on his side, and the other justice.

P. 29, l.   6.   Olympias, support me; my grief is great.

l. 22.   And blood will resume its customary sway.

P. 30, l.   9.   But a son is left to me; and I feel that I love him, rebel and even my rival as he is.

l. 14.   There is no fortune equal to my happiness, and in me you are about to see, on this auspicious day, the man of ambition on the throne, and the lover crowned.

l. 20.   The throne has always been my dearest passion . . . I take no step that does not lead to sovereignty.

l. 26.   What? you love her, Sire?—Do you expect me at my age to serve the base apprenticeship of love?

P. 32, l. 10.   How do you want me to treat you?—As a king.

l. 13.   Be neither.—And what shall I be?—A king.

P. 33, l. 18.   So many states, so many seas that are about to separate us will soon efface me from your memory. When one day the uneasy ocean sees you complete the conquest of the world on his waves, when you see kings fall on their knees, and the quaking earth hushed in your presence, will you remember, Sire, that a young princess in the depths of her states regrets you ceaselessly, and recalls in her heart the blissful moments when that great conqueror assured her of his love?

P. 34, l. 26.   I was deluding myself.

l. 27.   More than a hundred times.

l. 29.   In this extreme turmoil marry her he hates and punish her he loves.

l. 33.   Always ready to depart, and always remaining.

P. 35, l. 2.   See p. 16, n. 13 above.

l. 7.   But the ingrate merely wishes to insult me.

l. 12.   Ah! I did not think he was so close at hand.

l. 19.   See p. 16, n. 14 above.

l. 25.   Henceforth my heart, if it does not love passionately, must hate violently.

P. 36, l. 1.   Ungrateful as he is, death with him will be sweeter to me than life with you.

l. 6.   What a pleasure to revenge my insult myself, to draw back my hand stained with the false one's blood, and, in order to intensify his sufferings and my pleasure, to hide my rival from his dying glances.

l. 17.   Love does not govern the fate of a princess: the glory of obedience is all that remains to us.

l. 26.   Let us save him. Our efforts would become impotent if he were to recover his fury with his consciousness here.

n. 13.   Were you looking for me, madam?—I was on my way to my son's place of captivity.

P. 37, l. 5.   I did not love you, cruel man? What, then, did I do?

l. 13.   You were coming to observe the pallor of my brow, in order to go and laugh in her arms at my suffering.

l. 18.   See p. 15, n. 11 above.

l. 27.   He was never better loved.

l. 30.   Ah! do not wish for Pyrrhus's destiny: I should hate you too much.—You would love me all the more.

P. 38, l. 6.   He would have forfeited your love, if he could have forfeited your love.

P. 39, l. 7.   Must I forget Hector, deprived of funeral rites and dragged ignominiously round our walls?

l. 21.   Hector fell at his hands; Troy expired at yours.

l. 25.   The valour of Hector's aged father struck down at

the feet of his family, expiring in his sight, while your arm, buried in his breast, sought a remnant of blood frozen by age; burning Troy plunged into streams of blood; Polyxena slaughtered by your own hand before the eyes of all the Greeks, indignant with you: what can one deny these courageous blows?

P. 40, l. 13.   I recall what this city was formerly, so proud with its ramparts, so rich in heroes, mistress of Asia; and then I consider what Troy's fate has been and what its destiny is. I see only towers covered with ashes, a river stained with blood, a deserted countryside, a child in fetters.

P. 43, l. 24.   His wrinkles have engraved his deeds on his forehead.

P. 45, l. 26.   I, daughter, wife, sister, and mother of your masters.

n. 5.   Perhaps your pen owes to the censors of Pyrrhus the noblest characteristics with which you portrayed Burrhus.

P. 46, l. 16.   My orders brought the senate together in the palace, and behind a curtain, invisible and present, I was the all-powerful soul of that great body.

l. 22.   Rose to forestall me, and hastening to embrace me, led me away from the throne on which I was about to seat myself.

P. 48, l. 15.   I must hold the balance between them and me, so that some day, in the same way, Britannicus may hold it between my son and me.

l. 28.   Monster coming to birth.

l. 30.   Everything: Octavia, Agrippina, Burrus, Seneca, all Rome, and three years of virtue.

P. 49, l. 3.   In his face I discern the sullen and savage humour of the cruel Domitii. With the haughtiness that he has taken from their blood, he mixes the cruelty of the Neros that he has drawn from my body.

l. 12.   I even loved her tears, of which I was the cause.

l. 17.   Nero will not be jealous with impunity.

l. 25.   She loves my rival, as I am well aware; but I shall take delight in driving him to despair. I cherish a charming vision of his anguish.

P. 53, l. 23. Almost the whole of the East is about to submit to her sway.

l. 34. I hope that when I come back she will no longer be able to doubt my love.

P. 54, l. 2. I came to you without knowing my purpose: my love drew me on; and I was perhaps coming to seek myself and to know myself.

l. 15. All my moments are but an eternal transition from fear to hope, from hope to fury.

l. 28. In the empty East how my grief grew!

l. 31. I flee abstracted eyes that, seeing me always, never saw me.

l. 35. Struggles from which my heart will bleed for more than one day.

P. 55, l. 15. For ever? Ah! Sire, are you thinking in your heart how terrible that cruel word is when one is in love? In a month, in a year, how shall we allow, Sire, so many seas to separate me from you? the day to begin and the day to end without Titus's ever being able to see Berenice, without my ever, all day long, being able to see Titus!

l. 28. You are Emperor, Sire, and weeping.

P. 56, l. 7. Let us all three serve the universe as an example of the most tender and the most unhappy love of which it can preserve the doleful history.

l. 30. You won no great victory, false man, when you deluded this prepossessed heart, which itself was afraid of being undeceived.

P. 57, l. 1. You, Zatima, keep my rival here. Let him, as he dies, have only her cries as a farewell. Let her meanwhile be faithfully tended. Take care of her: her life is necessary to my hatred. Ah! if she was so easily filled with concern for my lover that fears for his life brought her to the brink of death, what additional vengeance and fresh delight to show him to her, pale and dead, to see her looks fixed on that object repay me for the pleasure that I afforded them!

l. 16. My joy and my happiness depend on you.

l. 28. So at last it is all over; and by my wiles, my unjust suspicions, my unlucky whims, I have at last reached the grievous moment when I see my lover dying as the result of my crime.

P. 58, l. 19.   That slave is no more. An order, dear Osmin, caused him to be hurled into the depths of the Black Sea.

P. 59, l. 20.   Bajazet is worthy of love. He saw that his salvation depended on winning her, and he soon won her.

   l. 27.   At last, with eyes that revealed her soul, she held out her hand as a pledge of her love. He, with eloquent glances, full of love, assured her in his turn of his passion, madam.

   n. 20.   As for me, I use this passion only in so far as it serves my ambition.

P. 60, l. 23.   If he goes out, he dies.

   l. 25.   And if ever I was dear to you. . .

   l. 26.   Go.

P. 62, l. 28.   My virtue mistrusts my weak efforts. I know that on seeing you a fond memory may wring an unworthy sigh from my heart, that I shall see my soul, secretly torn in twain, fly back to the lover from whom it is separated.

   l. 35.   Father, I am a woman, and I know my weakness; I already feel my heart taking pity on him; and I shall, no doubt, despite my marriage vows, give vent to a sigh unworthy of you and of me.

P. 63, l. 33   Heaven will suggest to me what course I must adopt.

   l. 36.   Heaven will suggest to me what I now must do.

P. 64, l. 1.   A hand dear to me.

Fearing the treachery of the dearest hands.

   l. 4.   A hand that was very dear to us thus pays us out for refusing to strike too inhuman a blow.

   l. 14.   This victorious son, this enemy of Rome, and this other self of yours, this Xiphares.

P. 67, l. 10.   That Achilles, the author of your sufferings and of mine, whose bloody hand carried me away a prisoner, who with one blow snatched my birth and your father from me, everything about whom, even his very name, should be hateful to me, is the dearest of all mortals in my eyes.

l. 21.   As soon as her blood flowed and stained the ground red, the gods caused thunder to be heard on the altar; the winds sent welcome tremors through the air; and the sea answered them with its roar. The distant shore moaned, white with foam. The flame of the pyre kindled itself of its own accord. The sky glared with lightning, opened, and spread a holy awe amongst us that reassured us all. The astonished soldiery says that Diana in a cloud came right down to the pyre, and believes that, as she rose through its flames, she bore our incense and our prayers to heaven.

P. 68, l. 4.   To complete my unhappiness, the gods every night, as soon as a light slumber suspended my anxieties, the gods, deprived of their altars' bloody privilege and revengeful, came and reproached me with my sacrilegious pity. Presenting the thunderbolt to my troubled mind, their arms raised in readiness, they threatened my obduracy.

l. 18.   You are not untrue to an ill-starred race. Yes, you are the blood of Atreus and Thyestes.

l. 22.   Your eyes will behold me again in Orestes, my brother. May he, alas! bring less sorrow to his mother!

l. 30.   Ready to confirm their august alliance.

P. 73, l. 8.   Aricia must be destroyed.

l. 17.   A dying woman, seeking to die.

l. 29.   Ye gods! why am I not sitting in the forests' shade! When shall I be able, through a cloud of noble dust, to gaze after a chariot flying through the arena?

l. 34.   Whither am I allowing my wishes and my mind to stray?

P. 74, l. 3.   He is not dead, since he breathes in you. Before my eyes, I forever think I see my husband. I see him, I speak to him, and my heart. . . I wander, Sire; my fond passion bursts forth in spite of myself.

l. 11.   Do you think this so shameful admission voluntary?

l. 17. What am I doing? Where is my reason straying? I jealous! And I am appealing to Theseus!

P. 75, l. 14. No, great gods! let this horrible secret remain buried in profound oblivion.

l. 18. I have been unable to conceal from you—judge if I love you—everything that I wanted to conceal from myself.

l. 28. But innocence after all has nothing to fear.

l. 30. Let us have the courage to rely on the justice of the gods.

l. 34. I hate even the protection with which the gods honour me, and I am withdrawing to bewail their deadly favours.

P. 76, l. 15. Wretched creature! and I live? and I tolerate the sight of the sacred sun from whom I am descended? I have as my grandfather the father and the master of the gods; the heavens, the whole universe, are full of my ancestors. Where can I hide? Let us flee into the darkness of Hell. But what am I saying? My father holds the urn of destiny there; fate, it is said, has entrusted it to his stern hands: in Hell, Minos judges all the pallid members of the human race.

l. 36. In proud revolt against love.

l. 37. From earliest youth opposed to love.

P. 77, l. 13. My eyes recognized him in his father's features.

l. 22. Neptune protects him, and that tutelary god will not be besought in vain by my father.

l. 29. Although you have only a faint glimmer of life left, my soul shall go down to the dead first. A thousand open paths always lead thither, and my just grief will choose the shortest. Cruel woman, when did my loyalty ever betray you?

P. 78, l. 3. When you know my crime, and the fate that overwhelms me, I shall die none the less; I shall die more burdened with guilt.

l. 9. The Cretan monster would have perished at your hands.

l. 13. I shall not see a rival preferred to me.

l. 15. Allow the lasting memory of a brave death, immortalizing a life so nobly ended, to prove to all posterity that I was your son.

l. 23. Sire, he was bidding me an eternal farewell.

l. 32. Given up to cruel monsters by this barbarian.

P. 79, l. 1. He maintains that Aricia has his heart, his love, that he is in love.

l. 6. Hippolytus is capable of feeling and feels nothing for me! Aricia has his heart! Aricia has his love!

l. 10. My murderous hands, eager to avenge me, burn to plunge themselves into innocent blood.

l. 14. Heaven be thanked, my hands are not criminal.

l. 18. Remember that, as a reward for my fortunate efforts, you promised to grant the first of my wishes.

l. 22. Be afraid, Sire, be afraid lest implacable heaven hate you enough to grant your wishes.

l. 30. I am in love! Do not think that at the moment I love you, I deem myself innocent and approve of myself; nor that my dastardly self-indulgence has nourished the poison of the crazy love that disturbs my reason.

P. 80, l. 2. Ye gods! What will the King say? What a baneful poison love has poured over his whole house!

l. 6. A fatal and profaned place where virtue breathes a poisoned air.

l. 14. Ye gods! why am I not sitting in the forests' shade!

l. 17. I was trying to safeguard my reputation by dying, and to remove such a black flame [i.e. shameful passion] from the light of day.

l. 20. Let us flee into the darkness of Hell.

l. 26. So far no monsters subdued by me have given me the right to err like him.

l. 32. Worthy son of the hero who has given you birth, deliver the universe from a monster who irritates you. The widow of Theseus dares to love Hippolytus! Believe me, this dreadful monster must not escape you.

P. 81, l. 7. Your invincible hands have freed the human race from countless monsters; but they are not all destroyed, and you are allowing one to remain alive . . .

l. 17.   And death, depriving my eyes of light, restores to the light of day, which they sullied, all its purity.

P. 83, n. 1.   He knows that he owes everything to me.

P. 86, l. 6.   The band of the children of Levi, divided into detachments, is stationed in profound silence at the gates. They are all to rush out at the same moment and shout as a signal: "Long live King Joas!"

l. 23.   Sometimes, seeing her insatiable thirst for gold, he persuades her that, in a place known to you alone, you are hiding treasures amassed by David.

l. 28.   It is true, one of David's treasures has been preserved.

P. 87, l. 13.   The terror of vain remorse perturbs that great soul. She wavers, she hesitates; in short, she is a woman.

l. 21.   I see the bearing and the gestures of Ahaziah.

l. 27.   An instinct impelled me to enter the temple of the Jews, and I conceived the notion of appeasing their God.

l. 31.   I do not know whether the angel of God, unveiling himself, came and displayed a glittering sword to her; but her tongue straightway froze in her mouth, and all her audacity seemed to be laid low. Her eyes, as if terrified, dared not look away. Eliacin, above all, seemed to alarm her.

P. 88, l. 3.   Deign, great God, deign to put your wisdom into his mouth.

l. 6.   The untimely memory of God whom I have deserted still casts a remnant of terror in my soul; and that is what increases and nourishes my fury.

l. 15.   Implacable God, you alone have brought everything about. It is you who, deluding me with [hopes of] easy revenge, have set me against myself a score of times a day, now awakening my remorse on behalf of a child, now dazzling me with your rich treasures, which I was afraid to give up to flames and pillage.

P. 93, l. 8.   In Heaven, Kings have a stern judge, innocence an avenger, and the orphan a father.

P. 95, l. 21.   Dazzled by his glory when the ambassadors of so many different kings came to pay homage to him in the name of the universe.

P. 96, l. 6. Your countenance is discomposed.

l. 7. See p. 73, l. 17.

l. 25. The blow that destroyed him came from him alone.

P. 97, l. 3. Behold the supreme justice of these great gods! They lead our steps to the brink of a crime; they make us commit it, and do not excuse it!

l. 21. Since, after so many efforts, my resistance is useless, I give myself blindly up to destiny, which is sweeping me along.

l. 29. I do not know what unjust power from time immemorial has left crime in peace and harried innocence. From wherever I turn my eyes upon myself, I see only misfortunes that condemn the gods.

l. 34. Thanks to the gods! My misfortune exceeds my hopes: yes, I praise you, oh Heaven, for your perseverance. Ceaselessly bent on the task of punishing me, you have brought me to the pitch of misery; your hatred has delighted in shaping my wretchedness; I was born to serve your wrath as an example, to be a perfect model of wretchedness.

P. 98, l. 18. I am an unhappy man, harried by destiny.

l. 27. You are in love. One cannot overcome one's destiny. You were led on by a fatal charm.

P. 99, l. 24. Do benefits counterbalance love in a heart? And without looking further, when the ingrate succeeded in winning my heart, was I any more grateful for his brother's favours?

l. 31. I am no doubt providing you, cruel man, with weapons against myself, and I ought to control my weakness; you are going to triumph over it. Yes, I confess to you, I affected a false cruelty in your presence. My joy and my happiness depend on you.

P.100, l. 17. She spends her days, Paulinus, asking for nothing but an hour to see me, and the rest to wait for me.

l. 20. A sigh, a glance, a word from your mouth, that is the ambition of a heart like mine.

l. 27.   She hears neither tears, nor advice, nor reason; with loud cries she implores a sword and poison.

P.101, l. 1.   As long as I breathed, your eyes are my witnesses that your danger alone was the object of my solicitude; and since it could terminate only with my life, I sacrifice it without regret. True, if Heaven had listened to my prayers, it might have granted me a happier death. You would still have married my rival: you could have promised her your hand in marriage, but you would not have added to the title of husband all those pledges of love that she has received from you.

l. 17.   Not that, weakly charmed by the eyes alone, I love in him his beauty, his so much vaunted grace, gifts with which nature has taken pride in honouring him, which he scorns himself, and of which he seems unaware. In him, I love, I prize nobler riches, the virtues of his father, not his weaknesses.

P.105, l. 26.   Our ships are quite ready, and the wind calls us. I know all the obscure windings of the palace; you observe that the sea washes up to its walls.

P.106, l. 7.   Can the winds have granted our prayers during the night? But everything sleeps, the army, and the winds, and Neptune.

l. 12.   See p. 67, l. 22.

l. 19.   We were compelled to stop, and the useless oars vainly beat a motionless sea.

l. 24.   See all the Hellespont white beneath our sails.

l. 26.   Already the sails are spread on the ships; already they are turning towards Troy at his command.

l. 30.   Already the prow of his ships was turned, and the sails, unfurled, were bellying in the winds.

P.107, l. 27.   I know a secret door, by which, without anyone seeing him, and unnoticed, crossing the brook Cedron with him, I shall reach the desert.

P.108, l. 4.   Perfidious Troy given up to the flames, its inhabitants in your chains, Priam at your knees, Helen restored to her husband by your hands. Behold the wreathed sterns of your ships, back with you in this same Aulis.

l. 25.   Would to the gods that this were the last of his crimes!

l. 31.   A door less familiar to the public.

l. 33.   This splendid, solitary closet is often the depository of Titus's secrets. Here sometimes he hides from his court, when he comes to tell the Queen of his love. This door is close to his apartments, and that other one leads to those of the Queen.

P.109, l. 6.   I can keep him here. But if he goes out, he is dead.

l. 10.   In a vestibule in the apartments of the high priest.

l. 36.   I thank Heaven that your indifference apprises me of the innocence of my successful suit.

P.110, l. 17.   He will not see me again.—Madam, here he is.

l. 20.   I can serve sultans faithfully; but I leave it to the vulgar to worship their whims, and I do not pride myself on the fond scruple of blessing my death when they have ordained it.

l. 28.   Why ask, since you know?

l. 32.   You know, and Calchas has told you a thousand times, that a secret marriage placed that prince in her bed, and that he had of her as a pledge a young princess whom her mother hid from the rest of Greece. But no, the love of a brother and his tarnished honour are the last of the cares that beset you.

P.112, l. 15.   Come, Narcissus. Let us go and see what we must do.

P.113, l. 12.   Here is Britannicus. I make way for him.

P.115, l. 9.   And while she displays the prophet's dreaded standard to the terrified populace, and Bajazet prepares to march after me, I am going to make known the cause of this signal, to fill the minds of all with just terror, and finally to proclaim the new emperor.

P.116, l. 6.   Powerful allies will take up our cause; Argos invites us, and Sparta calls us. Let us carry our just grievances to our common friends; let us not allow Phaedra, gathering together our remnants, to chase us both from our fathers' throne, and to promise her son my inheritance and yours. The occasion is favourable; we must seize it.

l. 18.   He marries Hermione to-morrow, he says; to honour me, he wants to receive her from my hand. Ah! this hand rather in the barbarian's blood. . .

l. 24.   I shall defend his life at the expense of my own.

l. 29.   Away from her eyes, I command, threaten, listen to your advice, have the courage to approve it; I work myself up against her, and try to defy her. But (I am now laying my soul bare before you) as soon as my ill-luck brings me back into her sight, my Genius, abashed, quakes before hers.

P.117, l. 6.   My flight will put an end to your fatal discord; Sire, I shall go and swell the number of the Vestals.

l. 10.   Britannicus is in his way, Albina.

l. 12.   See above, p. 49, l. 17.

l. 14.   You can imagine that I shall sell him dear the pleasure of seeing her.

l. 17.   And his destruction will be the infallible consequence of a gesture or a sigh that escapes to cheer him.

l. 20.   These sombre glances, straying at random.

l. 21.   I suffer too much, away from Junia.

l. 26.   Your death will be followed by my bloody death.

l. 32.   I could not check a jealous impulse.

P.118, l. 1.   Perhaps Bajazet, complying with your wishes, will take more care of his life than you want.

l. 8.   The King, always abounding in dangerous wiles, will arm himself against us with our least remarks.

l. 12.   Do not rely on the love he bears you: his jealous fury will be only the more violent for it.

l. 15.   Let her not drive this same affection—what shall I say?—to a fury of which my outraged heart would not repent until after it had taken its revenge.

l. 19.   You are here in the power of a violent hand, which rarely shrinks from the dearest blood; and I dare not tell you to what cruelty Mithridates's jealousy has often been carried away.

l. 32.	As if, in the depths of that vast edifice, God were concealing an avenger armed to kill her.
P.119, l. 1.	Oh, happy day for me! How ardently I should go and pay homage to my King.
l. 10.	Children, may you always be thus united!
l. 21.	Far from separating you, I intend to unite you and him to-day with eternal bonds.
l. 24.	I alone have woven the unhappy bond whose hateful knots you have just experienced.
P.120, l. 1.	Ever watchful over my conduct.
l. 6.	Examine their eyes, observe their remarks.
l. 11.	See above, p. 18, n. 16.
l. 15.	What! even your glances have learnt to be silent? What do I see? You are afraid to meet my eyes?
l. 20.	Everyone seems to approve my wrath with his eyes.
l. 25.	Your eyes, your sad eyes turn long glances towards heaven.
l. 32.	Allowed his displeasure to display itself on his face.
P.121, l. 2.	See above, p. 117, l. 21.
l. 5.	His unsteady eyes dare not raise their distraught glances towards heaven.
P.124, l. 1.	Forgive this transport, madam. I am going to help him if I can, or to follow him.
P.126, l. 34.	Nero was the first to allow laurel-crowned fasces to be borne before his mother.
P.127, l. 1.	On a hundred occasions you have seen our irate soldiers bear their eagles before you, grumbling.
l. 13.	As his only ambition, his singular virtue, he excels at driving a chariot in the arena, at competing for prizes unworthy of his hands, or offering himself as a spectacle to the Romans, at coming and lavishing his voice upon a stage, at reciting poems for which he exacts extravagant praise.
P.131, l. 9.	Always of my fury interrupting the course.
l. 14.	Of his fatal marriage I was cultivating the fruits.
l. 17.	I expected her . . . to come and free me from an irksome life, and to cut short an existence to which the grief of surviving my kings should a thousand times have put an end.

l. 25.   Captive, always sad, a burden to myself, can you desire Andromache to love you?

P.132, l. 3.   What charms for you have luckless eyes that you have condemned to eternal tears? No, no, to respect the wretchedness of an enemy, to preserve unhappy creatures, to restore a son to his mother . . . those, Sire, are cares worthy of the son of Achilles.

l. 10.   To marry what [i.e. her] he hates and punish what he loves.

l. 13.   Forgive [me], Acomat. With good cause, I pity hearts whose too ill-rewarded kindness had taken me as the object of all their thoughts.

l. 19.   Fatal blindness! Treacherous jealousy! False report! Suspicions that I was unable to conceal! Was it necessary to hearken to you, or was it necessary to speak?

l. 32.   Bajazet confused! Atalida alarmed!

P.133, l. 1.   I loved him in Lesbos, and I love him in Aulis.

l. 3.   Let us observe Bajazet; let us alarm Atalida; and let us crown the lover or destroy the deceiver.

l. 6.   See above, p. 79, l. 6.

l. 17.   Yes, like his exploits we admire your blows: Hector fell at his hands; Troy expired at yours.

l. 20.   Hecuba near Ulysses lived out her wretchedness; Cassandra to Argos followed your father.

l. 23.   Passionate in love but unrelenting in jealousy, his hatred always goes further than his love.

l. 33.   No, father, this heart (I have too long concealed it from you) has not disdained to burn with a chaste love. At your feet I confess my true offence; I am in love, I am in love, it is true, in defiance of your prohibition. Aricia holds my affections in thrall to her commands: the daughter of Pallas has conquered your son. I adore her, and my soul, rebelling against your orders, can neither sigh nor burn for any but her.

P.134, l. 12.   Creon even, Creon is on the side of peace!

l. 14.   Think, Cephisa, think of that cruel night.

l. 16.   I loved, Sire, I loved: I wanted to be loved.

l. 27.   Epirus will preserve what Troy preserved..

l. 29.   Before he betrayed me, you had all betrayed me.

l. 31.   See above, p. 20, n. 18.

l. 33.   See above, p. 79, l. 6.

P.135, l. 1.   It is he who is activating Pyrrhus's wrath. If Pyrrhus is to be softened, who can do it better than you?

l. 4.   I shall die; but at least my death will avenge me. I shall not die alone, and someone will follow me.

l. 7.   The deserts, formerly peopled by senators, are no longer inhabited except by those who betrayed them.

l. 13.   Must my sighs ask you for his life? Must I embrace your knees on his behalf?

l. 16.   Hippolytus asks to see me here? Hippolytus seeks me, and wishes to bid me farewell?

P.137, l. 12.   Phenissa is not coming? Too rigorous moments, how slow you seem to my rapid desires! I am restless, I rush about, languishing and dejected; strength leaves me, and repose irks me. Phenissa is not coming? Ah! how this delay alarms my heart with a foreboding of disaster! Phenissa will have no reply to bring me.

l. 31.   He owes it to me, Albina: everything, if he is generous, places this obligation on him; but everything, if he is ungrateful, speaks to him against me.

P.138, l. 1.   For in short this cruel man whom you are about to defy, this barbarous, unjust, bloody enemy, remember, whatever he has done, remember that he is my father.

l. 8.   Achilles has changed his mind about marrying you.

l. 11.   We are too well informed of your secret intentions, and it is not Calchas whom you are seeking here.

l. 16.   Achilles has changed his mind about marrying me; I must ignominiously retrace my steps; and you are seeking someone other than Calchas here?

P.139, l. 3.   See above, p. 17, n. 15.

l. 7.   See above, p. 80, l. 18.

l. 12.   Your blood, swallowed up by its furrows, has made the field from which it arose steam long enough.

l. 20. He brings back to you a heart that he has been unable to take away from you.

l. 22. Your heart, eager to see your Trojan moppet again.

l. 26. See above, p. 132, l. 3.

l. 29. See above, p. 54, l. 31.

P.140, l. 1. And still your mouth, mute in such great sorrow, has not deigned to open to complain about him.

l. 5. Since this fatal blow, Agrippina's power has daily been taking great strides towards its downfall.

l. 10. Seems to disdain the inconstancy of her lover, and thinks that, too happy to soften her rigour. . .

l. 15. Believe that to vanquish so great a love has cost me struggles from which my heart will bleed for more than one day.

l. 20. Favourable perils! Useless hope!

l. 24. His answer is dictated, and even his silence.

l. 26. Have you pitilessly relegated me to my court?

l. 28. Madam, without dying, she is dead to him.

l. 30. My reign will be only a long banishment.

l. 32. Shall I so often die without leaving life?

P.141, l. 3. See above, p. 106, l. 8.

l. 6. But faithful, proud, and even a little retiring, charming, young, trailing all hearts after him.

n. 9 Britannicus dying [i.e. the death of Britannicus] will arouse the zeal of his friends.

n. 10. For whom are those snakes hissing over your heads?

P.143, l. 5. Porus is doing his duty, and I shall do mine.

l. 9. Yes, madam, I want my gratitude henceforth to engrave your power in all hearts.

l. 13. See above, p. 119, l. 21.

l. 20. You will be there, daughter.

P.144, l. 14. See above, p. 81, l. 9.

P.145, l. 11. I swear by Heaven, which sees me confounded, by those great Ottomans from whom I am descended, and who are all on their knees beside me, pleading for the purest of the blood that they transmitted to us; Bajazet, sooner or later more sensible of your attentions, would not have been proof against so many charms.

l. 26.   I loved you fickle, what would I have done [if you had been] faithful?

l. 28.   Too present to my eyes, I thought I was speaking to her.

l. 30.   Present, I shun you; absent, I find you.

P.146, l. 1.   Speak.—Rome . . . The Empire . . .—Well?—Let us go, Paulinus; I can say nothing to her.

l. 6.   I burn, I adore her; and far from banishing her. . . Ah! that is another crime for which I want to punish her.

l. 14.   Unhappy people want lesser favours, Sire: it is for exile that my tears are asking you.

l. 19.   You want me to flee from him. Very well, nothing detains me: let us go. Let us no longer envy his unworthy conquest; let his captive extend her power over him. Let us flee. . . But if the ingrate were to return to his duty! If fidelity were to find some room in his heart again! If he were to come and ask my forgiveness at my feet! If, Love, you could subject him to my authority! If he wanted! . . . But the ingrate only wants to insult me. Let us remain, nevertheless, to disturb their bliss; let us take some pleasure in being a nuisance to them; or compelling him to break such a solemn engagement, let us make him criminal in the eyes of all the Greeks. I have already drawn their ire on to the son; I want them also to come and ask him for the mother. Let us inflict on her the torments that she is making me suffer; let her lose him, or let him destroy her.

P.147, l. 12.   If, in this high degree of greatness and power, you remember the places where you were born, madam, you remember that my heart received in those places the first shaft that came from your eyes. I loved. . .

l. 19.   Sire, since I must tell you, he is one of those captives destined to perish, brought from the banks of the Jordan to the Euphrates.—So he is a Jew?

l. 28.   But, Sire, what if he marries Andromache?—Oh, madam!—Think what a disgrace for us if he were to become the husband of a Phrygian.

P.148, l. 4.   The time is past, Phenissa, when I could be afraid.

Titus loves me; he is omnipotent; he has now but to speak. He will see the senate paying me homage, and the people placing wreaths of flowers on his statues.

Did you see last night's splendour, Phenissa? Are your eyes not full of his greatness? Those torches, that pyre, that blazing night, those eagles, those fasces, that throng of people, that army, that host of kings, those consuls, that senate, all borrowing their lustre from my lover; that purple, that gold, heightened by his glory, and those laurels still testifying to his victory; all those eyes that one could see coming from all quarters to mingle their avid glances on him alone; that majestic bearing, that sweet presence . . . Heavens! with what respect and what satisfaction all hearts secretly pledged their loyalty to him. Speak: can one see him without thinking, like me, that, even if fate had caused him to be born in utter obscurity, the world on seeing him would have acknowledged him as its master? But, Phenissa, whither does such a charming memory carry me?

Meanwhile, all Rome, at this very moment, is praying for Titus, consecrating by sacrifices the first fruits of the early days of his reign. Why do we dally? Let us go and offer up our prayers, too, for his happy reign to Heaven, which protects him. Immediately, without waiting for him, and without being awaited, I shall come back and seek him out, and in that interview say all that feelings so long held in check suggest to hearts content with each other.

P.152, l. 21.   Try to believe nothing of all that you see; believe that I am no longer in love; praise my victory to me; believe that my heart is inflexible in its displeasure, alas! and if possible, make me believe it, too!

P.153, l. 9.   Someone is coming; I can see Theseus.—Ah! I can see Hippolytus.

l. 19.   Speak to him every day of the virtues of his father, and sometimes, too, speak to him of his mother.

l. 22.   Titus cherished you; you admired Titus. On a hundred occasions I have taken the greatest delight in talking to Titus in another self.

l. 27.   With what insolence and what cruelty they were both laughing at my credulity.

P.154, l. 1.   Think, think, Cephisa, of that cruel night, which for a whole people was eternal night. Imagine Pyrrhus, his eyes gleaming, entering by the light of our blazing palaces, scrambling over my dead brothers, and, all covered with blood, encouraging the slaughter. Think of the shouts of the victors, think of the shouts of the dying, muffled by the flames, cut short by the sword. Imagine Andromache distracted amidst these horrors: that is how Pyrrhus first presented himself to my eyes.

Chronological Table

Note: Plays marked with an asterisk probably appeared late in the
year to which they are ascribed, or early in the following year.

	Plays	*Other Events*
1606		Corneille born
1610		Assassination of Henry IV; accession of Louis XIII
1622		Molière born
1625		Thomas Corneille born
1629	* Corneille, *Mélite*, comédie	
1635		Quinault born
1637	Corneille, *Le Cid*, tragi-comédie	
1639		Racine born
1640	Corneille, *Horace*, tragédie	
1642	Corneille, *Cinna*, tragédie * Corneille, *Polyeucte*, tragédie	Death of Richelieu
1643	* Corneille, *Pompée*, tragédie	Death of Louis XIII; accession of Louis XIV (regency of Anne of Austria)
1644	* Corneille, *Rodogune*, tragédie	
1648		The Fronde begins. Treaty of Westphalia
1649		Execution of Charles I
1651	Corneille, *Nicomède*, comédie héroïque * Corneille, *Pertharite*, tragédie	

	Plays	*Other Events*
1653		End of the Fronde
1654	Quinault, *La Généreuse Ingratitude*, tragi-comédie pastorale	
1655	Thomas Corneille, *Les Illustres Ennemis*, comédie Quinault, *Les Coups de l'Amour et de la Fortune*, tragi-comédie	
1656	Quinault, *Le Fantôme amoureux*, tragi-comédie (Nov. ?) Thomas Corneille, *Timocrate*, tragédie	
1657	Thomas Corneille, *Bérénice*, tragédie Thomas Corneille, *La Mort de l'empereur Commode*, tragédie Quinault, *Amalasonte*, tragi-comédie	
1658	Quinault, *Le Feint Alcibiade*, tragi-comédie (Summer) Quinault, *Le Mariage de Cambyse*, tragi-comédie * Thomas Corneille, *Darius*, tragédie * Quinault, *La Mort de Cyrus*, tragédie	
1659	(Jan. 24) Corneille, *Œdipe*, tragédie (Nov. 18) Molière, *Les Précieuses ridicules*, comédie	Treaty of the Pyrenees
1660	(Jan. 2) Quinault, *Stratonice*, tragédie (Jan. 27) Thomas Corneille, *Stilicon*, tragédie (Nov.) Corneille, *La Toison d'Or*, tragédie	Restoration of Charles II Marriage of Louis XIV and Maria Theresa of Spain
1661	(Jan. 28) Thomas Corneille, *Camma*, tragédie (June 24) Molière, *L'Ecole des Maris*, comédie (Aug. 17) Molière, *Les Fâcheux*, comédie	Death of Mazarin. Marriage of Philip of Orleans (Monsieur) with Charles II's sister, Henrietta (Madame)

Plays	Other Events
1662 (Feb.) Corneille, *Sertorius*, tragédie	Death of Pascal
(Feb.) Thomas Corneille, *Maximian*, tragédie	
(late) Quinault, *Agrippa*, tragédie	
(Dec.) Thomas Corneille, *Persée et Démétrius*, tragédie	
(Dec. 26) Molière, *L'École des Femmes*, comédie	
1663 (Jan.) Corneille, *Sophonisbe*	
(late) Montfleury, *Trasibule*, tragi-comédie	
* Thomas Corneille, *Pyrrhus*, tragédie	
1664 (May 12) Molière, *Tartuffe*, comédie	
(June 20) RACINE, LA THÉBAÏDE, tragédie	
(July 31) Corneille, *Othon*, tragédie	
* Quinault, *Astrate*, tragédie	
1665 (Jan. 15) Molière, *Dom Juan*, comédie	
(Oct.) Quinault, *La Mère coquette*, comédie	
(Dec. 4) RACINE, ALEXANDRE, tragédie	
1666 (Jan. 9) Thomas Corneille, *Antiochus*, tragi-comédie	Death of Anne of Austria
(Feb. 26) Corneille, *Agésilas*, tragédie	
(June 4) Molière, *Le Misanthrope*, comédie	
1667 (March 4) Corneille, *Attila*, tragédie	Beginning of the War of Devolution
(Nov. 17) RACINE, ANDROMAQUE, tragédie	
1668 (Feb.) Thomas Corneille, *Laodice*, tragédie	Treaty of Aix-la-Chapelle. La Fontaine's *Fables*, Books I–VI
(Sept. 9) Molière, *L'Avare*, comédie	

	Plays	*Other Events*
	(latter half) RACINE, LES PLAIDEURS, comédie	
	(Nov. 16) Quinault, *Pausanias*, tragédie	
1669	(Nov.) Thomas Corneille, *La Mort d'Annibal*, tragédie	
	(Dec. 13) RACINE, BRITANNICUS, tragédie	
1670	(Oct. 14) Molière, *Le Bourgeois gentilhomme*, comédie	Death of Madame. Pascal's *Pensées*
	(Nov. 21) RACINE, BÉRÉNICE, tragédie	
	(Nov. 28) Corneille, *Tite et Bérénice*, comédie héroïque	
	* Quinault, *Bellérophon*, tragédie	
1672	(Jan.) RACINE, BAJAZET, tragédie	Beginning of the Dutch War
	(Feb. 26) Thomas Corneille, *Ariane*, tragédie	
	(March 11) Molière, *Les Femmes savantes*, comédie	
	(Nov. 14) Corneille, *Pulchérie*, comédie héroïque	
	(Nov. 16) Thomas Corneille, *Théodat*, tragédie	
1673	(Jan.) RACINE, MITHRIDATE, tragédie	Death of Molière
	(Feb. 10) Molière, *Le Malade imaginaire*, comédie	
	(Dec. 29) Thomas Corneille, *La Mort d'Achille*, tragédie	
1674	(Aug. 18) RACINE, IPHIGÉNIE, tragédie	Boileau, *Art poétique*
	(Oct.–Nov.) Corneille, *Suréna*, tragédie	
1677	(Jan. 1) RACINE, PHÈDRE, tragédie	
1678	(Jan. 7) Thomas Corneille, *Le Comte d'Essex*, tragédie	Mme de Lafayette, *La Princesse de Clèves*. La Fontaine, *Fables*, Books VII–XI
1683		Death of Colbert. Death of Queen of France; secret

	Plays	*Other Events*
		marriage of Louis XIV and Mme de Maintenon
1684		Death of Corneille
1685		Death of Charles II; accession of James II. Revocation of Edict of Nantes
1688		William of Orange lands in England; flight of James II to France. Death of Quinault
1689	RACINE, ESTHER, tragédie	Beginning of the War of the League of Augsburg. Expedition of James II to Ireland
1690		James II returns to France
1691	RACINE, ATHALIE, tragédie	
1694		La Fontaine, *Fables*, Book XII
1697		Treaty of Ryswick
1699		Death of Racine
1709		Death of Thomas Corneille
1715		Death of Louis XIV

Select Bibliography

Editions:
There are numerous editions of Racine's plays, both collected and separate. Two editions of his complete works (including the letters) are in print:—
Racine, *Œuvres complètes*, ed. R. Groos, E. Pilon, and R. Picard, 2 vols., Paris, Gallimard (Bibliothèque de la Pléiade), 1950–2;
Racine, *Œuvres complètes*, Paris, Editions du Seuil (Collection l'Intégrale), 1962 (inexpensive; double columns, but clear print).

Translations:
Racine, *Andromache and Other Plays*, translated and introduced by John Cairncross, Penguin Books, 1967;
   Iphigenia, Phaedra, Athaliah, translated and introduced by John Cairncross, Penguin Books, 1963;
Racine, *Complete Plays*, translated into English verse and with a biographical appreciation by Samuel Solomon, New York, Random House, 2 vols, 1967;
Racine, *Phèdre*, Edinburgh University Press, (Edinburgh Bilingual Library), 1971 (contains the text of *Phèdre*, together with an introduction and a translation by Professor R. C. Knight).

Life:
Brereton (G.), *Jean Racine*, second edition, 1973;
Picard (R.), *La Carrière de Racine*, 1956;
   Corpus racinianum, 1956 (invaluable collection of documents relating to Racine's life and works);

Supplément au Corpus racinianum, 1961;

Pommier (J.), *Aspects de Racine*, 1954 (discusses various biographical problems; also usefully corrects Cahen's book on Racine's vocabulary, listed below, and studies *Phèdre* and its forerunners);

Racine (Louis), *Mémoires sur la vie et les ouvrages de Jean Racine* (by Racine's younger son, contained in the editions of Racine's complete works mentioned above; often inaccurate and misleading, but interesting);

Vaunois (L.), *L'Enfance et la jeunesse de Racine*, 1964.

Critical Studies:

The following is only a selection of the many studies of Racine; it may easily be supplemented from the bibliographies contained in many of the books listed.

(1) *General*

Adam (A.), *Histoire de la littérature française au XVIIe siècle*, vol. 4, 1954;

Bénichou (P.), *Morales du grand siècle* (sections on Jansenism and on Racine), 1948;

Butler (P. F.), *A Student's Guide to Racine*, 1974;

Edwards (M.), *La Tragédie racinienne*, 1972;

Hubert (J. D.), *Essai d'exégèse racinienne*, 1956;

Knight (R. C.), (ed.), *Racine. Modern Judgments* (Macmillan's Modern Judgments series), 1969;

Lancaster (H. C.), *A History of French Dramatic Literature in the Seventeenth Century*, Part III, 2 vols., 1936, and Part IV, 2 vols., 1940;

Lapp (J. C.), *Aspects of Racinian Tragedy*, 1955;

May (G.), *Tragédie cornélienne, tragédie racinienne*, 1948;

Mourgues (O. de), *Racine, or the Triumph of Relevance*, 1967;

Vinaver (E.), *Racine et la poésie tragique*, revised edition, 1963 (translated into English by P. Mansell Jones, under the title, *Racine and Poetic Tragedy*, 1955);

Weinberg (B.), *The Art of Jean Racine*, 1963.

(2) *On particular aspects of Racine's work*:

Butler (P. F.), *Classicisme et baroque dans l'œuvre de Racine*, 1959;

Delcroix (M.), *Le Sacré dans les tragédies profanes de Racine*, 1970 (contains a useful survey of criticism of Racine);

Jasinski (R.), *Vers le vrai Racine*, 2 vols., 1958 (contains some useful information, though the main argument—that Racine's plays are based not only on his own life but on that of Louis XIV and the political situation of the time—is carried too far);

Knight (R. C.), *Racine et la Grèce*, second edition, 1974;

Pommier (J.), *Aspects de Racine*, 1954 (discusses *Phèdre* and its forerunners amongst other things; see also above).

(3) *Style:*

Cahen (J. G.), *Le Vocabulaire de Racine*, 1946 (for some rectifications, see Pommier above);

France (P.), *Racine's Rhetoric*, 1965;

Freeman (B.C.) and Batson (A.), *Concordance du théâtre et des poésies de Jean Racine*, 2 vols., 1968;

Sayce (R. A.), 'Racine's style: periphrasis and direct statement' in *The French Mind. Studies in honour of Gustave Rudler*, 1952; reprinted in *Racine. Modern Judgments*, ed. R. C. Knight (see above);

Spitzer (L.), 'Die klassische Dämpfung in Racines Stil' in his *Romanische Stil- und Literaturstudien*, vol. 1, 1931; may be read in French in his *Etudes de Style*, 1970.

Background:

Chevalley (S.), *Album Théâtre classique*, 1970;

Deierkauf-Holsboer (S. W.), *L'Histoire de la mise en scène dans le théâtre français à Paris de 1600 à 1673*, revised edition, 1960.
      Le Théâtre de l'Hôtel de Bourgogne, 2 vols., 1968–70;

Lancaster (H. C.), *A History of French Dramatic Literature in the Seventeenth Century*, Part III, 2 vols., 1936, and Part IV, 2 vols. 1940;
      (ed.), *Le Mémoire de Mahelot, Laurent et d'autres décorateurs de l'Hôtel de Bourgogne et de la Comédie Française au XVIIe siècle*, 1920;

Lawrenson (T. E.), *The French Stage in the XVIIth Century*, 1957.

Lough (J.), *Paris Theatre Audiences in the seventeenth and eighteenth centuries*, 1957;

Mongrédien (G.), *La Vie quotidienne des comédiens au temps de Molière*, 1966 (translated into English by Claire Eliane Engel under the title *Daily Life in the French theatre at the time of Molière*);

Schérer (J.), *La Dramaturgie classique*, 1950.

Index